AF352601

*Miracle as Modern Conundrum
in South Asian Religious Traditions*

*Miracle as Modern Conundrum
in South Asian Religious Traditions*

Edited by

CORINNE G. DEMPSEY
AND
SELVA J. RAJ

STATE UNIVERSITY OF NEW YORK PRESS

Published by
State University of New York Press, Albany

For information, contact State University of New York Press, Albany, NY
www.sunypress.edu

Production by Eileen Meehan
Marketing by Fran Keneston

Library of Congress Cataloging-in-Publication Data

Miracle as modern conundrum in South Asian religious traditions / edited by
Corinne G. Dempsey and Selva J. Raj.
    p. cm.
  Includes index.
  ISBN 978-0-7914-7633-8 (hardcover : alk. paper)
1. South Asia—Religion. 2. Miracles. I. Dempsey, Corinne G. II. Raj, Selva J.

BL1055.M57 2009
202'.117—dc22

                                                                    2008000123

*We dedicate this volume
in vivid memory of Selva Raj
(1952–2008)
and to his lasting inspiration on us all*

Contents

Illustrations

Acknowledgments

This volume emerges from a series of meetings and, sadly, a departing. Several contributors read early drafts of their chapters at the 2004 American Academy of Religion convention in San Antonio, Texas at a session entitled "Revealing and Creating through Miracles." Remaining chapters were selected from the first annual Conference on the Study of Religions of India in June 2005. That year's CSRI conference, organized and hosted by Selva Raj at Albion College, centered around the theme, "Modern Constructions of the Miraculous and the Mysterious." On March 15, 2008, Corinne received the final, copyedited manuscript from SUNY Press that she was to read and return with corrections. The task that remained for Selva and Corinne as an editorial team was to write these acknowledgments. Later that same day, Corinne received a phone call from Bill Harman with the unthinkable news that Selva had suffered a heart attack and died the night before. Rather than face, among other things, the writing of this volume's final piece by herself, which now must be a tribute to an exquisite scholar and human being, Corinne suggested to the volume contributors, a week after Selva's death, that they memorialize his life and work together. She thanks them for heartily agreeing to do so (as all of us are still in a state of shock) and for offering a loving, crowning contribution to their good work that constitutes this volume.

"Selva was, in my mind, a pioneer in the scholarly study of Christianity in India, one who helped establish it as a respectable and legitimate topic of research. He possessed an uncanny ability to be at the right place at the right time, and to bring home from India account after account of intriguingly complex Christian (and Hindu-Christian) religious phenomena. But most of all, I am grateful to Selva for the way that he helped forge together a *community* of scholars, never neglecting, as he planned the CSRI conferences, to leave ample time, as he put it, for our 'spiritual' development (which generally took place in a local watering hole)."

—Chad M. Bauman

"Selva devoted his life to humanizing and dialogue; his capacity for generating communal enjoyment and conversation—whether through conferences, edited volumes, or warm engagement with friends and colleagues—was nothing short of miraculous. These qualities also resound throughout his research and writing, in his attention to the ways everyday religious practices create interreligious dialogue that audaciously defies abstraction. Selva's commitment to dismantling ideological barriers and nurturing human connection will be missed terribly yet, in many ways, will live on."

—Corinne G. Dempsey

"In the immediate weeks before Selva passed away, he and I had had a discussion about the range of projects our Emory University religion graduate students were working on. He immediately began to think of kinds of conferences and panels that would encompass their work and give them an opportunity to participate. This was so typical of the gracious inclusivity that Selva extended to his friends, colleagues and students. He was a consummate visionary and programmatic architect, not for himself, but to make space for others to participate in and in which to create intellectual community."

—Joyce Burkhalter Flueckiger

"In a document dated June 3, 2006, I have a one-page list of what Selva Raj in his ever kindly way described as 'friendly suggestions' for my chapter. I am struck by the way he showered effusive praise on what I had done while pushing me persistently to exert myself just a little harder to make my contribution not only more readable but a better piece of the whole book. Who knows how many such gently crafted memos constitute an academic lifetime; Selva's was cut short but our gratitude for all he did endures."

—Ann Grodzins Gold

"Selva Raj, true to his beliefs, was a model of and for humility, generosity, honesty, and kindness. He practiced what he believed. He was a gentleman-scholar."

—Sunil Goonasekera

"In memory of Selvaji—my brother, my teacher, a man whose wisdom and kindness enrich my life in countless ways."

—William P. Harman

"Selva was a warm, caring, genuine, and completely unpretentious person. He expressed those qualities in informal settings and in professional contexts too, so that under his leadership the CSRI was just as much a gathering of cherished friends as a scholarly meeting."

—*Robin Rinehart*

"In the years that I knew Selva Raj, I was deeply impressed by his integrative worldview. He saw his service work and his scholarly work as being on a continuum and moved seamlessly between the two. The interdisciplinary nature of his scholarly work, where he meaningfully interwove theological interpretation and ethnographic research, will continue to provide a model for those who study the complex religious landscape of India."

—*Neelima Shukla-Bhatt*

We would also like to thank the people at SUNY who worked with us on this volume: Nancy Ellegate, Senior Acquisitions Editor for welcoming our project and shepherding it through to press, Eileen Meehan for her fine work as production editor, and Wyatt Benner for his superb copyediting work.

CHAPTER ONE

Introduction

Divine Proof or Tenacious Embarrassment? The Wonders of the Modern Miraculous

CORINNE G. DEMPSEY

There is nothing quite like a good miracle story. Miraculous accounts have the capacity to enrapture or repulse; they can be sought after or disdained with seemingly equal passion. Depending on the type of miracle and mode of belief, they can be monotonously plentiful, enticingly elusive, or utterly preposterous. Throughout history and across cultures, purported miracle events and narratives have been foundational to faith conviction as well as to skepticism, making and breaking religious careers and movements in their wake. Although scholars of modern religion in South Asia are not known to shy away from sticky subjects, it appears that many have managed to keep these pervasively complex phenomena at arm's length, often leaving them unnoticed if not unscrutinized. Indeed, as Mark Corner observes, the concept of the miraculous often remains—among scholars and nonscholars alike—"cordoned off like a terminally ill patient in the corner of the hospital ward," beyond repair or understanding in the modern secular world (Corner 2005, vii).[1]

This volume is an attempt to bring South Asian narratives and conceptions of the miraculous into the light, to give them some of the attention we feel they deserve. We acknowledge that, in spite of the prevailing prognosis, the condition of the modern miraculous is far from dire, and thus this collection reads nothing like a diagnosis of a disease or discovery of a cure; it neither seeks to explain away nor rescue miracles from their demise. Instead, volume contributors uncover the range and variation of colliding forces that have forged the miraculous into what it is today: a healthy conundrum.

Well-known challenges to miraculous worldviews, generally represented by modern, rationalistic, scientific sensibilities—also alive and well in different ways across the globe—take a certain shape in South Asian cultural and religious contexts. Several chapters in this volume discuss conundrums created when miracle events and expectations are encountered by members of an educated Indian or Sri Lankan elite, living in South Asia or abroad, who typically have little time for or interest in miracles. In other chapters we find that, somewhat ironically, the strongest critiques of the miraculous emerge from religious leaders within Hindu traditions as well as within institutional Islam and Christianity. Some religious authorities indeed work tirelessly to promote miraculous events and worldviews, while others appear strongly disdainful of the same. Still others promote miracle events selectively, depending on their religious resonance and the context in which they occurred. Adding a final layer of conundrum to the mix, several volume contributors have woven into their writing their own—somewhat fraught—reflections on ethnographic encounters with the miraculous.

By investigating miracle as conundrum, it is our hope that, rather than simply reinforcing the usual distinctions between science/religion, West/the rest, modern/traditional, establishment/popular religion, and ethnographer/ native, we instead illustrate how narratives and conceptions of the miraculous more often than not confound these traditional divides. This collection furthermore describes encounters with the miraculous that produce unanticipated conundrums and new perspectives—often by default—demonstrating how miracles are, by nature, unwieldy. While some understandably want to sequester the whole matter by consigning it to dark, hushed corners for the terminally ill, experience suggests that there is not always a choice.

Situating the Modern Miraculous

For our purposes, "miracle" has been defined broadly in this volume to involve an array of phenomena and contexts. Some events such as healings, punishments, mystical experiences, and visions emerge within officially designated sacred spaces such as churches, temples, or shrines. Other events such as the discovery of an impressive Shiva lingam, animal rescues from natural disaster, and healings (actual or promised) occur in locations not—or not yet—sanctified, such as a vacant suburban lot, a raging ocean, a hospital, or a television advertisement. Most miracle accounts are assigned specific dates within the past decades, while others exist as past events frozen in narrative time yet no less alive to their modern audiences.

Tying all these instances together are, to some degree, a sense of awe or surprise evoked in listeners or experiencers. In both European Christian and

Indic traditions, the words most closely associated with miraculous events are also associated with human surprise or wonder. The Latin *miraculum* emphasizes the wonder-causing aspect of an event and the Greek root word for miracle is *meidian*, "to smile." Likewise, the Sanskrit root *smi*, "to smile," is the derivative for the most common dictionary term for an astonishing, wondrous event: *vismaya*. Although no Indic words neatly translate as "miracle," the Hindi term *alaukika* describes phenomena that depart from the normal course of events, and *ashcharya* is the human condition of wonder and astonishment. The Tamil word most typically used for a miraculous event is *putumai* and literally translates as "novelty" or "newness," yet when used in a religious context *putumai* translates better as "wonderment" evoked by sacred powers. *Athputham*, the most commonly used term for "miracle" in Malayalam, has a literal translation similar to that of *putumai*.[2]

But not all miracle narratives incite wonder. In some instances they are meant not so much to evoke awe in the listener but to convey lessons about the awesome power of a saint or divinity. In some cases, efforts to assign significance to purported miraculous events can strip them of their wonder. As suggested by Carolyn Walker Bynum, medieval theologians described and analyzed designated miracle events so persistently and thoroughly that the freshness of the event and thus the amazement originally provoked by it dimmed (Bynum 1997, 3, 24). As some volume chapters demonstrate, contemporary narrators and producers of miracles can likewise emphasize the lessons to be learned by them to such an extent that their wondrous qualities fade into the background. Indeed, wonder is not the only—or even the most important—ingredient for the miraculous. A talking cow, for instance, does not necessarily constitute a miracle. Miracles can only be labeled as such if they are understood as the direct or indirect result of divine or saintly power and therefore as containing a particular purpose or meaning for humanity (Corner 2005, 5; see also Basinger 1986, 3).[3] A miracle event must be, for those who identify it as such, a sign that is, in many cases, also a wonder.

Although religious authorities can offer a significant, seemingly ironic, force for deflating the wonders of miracles—sometimes debunking the category of the miraculous itself—the strongest antimiracle strain emerges from a post-Enlightenment scientific, empirical worldview. This perspective on miracles gained particular influence during and after the eighteenth century and is best articulated by the Scottish philosopher David Hume's proposal that miracles violate the laws of nature. This is not to say, however, that pre-Enlightenment cultures did or do not understand nature to have laws and properties that can be verified through empirical study. For instance, Lévi-Strauss's *The Savage Mind* describes how Amazonian empirical rigor and rationality forged an understanding of the natural world that is in some ways more complex and comprehensive than the current store of information held in botany, zoology, and pharmaceutical science.[4] The difference between Amazonian and modern nonmiraculous worldviews thus has less to do with conflicting beliefs about the laws of nature than with a disagreement over the existence of a supernatural realm that can involve itself in the natural world. The post-Enlightenment shift is thus one in which worldviews that conceive of nature as an open system with which spirits can wondrously interact are challenged—and in some cases replaced—by a perception of the natural world as a closed and complete system that overrules not only the intervention but the existence of supernatural forces.[5]

In Hume's famous essay "Of Miracles" he identifies "irrational" miraculous worldviews not only with the premodern but also with the primitive Other. He proposes that miracles "are observed chiefly to abound among ignorant and barbarous nations; or if a civilized people has ever given admission to any of them, that people will be found to have received them from ignorant and barbarous ancestors." Hume optimistically concludes this thought with his forecast that miracles will wane "in proportion as we advance nearer the enlightened ages" (Hume [1748] 1989, 31). Hume's associations are clearly a product of their time, riddled with holes; his prediction for the future seems to have also fallen quite flat. Just as skeptical and miraculous worldviews do not strictly correlate with premodern and modern societies, respectively, so they do not—as is too often assumed—reflect fundamental differences between Hume's no doubt colonialist distinction between "us" and "them."[6]

Although Hume's associations may be largely anachronistic, they nonetheless are difficult to shake. In the midst of his excellent work on modern Indian religious traditions, for instance, Lawrence Babb seems to promote the view that Indian and North American worldviews are fundamentally different. He expresses this view through his reticence to apply the term "miracle" across cultural boundaries. As he describes it, "miracle" typically refers, in the West, to the "disreputable opposite of scientific rationality." This association, as he sees it, potentially distorts significant realities in the "Hindu world" that allow for deities or unseen beings to affect the realm of normal experience (Babb 1986, 176).[7] Although this assessment may in some cases be true, we find that, based on evidence reflected in this volume and beyond, it is too broad to be helpful.

In her attempt to remedy such assumptions, Susan Sered proposes that in order for the category "supernatural" to be useful for ethnographers, the assumed natural/supernatural opposition must be dismantled, not only because it is often misleading but also because the opposition assumes a contentious hierarchy. This hierarchy, she argues, supports embedded hierarchies found in related dualisms such as West/the rest, Christian/pagan, true/false, and superior/inferior. Sered proposes that if the category of the supernatural were instead "part of a shifting lexicon that helps us make sense out of the experiences and stories that comprise our work, we can begin to think in terms of a series of continuums" (Sered 2003, 217). If viewed as differently situated in a variety of contexts, the category of the supernatural—and, we submit, the miraculous—would be far more useful to our understanding.

An easy entrée into dismantling such assumed associations is to consider the increasing North American belief in a divinity or spiritual force who actively engages with our natural world. Since World War II the United States has experienced a surge of Neo-Pentacostalism that revels in charismatic gifts of the spirit, divine signs, and healings. The long lines of books on spirituality at any given mainstream bookstore today might, as neatly described by Mark Corner, "make the mystery religions of Rome look tame by comparison" (Corner 2005, 179). In a *Newsweek* poll released May 1, 2000, nearly half of the respondents claim to have personally experienced or seen a miracle. Eighty-four percent professed a belief that God performed miracles.[8] It is also important to note that in India both belief in and skepticism of the supernatural are alive and well and have been for centuries. The most notable ancient skeptics were adherents of the Charvaka and Lokayata traditions, who denied all nonempirical events and provided an important foil against which religiously oriented philosophical texts argued.

A stellar incident of misapprehension and collision between Indian skepticism and American and European credulity occurred through the meeting of the Indian Arya Samaj and the American and European Theosophists in the late 1800s. The two groups were briefly under the impression that they would, as proponents of Eastern spirituality, join forces. Swami Dayananda Saraswati, leader of the Arya Samaj and champion of Hinduism as a rationalistic and scientifically verifiable religion, abruptly broke with the Theosophist delegates Henry Olcott and Madame Blavatsky, from the United States and Russia, respectively, once he discovered their propensity, as Spiritualists, to communicate with spirits of the dead. This breakup was marked by Dayananda's publication of a pamphlet, *Humbuggery of the Theosophists*, in which he denounced the trickery and irrationality of Olcott and Blavatsky's practices (Van der Veer 2001, 55–57).

Efforts to relinquish assumed oppositions and hierarchies when discussing miraculous worldviews is not the same as obliterating distinctions completely, particularly in reference to premodern and modern beliefs in the miraculous. The most significant difference between premodern Amazonian and contemporary middle-class South Asian or North American miraculous worldviews is not an indebtedness—or lack thereof—to empiricism but the extent to which modern miracle advocates must defend their position. Although modern proponents of the miraculous likely do not agree with prevailing post-Enlightenment assumptions that render their worldview primitive or suspect, it is nearly impossible not to, on some level, engage with or respond to such assumptions. As noted by Ursula Rao in her discussion of the miraculous in contemporary urban north India, modernity is not, as is often presumed, an opposition to or replacement of tradition but rather "the struggle over traditions." The question of "whether to keep, abolish, rework or reinvent them [i.e., miraculous worldviews]—is considered to be part of the modern condition" (Rao 2002, 8). Miracles in the modern context thus rarely cease to be a conundrum for their supporters, who, more elaborately than their predecessors, must work to give validity and respectability to their beliefs.

Much ink has been spilt on the part of theologians, philosophers, scientists, and folklorists in their efforts to maintain a level of respectability for the miraculous in today's world. Among European and North American Christian theologians who argue in their defense, a sturdy bone of contention worthy of centuries of rebuttal is, as mentioned, the writings of David Hume. Prophesying the importance of his argument, Hume declared, "I flatter myself, that I have discovered an argument of a like nature, which, if just, will, with the wise and the learned, be an everlasting check to all kinds of superstitious delusions, and consequently, will be useful as long as the world endures" ([1748] 1989, 24). Although perhaps overly optimistic about the final impact his argument would have on what he considered to be the terminally ill modern miracle, Hume could not have overstated his lasting influence on the miracle debate. In an effort to understand the range of religious responses to Hume's assessment that miracles violate the laws of nature and are therefore irrational and that witnesses claiming to vouch for them must be untrustworthy or deluded, I have arranged miracle advocates into two camps: classical theists and nondualists. Although these camps are not necessarily mutually exclusive and miraculous worldviews are often too unwieldy to be perfectly accommodated by such categories, I find this schema helpful for sorting out not only how religious traditions (and traditions within traditions) defend the miraculous but also how they make room for miracles in the modern context.

Briefly put, modern miracle advocates in the classical theist camp acknowledge the laws and properties of an empirical, scientifically validated reality yet counter Hume's argument against Christian theism by contending that this reality is not the only one in existence. Divinity and divine powers are realities that reside in a separate realm that, under extraordinary conditions and largely in response to prayer or ritual activity, make their presence known—through blessings, healings, and occasional punishments—to the empirical world. Nondualists, in contrast, include adherents who are largely nontheistic in their religious orientation. Proponents tend to agree, for the most part, with Hume's view of nature as a complete system closed to outside forces. Yet they do not conclude that divine or "supernatural" power must therefore be nonexistent. Rather, seemingly extraordinary forces work through specially tuned humanity and within the laws of nature. "Miraculous" events thus often appear as such to the uninitiated who have yet to comprehend or discover aspects of the natural world that allow for these events. In spite of the fact that many nondualists understand the acquisition of extraordinary abilities such as fore-knowledge, spontaneous healing, and bilocation to be available through the natural processes of human proclivity and discipline, I nonetheless label their view miraculous, because the end product has religious significance that transcends the mundane.[9] Also, for those who stand outside his or her conceptual box, a nondualist's science will likely be viewed as pseudoscience.

Theologians and philosophers from the classical theist position tend to stave off Hume's accusation that miracles violate nature's laws by rendering this statement either irrelevant or erroneous. Cardinal Newman, for example, argued for the existence of a divine reality separate from the natural realm, a reality that can only be accessed by faith, not science. In Newman's mid-nineteenth-century sermon "Faith and Reason Contrasted as Habits of the Mind" (in which he refers to Hume not by name but as "a well known infidel of the last century") he does not attempt to defend two spheres of reality but, rather, two mutually exclusive types of minds. Newman agrees with Hume that no amount of empirical evidence can compel a person to have faith in miracles; rather belief in miracles has to do with "a 'habit of the mind' prior to and independent of examination of the material world" (quoted in Mullin 1996, 127). C. S. Lewis attempts to undermine Hume by describing divine and empirical realities as "naturally" interconnected. Using the analogy of the collaborative process of human conception, he reasons, "If Nature brings forth miracles then doubtlessly it is as 'natural' for her to do so when impregnated by the masculine force beyond her as it is for a woman to bear children to a man. In calling them miracles we do not mean that they are contradictions or outrages; we mean that, left to her own resources, she could never produce them" (Lewis 1947, 61–62). The analytic philosophers David and Randal Basinger argue that miracles, understood by classical theists to be fueled by divine forces, do not, as Hume contends, violate natural law. Responding to Hume's critique that miracles have no plausible proof, the Basingers note that since the cause of miracles is nonempirical, their proof can only be nonempirical: "Since natural laws can only tell us what will or will not happen under natural conditions, they cannot be used to predict or explain what will happen when nonnatural forces are present" (Basinger and Basinger 1986, 13).

Nondualist miracle supporters tend to challenge Hume by embracing the scientific approach, arguing for the natural occurrence of "miracles" or seemingly supernatural events. Alfred Russel Wallace, a nineteenth-century British biologist known for formulating the theory of evolution by natural selection,[10] levels his critique of Hume by making a case for Spiritualism and for supernatural forces that can be empirically measured and therefore proven. These supernatural "facts," rather than violating nature's laws, demonstrate that our current understanding of the laws of nature is incomplete. Wallace writes in his *Miracles and Modern Spiritualism* that "many phenomena of the simplest kind would appear supernatural to men having limited knowledge. Ice and snow might easily be made to appear so to inhabitants of the tropics. . . . A century ago, a telegram from three thousand miles' distance, or a photograph taken in a fraction of a second, would not have been believed possible, and would not have been credited on any testimony, except by the ignorant and superstitious who believed in miracles" (Wallace [1896] 1975, 39).[11] The Christian process theologian David Griffin echoes this view by arguing for the repeatability and therefore scientific validity of phenomena that suggest life after death, apparitions, extrasensory perception, and "apparent" precognition.[12] Griffin's view is based philosophically on a nondualistic association between mind and body, an association, he contends, that is supported by Hume's writings (Griffin 1997, 108–10).

Since nondualists tend to downplay the existence of a divinity who exists separately from yet is involved in the course of human history[13]—a foundational belief for mainstream Christians—most of its adherents in contemporary Europe and the United States include New Age practitioners, nontraditional Christians, and members of nontheistic religious traditions. In India, the modern nondualist approach that applies scientific terminology and methods to seemingly supernatural phenomena has emerged most significantly within Hindu nontheistic traditions, particularly in association with Neo-Vedantic philosophies and practices. Beginning in the mid-1800s, Hindu Renaissance leaders such as Vivekananda and Yogananda de-emphasized ritual practices and theism and promoted instead an ethical spirituality and experientially based meditational practices that showcased Hinduism as a scientifically verifiable religion. Mystical capabilities known as *siddhi*s, understood as by-products of yogic discipline, have for over a century been examined and explained through scientific means. H. C. Mathur, a former U.N. telecommunications expert, describes the capacity for reading minds, seeing hidden objects, healing the sick, and levitation as arising from a subconscious faculty of the brain that has been developed through discipline and practice. While *siddhi*s may seem miraculous (or faked) to the ordinary person, Mathur notes that "they are no more miracles than the scientific gadgets like radios, TVs or telephones which produce intelligent speech, music, or pictures out of nothing" (Mathur 1998, 3; see also Davis 1998, 10–11).

The nondualist's scientific approach to extraordinary events and capabilities has recently made inroads into classical theistic traditions in India, as well. As such, scientific language has become, for some, a means to legitimize an array of religious phenomena including communication with and actions of deities. Ursula Rao describes how terminology such as "proven fact" ascertained through "sensory experience" and "physical examination" has in north

India begun to replace traditional means of validation such as "belief" when referring to such events. As Rao puts it, scientific rhetoric has allowed traditional religious adherents to enter "the discourse of the elite and [has] deprived the elite of its claim to a language of superiority" (Rao 2002, 10). As she describes it, rationality can no longer be the domain of one privileged group, but of several groups in competition with and in seeming opposition to one another.

The miracle debate does not therefore simply rage between adherents of secular scientific and religious worldviews but can also be a fiercely contested intrareligious affair. As suggested above, those who hold the nondualist position within Hindu traditions can be disdainful of theistic Hindus who adhere to more conventional devotional practices. Neo-Vedantic gurus at the turn of the nineteenth century most starkly articulated this tension by deriding ritually based Hinduism and passionately arguing that science, not the miraculous, was the root of their tradition. This assertion did not necessarily rule out, however, the possibility of supernatural powers ascertained through yogic practices. Urban elite Sai Baba devotees likewise commonly associate miracle-prone traditional Hindu practices and beliefs with superstition yet align themselves, somewhat ironically, with a wonder-worker godman (Babb 1986, 200). On the North American front, miracle-prone Pentacostal groups who tend to dismiss postbiblical medieval (i.e., Catholic) miracles as "pagan supernaturalism" believe that, more recently, as phrased by Mark Corner, "the miraculous taps were turned on again on behalf of the Protestants" (Corner, 2005, 185).

Demonstrating a Christian perspective that stands in strict opposition to miraculous worldviews are mainline Protestant and Catholic theologians who, since the mid-nineteenth century, have ultimately agreed with Hume's assessment of miracles. Friedrich Schleiermacher (1768–1834), one of the first Protestant theologians to assert this position, argued that since nature is God's handiwork, any supposed violation would be a transgression of God's own work. Humanity's connection to and reliance upon God should not therefore be based upon miraculous events but upon a sense of awe and wonder invoked by nature taking its course (Corner 2005, 3). As stated by the Protestant theologian Rudolf Bultmann, the miraculous worldview reflected in the Bible, traditionally accepted by Christians, must be rejected by all believers who wish to stake their claim as members of contemporary—that is, rational—society: "[I]t is impossible to use electric light and the wireless and to avail ourselves of modern medical and surgical discoveries, and at the same time to believe in The New Testament world of miracles" (Bultmann 1972, 5, quoted in Corner 2005, 80).[14]

Although the pressures of scientific empiricism and religious rationalism have not ultimately succeeded in squelching modern conceptions of the miraculous, this is not to say that today's miraculous worldviews are not high maintenance. One could even argue that, in some contexts, miraculous worldviews are held against great odds and with considerable tenacity. As described by Robert Mullin, this tenaciousness seems due in part to the complexity of miracles, to the web of "cherished beliefs" woven into a belief in miracles. Upon challenging the existence of miracles, one also challenges the existence of the spiritual realm, the efficacy of prayer, and the availability of a personal God who cares for humanity (Mullin 1996, 4–5). Weaving a slightly different cherished web, the nondualists' miraculous view assumes a perception of a natural world that is imbued with spiritual energy and agency, one that lends deeper significance and contour to mundane understandings of the empirical world.

Skeptics' arguments for the nonexistence of miracles are no less complicated and no less wed to an array of related concerns. An antimiracle skeptic does not simply take a stance against irrationality but also against a host of troubles understood to be associated with irrationality and credulity. The Indian Science and Rationalists' Association, established in 1949 and known to many as "guru busters," explicitly aims to expose fraud among wonder-working gurus, astrological societies, and miracle events such as the internationally renowned Ganesh milk-drinking miracle in 1995. The stated purpose of the association is not simply to promote rationalism as an end in itself, but also to combat what they consider to be spiritualism's exploitation of the poor (Burns 1995). Joe Nickell, a former professional stage magician and private investigator who wrote *Looking for a Miracle: Weeping Icons, Relics, Stigmata, Visions and Healing Cures* likewise sets out, as he puts it, to expose "pious frauds." Nickell describes the task of exposing miracles as gravely serious due to the magnitude of miracle claims themselves as well as to the impact these claims have on the credulous masses. In the book's introduction, Nickell recounts the benefits that rational thought and enlightened endeavor have brought to our world, replacing "primitive authoritarianism" with "enlightened democracy." He concludes his statement with a sober reminder that "there are those whose beliefs and actions run counter to a rationalist ideal. Often seemingly contemptuous of science or, at best willing only grudgingly to acknowledge its benefits, they view the world in terms that hark back to the 'Dark Ages,' holding beliefs in myriad phenomena—from apparitions to weeping statues—that might generally be described as miraculous" (Nickell 1993, 9).

Based on the preceding accounts of classical theist and nondualist worldviews, it appears that modern supporters of the miraculous understand or contextualize science differently than Nickell but can hardly be considered "contemptuous" of it. The opposition Nickell sets up between secular scientific and miraculous views thus seems rather forced, and yet, as argued by the folklorist Gillian Bennett, who studies popular accounts of the supernatural in England, believers and skeptics often face one another in mutual incomprehension

(Bennett 1987, 15–16). In H. C. Mathur's introduction to his book exploring the *siddhi* powers of yogic adepts, he glumly notes this mutual incomprehension by describing how his work—mixing scientific theory with religion—has difficulty finding an audience: "The readers who are interested in Indian mythology with a religious bent of mind do not have enough knowledge of science to understand the theory of wave mechanics involved. On the other hand, readers with sufficient knowledge of science are just not interested in theological literature. So nobody found [my] first two books interesting" (Mathur 1998, vii).

Not only are staunch believers and skeptics typically indisposed to the perspectives of one another, but also these indispositions can be equally resolute. From today's mainstream rationalistic vantage point, it is easy to see a belief in miracles as tenacious. Yet when viewed from the opposing angle, from a context that allows for miracles, skeptics can seem just as loyal to culturally predetermined perceptions. Nickell, for instance, insists that he is objective in his investigation of miracles and does not decide ahead of time—based on wishful thinking—about their truth or falsity (1993, 9). Yet this assurance rings hollow when it directly follows the passage, partially quoted above, describing the perils of the "primitive authoritarian" miraculous worldview. In order to not be swayed by preconceived notions, Nickell suggests that miracle investigators make use of the principle of Occam's razor, which proposes that the simplest tenable explanation—the one laden with the fewest assumptions—is most likely the correct one (1993, 13). Based on Nickell's predisposition, it is clear from the outset that the most reasonable (i.e., simplest) explanation will be one that does not involve the supernatural. Yet, as argued by Bennett, an application of "common sense" in investigations of the supernatural can produce rationales far more elaborate than "simple" supernatural explanations themselves. Bennett offers a number of examples, including the rather extreme case of a man whose house was plagued by mysterious noises. His daughter, refusing to give in to the supernatural rationale of a haunting and apparently lacking any better reasoning, suggested that the sounds were "made by a fox which was trying to attract the hunt, so it would have an excuse to run about and get warm" (Bennett 1987, 14).[15]

My own experiences of similar—albeit less outlandish—"commonsense" explanations emerge from academic settings where I presented abbreviated versions of the chapter included in this volume. Briefly put, my presentations explored the subjective nature of the miraculous as experienced at a Hindu goddess temple in upstate New York. I argued that one person's routine experience is another's miracle and told the story of a friend of mine who, due to the touch of a guru, experienced an intense burning of the six chakra centers located up her spine—something she related to me later in textbook detail. My friend's religious training had been entirely in Christian and Jewish traditions, and thus she was not predisposed to the possibility of a guru's charged touch (known as *shaktipat*) or of the existence of chakra points in the body. As such, this experience, which may have been commonplace for others, seemed like a miracle to my friend. In the discussion following my presentation I was hoping to explore further how individual frameworks shape the meaning—not the actuality—of such events. Yet I was surprised at how, in both settings in which I told this story, some of the skeptics in the audience were eager to figure out the "real" cause of my friend's sensations. In one setting, a retired scholar deduced that since my friend was training to be a nun, she must have, at some point in her past, had access to a chart with the chakras on it. Although she may have forgotten, her subconscious mind fed her the pertinent information that led to her experience. In the other setting, a baffled participant suggested, half-humorously and after relinquishing his earlier hypothesis that her experience was imagined, that my friend was in fact experiencing menopausal hot flashes. Not everyone in the two settings seemed equally baffled by the event; my guess is that participants ran the gamut from true believers to true skeptics, with many in between. The vocal skeptics in the room seemed to take for granted that the yogic explanation was untenable and thus searched for another. If we applied Occam's razor to their "commonsense" explanations I'm not sure they would be the best choice. In the end, it was interesting for me to note how one person's routine experience is another's miracle is another's impossibility.

Without doubt, credulity can and has led to massive exploitation; "pious frauds" are not in short order, and the principle of Occam's razor does often militate against supernatural explanations. From a classical theist's perspective, a miraculous worldview must also answer to the problem of theodicy—how an omnipotent, beneficent God can be active in a world containing so much evil.[16] Defenders of miracles—often defenders of particular religious traditions, movements, and/or wonder workers—are often no less aware of the pitfalls of purported miracles than are their critics. Yet believers can speak eloquently, and to the right audience convincingly, on their behalf. As described by Cardinal Newman, the language often used to describe the realm of the miraculous is the language of faith, something that speaks from experience and often in defiance of an established logic. C. S. Lewis contends that miracles make sense in the same way that moments of inspired poetry can; in the most unexpected, jarring turns of phrase, poetry can illuminate if not create realities for those who understand: "[Miracles] will not be like unmetrical lumps of prose breaking the unity of a poem; they will be like that crowning metrical audacity which, though it may be paralleled nowhere else in the poem, yet, coming when it does, and effecting just what it effects, is (to those who understand) the supreme revelation of the unity in the poet's conception" (1947, 61).

Regardless of the credence one gives to modern miracle accounts, it is not hard to argue that they are—on a variety of levels—audacious, supremely revealing, and worthy of analysis. Because modern conceptions of the miraculous can never escape some measure of scrutiny, critique, and exaltation, they also cannot help but be a conundrum—especially if one stands far enough back to take in the full view. It is our hope that the chapters in this volume provide enough close scrutiny to illumine the critique and poetry embedded in South Asian conceptions of the miraculous; taken as a whole, we hope to paint a panorama that not only allows the reader to view the modern miraculous as a wondrous conundrum but to make some sense of it, as well.

Situating the Volume

Departing from generalizing theology, philosophy, and scripture—and thus from overt critique or support of miracles—the chapters that fill this volume offer, as a whole, a rather complicated view of the miraculous. Contributors' discussions and analyses of the modern miraculous tend to be anchored in particular narratives that invoke faces, names, and places that help to assuage abstraction. Whether viewed through the eyes of religious proponents or skeptics or conceived from the perspective of tentative born-again belief, savvy miracle marketing, or ethnographical consternation, the collection paints a richly variegated picture of a richly variegated subject matter. The organization of the volume into three parts, centered around contexts within which conceptions of South Asian modern miracles find their shape, is nevertheless an attempt to tease out important themes and trends that emerge when considering the modern miraculous in all its complexity.

Part 1, "Miracles and Modern Ambivalence," explores the complicated ways modern religious movements and sensibilities—both nondualist and classical theist—integrate and accommodate modern scientific worldviews. Here we find that in spite of the efforts of self-proclaimed modern rationalists to wrest the miraculous from their religious purview—and in so doing putting a safe distance between their religiosity and that of the credulous masses—miraculous experiences and interpretations find ways of creeping back in. Contributors to this section explore the dynamic and often unexpected ways that particular religious representatives of scientific rationalism—Neo-Vedantic swamis (in response to British colonial expectation), Christian medical missionaries, and mainstream urban sensibilities—selectively interact with, push against, and, in some instances, unwittingly (or covertly) give in to miraculous worldviews.

Part 2, "Making and Breaking Shrine Reputations," relates tales and experiences situated in particular localities associated with the miraculous—

shrine contexts and divinities known for (and, in various ways, dependent upon) miraculous events. In such instances, although miracle clientele can be indebted to mainstream modern sensibilities, purported miracles seem less challenged by institutional and modernist expectations. In comparison with part 1 and part 3, conundrums described in these chapters tend to be more nuanced, focusing on the often-confounding nature of divine activity in the world rather than skeptically confounded humanity. All three settings—rural Rajasthan, suburban middle-class Tamil Nadu, and upstate New York—involve Hindu traditions that differ significantly due to their location and clientele. As a result, each chapter describes varying conceptions of divine intervention that present a range of challenges for divinity as well as humanity.

The volume's final part, "Managing the Establishment: Miracles and Popular Expression," is similar to part 1 in its exploration of the fraught relationship between popular expectation and modernist/institutional reticence, but it views the interaction largely from the opposite perspective—from that of the miracle proponent. Here, miraculous worldviews are encased in and reliant upon modern institutions and media—constrained by post-Enlightenment rationalism, theological orthodoxy, or a combination thereof—that are, in turn, somewhat reliant upon miracles for their livelihood. We learn that popular support for miracles must often contend with the formalized contexts that help deliver them—and vice versa. This push-and-pull dynamic is viewed from the context of a Catholic pilgrimage site, of a Muslim healing center, and of advertisements for South Asian miracle workers aired on Zee TV. Those who experience, narrate, and promise miracles in these contexts uniquely respond to and in some ways defend against contrary expectations of the institutions and media to which they are, somewhat ironically, symbiotically tied.

Starting off the first part, "Miracles and Modern Ambivalence," Robin Rinehart discusses strategies employed by Swami Vivekananda and Swami Rama Tirtha—two late-nineteenth/early twentieth-century advocates of Neo-Vedanta—in making their case for Hinduism as a scientifically verifiable religion. Teaching at a time when Christian colonizers and missionaries accused popular Hindu practices of superstition, these men not only debunked purported miracles within the Hindu context but argued that such beliefs were not the "real" Hinduism. In spite of their efforts to keep the wondrous at bay, miracle accounts associated with these two men emerge when given the right conditions and distance from colonial suspicions. Set in the same time period are the interactions between Satnami-Christian and European and North American medical missionaries in Chhattisgarh, explored by Chad M. Bauman. Moving from Rinehart's view of an elite Indian response to colonial derision of Indian credulity, Bauman examines more closely colonial assumptions expressed and enacted by Western evangelicals. He finds that the missionary campaign to convince Satnami converts to forgo superstitious practices, particularly in the context of healing, was never complete and—more significantly—medical experts were not entirely devoid of their own reliance on supernatural forces in their healing practices. Bauman details how Western missionaries' assumed alliance with the purely modern was made possible through a heavily biased double standard. Sunil Goonasekera's chapter brings us to present-day Sri Lanka, to Hindu and Buddhist devotion to Kataragama Deiyo and to the immediate aftermath of the 2004 tsunami. The miracle narratives highlighted in this chapter delve into the accounts of two Western educated gentlemen who experience deliverance from calamity by a mysterious stranger and an alligator, respectively. Through their tales, these men wrestle with rationalistic expectations that are difficult to square with events that seem nothing short of miraculous. Discursive strategies such as sly suggestion and implication help them in their efforts to seem not taken in by something that has clearly taken them in. They articulate a fine balancing act, deftly executed in the face of conflicting impulses.

In part 2, "Making and Breaking Shrine Reputations," we begin with Ann Grodzins Gold's discussion of miracle narratives associated with deities residing at rural Rajasthani pilgrimage shrines. She compares these "real-time" narratives with a miracle story embedded in a women's worship tale from the same community. While shrine narratives tend to expose divinity as somewhat of a show-off—at times quarrelsome and bent upon garnering respect—Gold notes that the women's worship tale reflects a more remote, eternal divinity whose miraculous actions are, seemingly, taken for granted. Human wonder at such miracles can be less a sign of devoted affiliation than of obtuseness; yet it is human obtuseness that requires shrine deities to unleash powers in ways that shake their worlds—hopefully for the better. William P. Harman relates a temple-origin story from a middle-class suburb in central Tamil Nadu that hinges on a series of miraculous events. At the root of these events, many having to do with dream appearances of Lord Shiva, is the discovery of a sizeable Shiva lingam in a vacant lot in the form of a granite outcropping. Harman describes not only how such temple miracle accounts give power and credibility to the shrine, but explores the mechanisms that give the narrative telling its force and, indeed, a sacred reality its own that is difficult to discount—even in its modern suburban setting and in the eyes of a non-native ethnographer. My chapter relates miracle stories emergent at a Hindu temple in the town of Rush in upstate New York. The temple, whose members hail from a variety of backgrounds, has built a reputation for miraculous events and experiences. Founded on the Srividya tantric tradition that works to tap divine energy through ritual, the Rush temple also employs Neo-Vedantic scientific terminology to explain ritual energy and mystical experiences. I explore inherent tensions and resolutions in this setting where devotion is offered to a (partially) transcendent temple goddess and mystical and ritually powerful events are understood as scientifically verifiable.

Selva J. Raj begins the volume's final part, "Managing the Establishment: Miracles and Popular Expression," by guiding the reader through the miraculous as experienced at a Catholic healing shrine dedicated to St. Anthony and located in the rural village of Uvari in Tamil Nadu. The Uvari shrine, known for offering relief to victims of possession, attracts a significant number of Hindu as well as Catholic pilgrims. Raj relates two case studies of supernatural possession and healing and elaborates upon the ecumenical nature not only of the clientele but of the supernatural entities responsible for possession and healing. Experiencing significant strain from such complicated human-divine interactions are rationally minded Catholic clergy who nonetheless stand to gain from pilgrimage traffic to their religious site. Joyce Burkhalter Flueckiger tells stories of *karamat*—miraculous feats performed by Sufi saints—as related by a Sufi healer and her husband in the south Indian city of Hyderabad. Although a reputation for wondrous powers can elevate individuals to sainthood, it can also—if their story is framed the wrong way according to Islamic theology—brand them as heretics. Flueckiger describes how storytellers and miracle workers, in order to keep *karamat* within the realm of orthodoxy, must strike a balance between secrecy and revelation in their accounts of the miraculous. Neelima Shukla-Bhatt recounts the content and reception of television advertisements produced on behalf of three modern-day miracle workers, advertisements aired in North America and the United Kingdom. These commercials, guaranteeing immediate relief from life's problems, deftly conjure up nostalgia for traditional religious and cultural modes while incorporating new world images and business strategies. The reception of these ads is equally mixed: the fact that they air frequently suggests a certain appeal to segments of the diaspora community. Yet strong disdain, bandied about on Internet sites, tells another side of the story.

Notes

My thanks to Selva Raj for his insightful reflections and comments, which I have incorporated into this introduction. Thanks also to our anonymous reviewers for their keen suggestions and encouragement. I gladly accept responsibility for all remaining oversights.

1. The folklorist Gillian Bennett notes that this avoidance of the supernatural results in a vicious circle of sorts: no one will tackle the subject because it is disreputable, and it remains disreputable because no one will tackle it (1987, 13).

2. Selva Raj helped explain to me the finer points of *putumai*. See also Davis (1998, 4, 8).

3. The folklorist Jan Harold Brunvand suggests a similar set of necessary conditions for narratives to be urban legends that are survivable in our culture. They must have a strong story appeal, have a foundation in actual belief, and have a meaningful message or moral (1981, 10). Likewise Benedicta Ward notes that early Christian texts portray miracles as less wondrous than meaningful. Events such as healings or surprisingly ethical behavior of animals were considered significant because they were signs of God's Kingdom, not because they broke with any preset law of nature. Since these actions were celebrated as a "special manifestation of the powers of heaven, which constitute the world at all times," the question of "how" they occurred was not as important as "why" (1992, 540–42).

4. See Lingis 1994 for a discussion of science along these lines. Lingis argues that the basis for building community is shared reason.

5. For more on the post-Enlightenment shift that conceived of nature as a closed rather than an open system, see Nichols 2002.

6. Kirin Narayan's article about European and North American perceptions of Hindu holy men nicely fleshes out the propensity to project all things mysterious and strange onto Indian religious traditions. Amartya Sen furthermore argues that colonial associations of India with religiosity—for better and for worse—has affected India's self-perception and undermined the rationalist strains of Indian intellectual traditions. (See also Davis 1998, 8, and Corner 2005, 21.)

7. Similar to Bynum's reference to medieval miracles is Babb's remark that within this Hindu worldview a miraculous event is so naturally anticipated that it "lacks any element of truly radical surprise" (1986, 177).

8. Of the Americans polled, 90 percent of the Christians said they believed in miracles in comparison to 46 percent of non-Christians polled. These statistics also reflect a possible increase in a belief in miracles since the 1995 *Time Magazine* poll that found that 69 percent of Americans believe in miracles (Mullin 1996, 262–64).

9. In some cases, extraordinary powers are attributed to non-natural forces as a means to give them—and those who display them—special significance. For instance, devotees of the godman Sai Baba consider his miraculous powers to be intrinsic to his nature rather than mere *siddhi* powers gained naturally through human accomplishment and discipline. Some skeptics who accuse Sai Baba of being a fraud argue derisively that his powers are mere *siddhi*s and not miraculous (Babb 1986, 188, 192).

10. For a discussion of Wallace's unheralded contribution to Darwin's theory of evolution, see Shermer 2006, 202.

11. The folklorist Gillian Bennett likewise argues that folklore events associated with the supernatural are not necessarily "false" but are considered folklore because they are not accepted by mainstream society. To make her point, she lists a number of folk practices such as leaving apple rings and bread to mold for application on wounds and agricultural practices having to do with the waxing and waning of the moon, all of which ended up having scientific merit (1987, 12).

12. Griffin prefers the term "apparent precognition" to foreknowledge, since the capacity to know events in advance, he argues, has not to do with actually knowing

things before they happen but with the ability to transcend typical limitations of time in the same way that other paranormal capacities demonstrate the ability to transcend the typical constrictions of space (1997, 90).

13. The deistic position understands divinity as responsible for the creation of the world but maintains that, once the world is created, divinity stands remote from and unengaged in the natural realm. I do not include this position in my various descriptions, since it logically makes no room for the miraculous.

14. Interestingly, Bultmann here juxtaposes modern inventions with miraculous worldviews to argue for the latter's obsoleteness. In comparison, H. C. Mathur and Alfred Russel Wallace, as noted earlier, describe technological advances to argue that anything is possible—even a seemingly supernatural event—when one considers the unforeseen astonishing appearance of technological gadgetry.

15. See Corner for a similar suggestion that the most "reasonable" explanation for an event can, at times, be a supernatural explanation (2005, 24–28).

16. As described by the philosophers David and Randal Basinger, classical theists cannot have it both ways: they cannot maintain a belief in an omnipotent God capable of acting in the world while also accounting for God's goodness in the presence of evil. God's relationship to and responsibility for evil must also be accounted for (1986, 117). The theologian Mark Corner attempts to resolve the problem of theodicy within a miraculous worldview by proposing that God's omniscience is limited. He reasons that since, according to classical theology, God does not determine human choice, God cannot always know future events. Corner proposes an analogy in which God is a chess player in life's game of chess. Although unable to predict humanity's next move, God can nonetheless reach into the game to make moves that steer the game's course (2005, 55–57).

References

Babb, Lawrence. 1986. *Redemptive Encounters: Three Modern Styles in the Hindu Tradition*. Berkeley and Los Angeles: University of California Press.

Basinger, David, and Randal Basinger. 1986. *Philosophy and Miracle: The Contemporary Debate*. Problems in Contemporary Philosophy, vol. 2. Lewiston, NY: Edwin Mellen Press.

Bennett, Gillian. 1987. *Traditions of Belief: Women and the Supernatural*. London: Penguin.

Brunvand, Jan Harold. 1981. *The Vanishing Hitchhiker: American Urban Legends and their Meanings*. New York: W. W. Norton and Company.

Bultmann, Rudolf. 1972. "New Testament and Mythology." In *Kerygma and Myth*, edited by H. W. Bartsch. London: Society for the Propogation of Christian Knowledge.

Burns, John. 1995. "India's 'Guru Busters' Debunk All That's Mystical." *New York Times*, October 10.

Bynum, Carolyn Walker. "Wonder." *American Historical Review* 102, no. 1:1–26.

Corner, Mark. 2005. *Signs of God: Miracles and Their Interpretation.* Hampshire, England: Ashgate.

Davis, Richard. 1998. "Introduction: Miracles as Social Acts." In *Images, Miracles, and Authority in Asian Religious Traditions*, edited by Richard Davis, 1–22. Boulder, CO: Westview Press.

Griffin, David Ray. 1997. *Parapsychology, Philosophy, and Spirituality: A Postmodern Exploration.* Albany: State University of New York Press.

Hume, David. [1748] 1989. "Of Miracles." In *Miracles*, edited by Richard Swineburne, 23–40. New York: Macmillan.

Lewis, C. S. 1947. *Miracles: A Preliminary Study.* New York: Macmillan.

Lingis, Alphonso. 1994. *The Community of Those Who Have Nothing in Common.* Bloomington: Indiana University Press.

Mathur, H. C. 1998. *Siddhi: The Science of Supernatural Powers.* New Delhi: Shree Publishing House.

Mullin, Robert Bruce. 1996. *Miracles and the Modern Religious Imagination.* New Haven, CT: Yale University Press.

Narayan, Kirin. 1993. "Refractions of the Field at Home: American Representations of Hindu Holy Men in the 19th and 20th Centuries." *Cultural Anthropology* 8, no. 4:476–509.

Nichols, Terence L. 2002. "Miracles in Science and Theology." *Zygon* 37, no. 3:703–15.

Nickell, Joe. 1993. *Looking for a Miracle: Weeping Icons, Relics, Stigmata, Visions and Healing Cures.* New York: Prometheus Books.

Rao, Ursula. 2002. "How to Prove Divinities? Experiencing and Defending Divine Agency in a Modern Indian Space." *Religion* 32:3–11.

Schleiermacher, Friedrich. 1976. *The Christian Faith.* Edited by H. R. Mackintosh and J. S. Stewart. Edinburgh: T. and T. Clark.

Sen, Amartya. 1993. "India and the West: Our Distortions and Their Consequences." *New Republic*, June, 27–34.

Sered, Susan Starr. 2003. "Afterword: Lexicons of the Supernatural." *Anthropological Forum* 13, no. 2:213–18.

Shermer, Michael. 2006. *In Darwin's Shadow: The Life and Science of Alfred Russel Wallace.* New York: Oxford University Press.

Van der Veer, Peter. 2001. *Imperial Encounters: Religion and Modernity in India and Britain.* Princeton, NJ: Princeton University Press.

Wallace, Alfred Russel. [1896] 1975. *Miracles and Modern Spiritualism.* New York: Arno Press.

Ward, Benedicta. 1992. *Signs and Wonders: Saints, Miracles, and Prayers from the 4th Century to the 14th.* Hampshire, England: Variorum.

PART I

Miracles and Modern Ambivalence

CHAPTER TWO

The Neo-Vedanta Miracle

ROBIN RINEHART

Can miracles be proven? If so, what, if anything, do miracles themselves prove? What relevance do miracles have to spiritual advancement? Such questions recur throughout the works of Swami Vivekananda and Swami Rama Tirtha, two late nineteenth-century/early twentieth-century advocates of Neo-Vedanta. In their all-too-brief lives, both swamis traveled and lectured throughout the United States and India, and both sought to create a kind of "practical" Vedanta that captured what they considered to be the essential core not just of Hinduism, but also of all the religions of the world. And, they argued, this Vedanta did not contradict any principles of science. Each proposed a new way to define and evaluate miracles, and their assessment of miracles was a key component in a rhetoric that sought to demonstrate that their Practical Vedanta could provide a model for every aspect of life.

Both swamis received Western education in colonial India. Swami Vivekananda (1863–1902) is the better known of the two. Raised in Bengal, he was attracted to the teachings of the Brahmo Samaj as a young man, but became a close disciple of Ramakrishna (1836–86), and then helped establish the Ramakrishna Mission in his guru's memory. Swami Vivekananda's lectures on Hinduism at the Chicago World's Parliament of Religions in 1893 won him fame in the United States and India. During his travels in the United States, he also established branches of the Vedanta Society, many of which are still in existence. It was he who first spoke of "Practical Vedanta"; Swami Rama Tirtha apparently adopted the term later.

Swami Rama Tirtha (1873–1906) was a somewhat younger contemporary of Swami Vivekananda. A Punjabi Brahmin from a small village who became a mathematics professor, he began his career as a religious leader lecturing

FIGURE 2.1. Swami Vivekananda, 1863–1902. Photo courtesy of the Vedanta Archives.

about Krishna devotion for the Sanatana Dharma Sabha ("Eternal Dharma Society"—a loosely affiliated set of organizations in north India that sought to defend traditional devotional Hinduism against the reforms of groups such as the Arya Samaj, which opposed image worship). His passionate devotion to Krishna gradually gave way to the nondual approach of Advaita Vedanta, and he became a renouncer around 1900. Like Swami Vivekananda, Swami Rama Tirtha initiated himself as a sannyasin or renunciant. He too traveled outside India—in fact, the maharaja of Tehri sent him to Japan after hearing there was to be another parliament of religions there, and hoped that Swami Rama Tirtha could achieve the same fame as had Swami Vivekananda. The story about another parliament of religions turned out to be a false rumor, but the

FIGURE 2.2. Swami Rama Tirtha, 1873–1906. Photo courtesy of the Vedanta Archives.

journey to Japan proved fortuitous, for there Swami Rama Tirtha cast his for-
tunes with an Indian circus troupe on its way to the United States. He ended
up spending a couple of years in the United States giving lectures, mainly on
the West Coast. When he returned to India, the swami's followers encouraged
him to take a public role as a religious leader and found some sort of organization, but he was uncomfortable with such plans and soon retired to the
Himalayas. He drowned while bathing in a river in 1906 at the age of thirty-
three. His followers later established the Swami Rama Tirtha Mission, which,
like the Ramakrishna Mission, advocates social service as part of individual
spiritual practice.

Swami Vivekananda and Swami Rama Tirtha apparently met briefly in
Lahore in 1897 when Swami Vivekananda gave a lecture there. Otherwise,
there is no formal connection between the two or the organizations that carry
on their work. The extent to which Swami Rama Tirtha's views about Vedanta
may have been influenced by Swami Vivekananda is unclear. According to his
early biographers, Swami Rama Tirtha's focus shifted from Krishna devotion

to Vedanta under the influence of Swami Madhva Tirtha, who was the head of the Dwarka Monastery, said to have been established by the great Advaita philosopher Shankara. Still, as their ideas about miracles will show, the two swamis thought along similar lines. Certainly the fact that Swami Rama Tirtha traveled abroad in hopes of addressing a parliament of religions suggests that he had some thought of duplicating Swami Vivekananda's successes.

For the followers of both swamis, the fact that each spent time lecturing in the United States and attracted media attention in both the United States and India is very important. The collected works of each swami contain a large number of lectures, newspaper reports, and other materials from travels abroad. Many of the newspaper articles in particular report question-and-answer sessions in which members of American audiences asked the swamis what they thought about particular aspects of Christianity. In many of their lectures, the swamis insisted that Practical Vedanta already contained whatever relevant insights Christianity might have for the spiritual seeker. American audiences were also curious to find out whether the swamis could perform the kinds of miracles (such as levitation) popularly attributed to Indian yogis. In an era in which many Americans perceived a growing rift between religion and science, both the power to perform miracles and the power to disprove claims of miracles were central to debates about claims to religious truths.

Both Swami Vivekananda and Swami Rama Tirtha advocated a point of view that scholars now typically term Neo-Vedanta—and which the swamis themselves called Practical Vedanta. By "Practical" they meant that it was a Vedanta suited for the modern world, useful and applicable to every part of life. As such, they distinguished it from classical forms of nondual or Advaita Vedanta philosophy, the implication being that such classical forms were more given to arcane philosophical disputation than to providing a model for daily activities. Of particular importance was their view that Practical Vedanta, by asserting the fundamental unity of all humankind, established the ethical basis for social service (a central activity of both the Ramakrishna Mission and the Swami Rama Tirtha Mission). Another key component of their Practical Vedanta was that it was suitable for everyone in the world, not just Hindus; in fact, the swamis both argued that Practical Vedanta was at the heart of all religion. For their followers, the records of the swamis' successes abroad provide convincing evidence for the argument that their teachings were applicable beyond the realm of India.

In explaining Practical Vedanta, both swamis emphasized that it was not a faith, but rather something akin to a scientific method. They asked their audiences to test the hypotheses they presented and confirm them for themselves, and not just accept Practical Vedanta on the swamis' authority. This notion of reproducible results is central to their understanding of miracles, which is based in part on a reinterpretation that challenges the typical way miracles are defined. The *Oxford English Dictionary* defines a miracle as: a marvelous event occurring within human experience, which cannot have been brought about by human power or by the operation of any natural agency, and must therefore be ascribed to the special intervention of the Deity or of some supernatural being; chiefly, an act (e.g., of healing) exhibiting control over the laws of nature, and serving as evidence that the agent is either divine or is specially favored by God (*Compact Edition of the Oxford English Dictionary*, S.V. "miracle").

In the context of Practical Vedanta, the key elements of this definition are that miracles "cannot be brought about by human power or natural agency" and that they demonstrate "control over the laws of nature." Thus according to a standard definition, a person who performs a miracle is not doing it himself or herself, unless he or she is divine or favored by God. At issue here is what powers humans are capable of attaining, what humans know about the laws of nature, and the nature of divinity itself. From the Practical Vedanta standpoint, all humans have within them the *atman* or eternal soul that is a part of the underlying unity of all creation, and are therefore all themselves divine if they realize their true nature. Thus, an apparent miracle need not depend on a deity's special intervention, but instead could be performed by a human. In addition, both swamis taught that the practice of yoga, which they likened to a science, brought an understanding of and control over the body and nature far beyond that of the ordinary human being. What might seem like a miracle to an ordinary person could be explained by laws that only an accomplished practitioner of Practical Vedanta could understand and control. Both points are crucial to the interpretive model the swamis presented for assessing miracle claims. Neither was willing to accept that an event deemed a miracle might remain a conundrum—in the Practical Vedanta view, there was an explanation for everything, however miraculous it might seem to the ordinary person. Miracles then could only lie in the eye of the beholder, and any such beholders would by Practical Vedanta's definition necessarily have misinterpreted the "miracles" they perceived, because they did not understand the laws according to which the seeming miracle was performed. When interpreters of religious miracles assert that a miracle serves as evidence of supernatural or divine power, and the miracle's power therefore to some extent lies in its very inexplicability, they are in part asking for an act of faith in accepting the miracle as miracle as well as the power behind the miracle. In contrast, the swamis' arguments that apparent miracles can be explained according to Practical Vedanta appears designed to strike at the very foundation of religious notions of divine power predicated on faith over provability.

In 1894, when an American newspaper requested that Swami Vivekananda work a miracle to prove his religion, he replied:

> I cannot comply with the request of the news to work a miracle in proof of my religion. . . . In the first place, I am no miracle worker, and in the second place the pure Hindoo religion I profess is not based on miracles. We do not recognize such a thing as miracles. There are wonders wrought beyond our five senses, but they are operated by some law. Our religion has nothing to do with them. Most of the strange things which are done in India and reported in the foreign papers are sleight-of-hand tricks or hypnotic illusions. They are not the performances of the wise men. These do not go about the country performing their wonders in the market places for pay. They can be seen and known only by those who seek to know the truth, and not moved by childish curiosity. (Vivekananda 1964–68, 3:495–96)

Thus, for Swami Vivekananda, the pure Hindu religion is not based on miracles—any apparent wonders are caused by some law, and anyone who can perform real wonders will not be doing so in public. The newspaper presumably was thinking of the kinds of "miracles" popularly attributed to Indian yogis, and therefore associating Hinduism itself with such feats. Swami Vivekananda, however, was careful to point out that such notions of Hinduism were a misunderstanding, and that in its true form, Hinduism was governed not by a faith engendered by miracles, but by laws. He also distinguished between apparent miracles that are really "sleight-of-hand tricks" and "the performances of the wise men." Thus, he was suggesting that there are miracles—albeit caused by some law—that wise men or "truth-seekers" can perform.

Both Swami Vivekananda and Swami Rama Tirtha described yoga as a type of science, a time-tested technique that one could follow to gain spiritual insight. Following the classical Indian understanding of yoga and the powers attained through yoga (known as *siddhis*), they both asserted that the yogi at certain stages in his or her practice could perform feats that appear to exhibit control over nature. For example, in a lecture he gave in Faizabad in 1905, Swami Rama Tirtha described some of the powers he attained during the months after he had left his teaching post in Lahore, but before he took the vows of renunciation or *sannyasa*. He was wandering in the Himalayas, and found that for about six months, seemingly miraculous things happened. If he needed a particular book, someone would just bring it to him. He explained, in his typical style of referring to himself in the third person, "At that time Rama's condition was so much changed that if he ordered air to blow, it would start blowing. All the elements of nature would obey" (Rama Tirtha 1978–90, 4:299). Importantly, he explained, anyone could acquire the same power—so there was nothing truly miraculous about it after all, and any validation of such an apparent miracle was to come from replicating his results and not through faith in the swami's own powers.

In his explanations of Practical Vedanta, Swami Rama Tirtha often drew on his mathematics background; he told one audience that in order to understand Vedanta, one must start at the beginning, just as one cannot explain Euclid's forty-seventh proposition without the listener knowing the previous ones. He told an American audience, "A science should not be attacked in a state of confusion; it ought to be attacked systematically, with method, with order. This Vedanta Philosophy, this Religion, is a religion as well as a science. In Europe you have a conflict between Science and Religion, but this teaching which Rama brings to you reconciles them; in fact it reconciles Philosophy, Science and Religion" (Rama Tirtha 1978–90, 3:99). Swami Rama Tirtha was effectively arguing for a sort of science of yoga, or as he put it, a science of religion that explained both material and spiritual laws. In one lecture, he noted that one could prove the reality of the soul or *atman* through the experience of deep sleep, but provided no further details about how to go about this (4:25–26). He once wrote that "religious experiences are as convincing as any direct sensible experience can be, and they are, as a rule, much more convincing than results established by mere logic ever were" (7:308). Thus one's own spiritual experience, or experiments, observations, induction and deduction, using the analogy with science, are the best form of proof of Vedanta—not miracles.

Swami Vivekananda similarly linked yoga and science. During a discussion of meditation, someone asked him about a person who had power over his body such that he could resist injury when someone hit him. The swami answered that if someone had stumbled on this power by chance, it might appear to be a miracle, but that if someone learned this power scientifically, it is yoga (Vivekananda 1964–96, 4:229). Swami Vivekananda explained, "I have seen people healed by the power of mind. There is the miracle worker. We say he prays and the man is healed. Another man says, 'Not at all. It is just the power of the mind. The man is scientific. He knows what he is about'" (4:230). In an interview with a Memphis newspaper, whose reporter asked him about yogis who can live in a state of suspended animation, Swami Vivekananda proposed that the yogis had developed the technique to do so by observing hibernating animals (5:184). Thus, a yogi who could survive long periods of time buried underground was not performing a miracle, but had perfected a technique "under the operation of natural laws" already available to other creatures in the natural world (5:183). Miracles, therefore, are in the eye of the beholder: the scientific person understands that yoga operates according to laws of nature of which the ordinary person is unaware. In his writings on raja yoga, Swami Vivekananda explained, "When the Yogi becomes perfect, there will be nothing in nature not under his control. If he orders the gods or the souls of the departed to come, they will come at his bidding. All the forces of nature will obey him as slaves. When the ignorant see these powers of the Yogi, they call them the miracles" (1:148).

Both the witness of such "miracles" and the person who acquires such powers through yoga run the risk of being diverted from the goal of Practical Vedanta—self-knowledge. Swami Vivekananda explained that his teacher Ramakrishna had taught him of the dangers of miracles.

> . . . Shri Ramakrishna used to disparage these supernatural powers; his teaching was that one cannot attain to the supreme truth if the mind is diverted to the manifestation of these powers. The human mind, however, is so weak that, not to speak of householders, even ninety per cent of the Sadhus happen to be votaries of these powers. In the West, men are lost in wonderment if they come across such miracles. It is only because Shri Ramakrishna has mercifully made us understand the evil of these powers as being hindrances to real spirituality that we are able to take them at their proper value. (6:515–16)

Swami Rama Tirtha too cautioned against "miracles" that served no long-term spiritual goals, or even short-term gain. In a San Francisco lecture, he described a friend in India who could read and transcribe books on mathematics while blindfolded. The swami did accept that this was possible, but of little use, since the friend was neither holy nor happy (Rama Tirtha 1978–90, 2:39). He told another story of a man who spent seventeen years acquiring the power to walk on water, only to be told by a "real saint" that he had wasted seventeen years acquiring a power worth precisely two cents, the cost of being ferried across a river (2:40)—an impractical miracle indeed.

During their travels in the United States, both Swami Vivekananda and Swami Rama Tirtha were often asked about the claims of religious movements then popular in the United States. The late nineteenth and early twentieth centuries were a time of great interest in alternative forms of spirituality and healing, many of which explicitly claimed to unite religion and science. The discovery of magnetism, and Franz Mesmer's ideas about animal magnetism, which date to the late eighteenth century in Austria, had spawned a thriving trade in magnetic healing. Interest in spiritualism had swept the country after the Fox sisters asserted in the mid-nineteenth century that they were communicating with the spirit of a peddler murdered years earlier in their New York home. Spiritualist mediums offered messages from the dead through séances, spirit writing, spirit painting, and the occasional materialization. While much of this activity was the subject of media ridicule (and a fair number of mediums were exposed as frauds), noted Spiritualists such as Sir Arthur Conan Doyle argued that they had scientific proof that they could communicate with the spirits of the dead (Doyle 1926). These were also the early decades of Christian Science, which Mary Baker Eddy founded in 1875 after Bible reading cured her of injuries suffered in a fall. Events that might earlier have been deemed miracles, such as Mary Baker Eddy's healing, were now being seen as some kind of science—that is, something fully explainable and within ordinary human beings' power. Enthusiasts for many of these new movements were typically the main audience for swamis such as those under our consideration.

Although Christian Science, as its name suggests, advocates a scientific approach to religion, Swami Rama Tirtha ranked its healing on roughly the same level as that of the Indian saint who could walk on water. He saw Christian Science healing as ultimately doomed to failure (because of what he believed to be its misguided emphasis on the physical body), and no more effective than keeping someone awake artificially for hours (Rama Tirtha 1978–90, 7:99). Swami Rama Tirtha also questioned the practicality of attaining psychic powers, then a very popular pursuit and the topic of many questions from his American audiences, so much so that he prepared a lecture entitled "True Spirituality and the Psychic Powers" while he was in San Francisco. In this lecture, he explained that there are three worlds: the gross material world or *pratyaksa samsara*, the psychic/astral world or *manasik samsara* (which he likened to the Christian heaven and hell, Muslim paradise, and Hindu heaven or *swarga*), and the unknown world or *avijnata samsara*, which can be approached to a limited extent through deep sleep. The communication with the dead so prized by spiritualists was a matter of the realm of the psychic or astral world, and nothing particularly special in terms of spiritual progress (2:38–39). One could train to acquire such powers much as one might train to be an engineer (2:44); such powers were useful only within the material world. In another lecture on Vedanta and hypnotism, he similarly argued that being hypnotized was not a profound spiritual experience (3:90–93). Many of the events deemed miracles, then, were not important to Practical Vedanta, and clearly of a lower order of spirituality. Nonetheless, he did assert that movements such as Christian Science and Spiritualism were imbibing the spirit of Vedanta (2:126), insofar as they would eventually lead people to explore what he believed to be the higher level of Vedantic truth.

Swami Vivekananda too was dismissive of many popular American spiritual pursuits, though at the prompting of Josephine McLeod, an American admirer, he underwent magnetic healing therapy. In an 1899 letter to his disciple Sara Bull, he indicated a skeptical attitude: "Joe has unearthed a magnetic healing woman. We are both under her treatment. Joe thinks she is pulling me up splendidly. On her has been worked a miracle, she claims. Whether it is magnetic healing, California ozone, or the end of the present spell of bad Karma, I am improving" (Vivekananda 1964–96, 8:486). He wrote from Boston to his brother disciples of Ramakrishna in India that he had not reached a final conclusion on the spiritualists' claim to communicate with the dead, but he was leaning toward finding their work a hoax (6:270).

In the same letter, he was dismissive of American spirituality as a whole: "This is a thoroughly materialistic country. The people of this Christian land will recognise religion only if you can cure diseases, work miracles, and open up avenues to money; and they understand little of anything else" (6:270).

In addition to asking the swamis to perform miracles themselves, Americans also asked them what they thought about the miracles central to Christianity, such as Jesus's birth to a virgin mother, his acts of healing, and his resurrection. Swami Rama Tirtha's explanation of the virgin birth was that once when Mary and Joseph were deep in samadhi or spiritual absorption, they conceived a child, but forgot what they had done when they emerged from the spiritual state. "The Laws of Nature," suggested the Swami gently, "were at that time just the same as they are now . . ." (Rama Tirtha 1978–90, 1:314–16). When asked about Jesus's crucifixion and resurrection, Swami Rama Tirtha opined that Jesus, like his parents when he was conceived, was in a state of samadhi when he was crucified. But he did not die on the cross; instead, he went to Kashmir and there acquired teachings (1:195).[1] In the question-and-answer session following a lecture, Swami Vivekananda was once asked if he believed in Christ's resurrection. He replied that since Jesus was God incarnate, he could not really be killed, and the body that was crucified was only "a semblance, a mirage" (Vivekananda 1964–96, 1:328). The audience member then suggested that if Jesus had been able to produce a body that was a mirage, that in and of itself would have been "the greatest miracle of all." Swami Vivekananda responded, "I look upon miracles as the greatest stumbling blocks in the way of truth. When the disciples of Buddha told him of a man who had performed a so-called miracle . . . he . . . told them never to build their faith on miracles, but to look for truth in everlasting principles. . . . Miracles are only stumbling-blocks" (1:328). Thus, in evaluating the virgin birth and crucifixion of Jesus, both swamis proposed that these seeming miracles were really explainable according to laws of nature—Swami Rama Tirtha, for example, argued that the laws of nature do not allow for virgin birth, and that the resurrection could not have happened, because Jesus did not die on the cross. Swami Vivekananda's explanation of the crucifixion differed in that he argued that Jesus was not an ordinary, embodied human being, but an incarnation, though subject to particular laws. Neither Swami believed that miracles should be the basis for faith, or indeed even that faith should be the goal of spiritual practice.

Swami Rama Tirtha addressed the issue of Jesus and miracles in another American lecture on Vedanta. The swami was fond of saying that since everyone shared in the same essential soul, everyone effectively was Jesus, the Buddha, Muhammad, and so on. Some Christians objected to Swami Rama Tirtha comparing himself to Jesus, and demanded that he prove his claim by performing miracles as had Jesus. The swami first noted that performing miracles did not necessarily make people believe in Jesus, and that any miracles performed by a person through bodily action were irrelevant to divinity in any case. He feared that if he were to perform miracles, people would "make a God of this body" when instead they should make a god of their own selves and not look to some outside source of authority. "Rama does not wish to take away your freedom by working miracles and imposing this particular personality on you. Rama should not enslave you and take away your independence, as was done by the previous prophets" (Rama Tirtha 1978–90, 3:109–10). The swami had concluded that miracles do not really make anyone believe anything (though it should be noted he did not deny the possibility that he could perform acts his audience would deem miracles)—thus, they are not practical in terms of generating a faith that can lead to spiritual advancement through a gradual understanding of the laws of nature. Even if bodily miracles are possible, they have no connection with one's true identity, the self or *atman*. Those who do perform miracles mislead people into becoming focused on them as persons rather than on the truths they have discovered.

Similarly, in a lecture on devotional or bhakti yoga, Swami Vivekananda argued that Christ's miracles were "low, vulgar things that He could not help doing because He was among vulgar beings." Any fool can perform miraculous healings, said the swami; "these are powers, truly, but often demoniacal powers" (Vivekananda 1964–96, 4:32–33).

Swami Vivekananda also argued that attempting to prove biblical miracles through science would pose an insurmountable challenge to traditional Christian ideas about God's power. He described a conversation he had had with a Christian missionary while both were on a ship sailing the Red Sea. The missionary explained that science could now prove that Moses had parted the Red Sea to lead his people out of Egypt. Swami Vivekananda, however, pointed out that if a scientific explanation could show that the sea parted in accordance with some natural law, then the story lost some of its force, because the parting of the sea could no longer be directly attributed to God's great power. He explained, "A great dilemma!—If they are opposed to science, those miracles are mere myths, and your religion is false. And even if they are borne out by science, the glory of your god is superfluous, and they are just like any other natural phenomena" (7:345).

For both swamis, miracles that brought about bodily transformations, such as healing, were certainly possible but unimpressive insofar as they made no contribution towards the Vedanta goal of transcending bodily identity and gaining direct knowledge of the eternal soul. And because such apparent miracles were to their understanding fully explicable, they were not particularly miraculous after all. Miracles meant to demonstrate the power and greatness of God, such as the parting of the Red Sea, were compelling only if they were indeed "miraculous" or inexplicable in some way; asserting a scientific explanation for them robbed either the miracle itself or the god of his power. Both swamis' discussions of miracles in the context of Christianity show that Americans were keen for them to show some evidence of their own powers to prove their claims about Vedanta, and that they were interested to learn what the swamis thought about Christianity and its miracles. But both suggested that miracles, or events that appear to be miracles, are obstacles to genuine spiritual realization. There is certainly an implicit critique of Christianity in such comments, given the centrality of Christian belief in the miracle of Christ's virgin birth, crucifixion, and resurrection.

While many of the two swamis' comments on miracles are tailored to the concerns of American audiences—largely because records of their travels in the United States form substantial portions of both their recorded works—it is important to note that their views on miracles are also part of late nineteenth-century and early twentieth-century colonial Indian religious discourse. Both swamis were familiar with some of the major Hindu reform movements of their day, such as the Brahmo Samaj and the Arya Samaj. The Practical Vedanta teachings the two swamis developed addressed the same issues highlighted by these and many other Indian religious reformers (such as education and reform of particular social practices) and followed the typical reform strategy of identifying key aspects of Hinduism as comprising its essence, and discarding others.[2] The Arya Samaj, for example, argued that the Vedas were the essence of Hinduism, and that any practice not in accord with the Vedas must be discarded. Within the swamis' Practical Vedanta framework, just as they rejected the miracle claims of Christianity, they could similarly explain or reject the miraculous tales of Hindu mythology.

For these two advocates of Practical Vedanta, then, there are various events that people—whether in the United States or India—may judge to be miracles. What is significant about such events is that despite their apparent inexplicability, Practical Vedanta, with its "scientific" approach to spirituality, purports to explain them thoroughly. Thus miracles can be "proven" to exist insofar as certain people perceive particular events to be miracles, but by proving them—or explaining how they occurred—Practical Vedanta makes the miracles lose their miraculous quality. Some people can acquire seemingly miraculous powers and walk on water and the like—but this has no connection with practical or true spirituality. Some religions, notably Christianity, may base their theology on miracles, but those events may be explained in other ways not involving the notion of miracles. A religion based on miracles is not as effective as a religion based on the scientific method of Practical Vedanta, which explains miracles with its advanced understanding of both the material and the spiritual. Once such miracles are demonstrated to be the result of powers fully explicable through the acquisition of yogic power, they no longer carry any compelling weight in convincing a person to have faith;

instead, their power is presented as something convincing only to people of a low level of spiritual insight who fail to see that there is a perfectly reasonable explanation for miracles in the "science" of Practical Vedanta.

The fate of these swamis' explication of miracles shows how important social and historical context are in determining whether a particular teaching persists. Swami Vivekananda regularly argued against miracles as a part of religious practice in both the United States and India. He also fought a tendency among Ramakrishna's followers in India to focus on miracles attributed to Ramakrishna. For example, in an 1894 letter, he instructed an Indian colleague to write a sketch of Ramakrishna's life "studiously avoiding all miracles" in favor of illustrating only what he taught (Vivekananda 1964–96, 4:359); Swami Vivekananda was clearly troubled by the prospect of Ramakrishna's fame spreading through miracle stories. After Swami Vivekananda's own death, people have asserted that Swami Vivekananda spoke to them or appeared to them in miraculous visions. Sri Aurobindo, for example, reported that he heard Swami Vivekananda's voice for a couple of weeks while he was in jail (Dhar 1975, 499). More recently, the physician A. Chandrashekhara Udupa reported that he sought a vision of Swami Vivekananda, and early in 1971 "the long awaited miracle happened." Dr. Udupa saw a flash of light and then "had the vision of the resplendent face of Swami Vivekananda" ("the Genesis," at www.divinepark.org). While there may well be a Practical Vedanta explanation for such visions, it is significant that people describe them as miracles.

The tendency to focus on miracles is even more marked in the traditions about Swami Rama Tirtha that have developed in the century since his death. Swami Rama Tirtha had always directed his followers to take nothing about him on faith, and instead to confirm everything he taught through one's own practice. But one miracle that followers now report dates to the days of Swami Rama Tirtha's teaching of mathematics, before he had adopted Vedanta and become a renunciant. He was so absorbed in devotion to Krishna one day that he forgot to teach his mathematics class. But when he finally showed up at work, his students told him, much to his surprise, that his lecture that day had been his best ever. At the college office, he saw that his name was signed on the register for the day. It slowly dawned on him that Krishna himself had taught the lecture (Rinehart 1999, 111–12). Another miracle, widely reported in the post-Indian independence publications of the Swami Rama Tirtha Mission, is a statement attributed to Swami Rama Tirtha, made January 1, 1900, that he would ensure that India would become free within fifty years. The miracle, of course, is that Swami Rama Tirtha is revealed to be the driving force behind India's independence from the British—he predicted when independence would happen and at that point had already set in motion the forces that brought it about (Rinehart 1999, 169–74).

Why did these miracles become important when Swami Rama Tirtha himself discouraged people from focusing on a person's ability to perform miracles? In the earliest sources for the well-documented life and work of Swami Rama Tirtha, there is no evidence for either miracle—for Krishna teaching his mathematics class, or the swami being so powerful that he could predict and set in motion the process of India's becoming independent even before he had taken formal vows of renunciation. While it may seem ironic that miracle stories should surface in the traditions surrounding these Practical Vedanta swamis, their appearance reflects the changing contexts in which the swamis' followers operate, and the role that miracles play in religious discourse.

Swami Vivekananda and Swami Rama Tirtha taught at a time when Hinduism had been under fire by Christian missionaries. In Swami Rama Tirtha's home region of the Punjab, in particular, there was a sense of competition between different religious traditions, a competition heightened by British census-taking that tracked religious affiliation and showed increasing numbers of Christian converts. At the same time, all religions faced the challenge of a growing body of scientific knowledge that threatened to dislodge traditional religious accounts of how the world came to be and how it functioned. In colonial India and in the United States, both Swami Vivekananda and Swami Rama Tirtha set out to demonstrate that Practical Vedanta was the heart and soul of "pure" Hinduism and indeed pure religion, and could unite religion and science, even religion and philosophy. As such, it was far superior to Christianity, and showed that India could compete on the world stage, and even reshape the competition itself by uniting what to the West were separate entities. In an era in which many typical Hindu practices were denounced as superstition and mindless ritual, Practical Vedanta revealed a "modern" and useful, practical form of religious practice—which nonetheless derived from ancient Indian thought, showing that India had once been in far better circumstances than it was during the colonial period.

In independent India, however, the context is different. While claims for the universality of Practical Vedanta are as popular as ever, the debate is not so focused on degenerate, superstitious forms of Hindu religious practice— the target of Christian missionary's criticisms of Hinduism. Nor does there seem to be as much concern with refuting specific Christian theological claims. Instead, in the contemporary secular arena in which the Ramakrishna Mission and the Swami Rama Tirtha Mission both function, it is more common to name Christianity as one of many paths—albeit a less effective one— leading to the same goal.

Miracle stories, despite the Practical Vedanta swamis' own misgivings about their relevance, remain a powerful rhetorical tool for communicating a swami's power. While such miracles had little place in the context of colonial Practical Vedanta (which valued explicability), in independent India miracles are now likely to be presented as legitimate not so much because they can be explained with a superior understanding of universal laws, but because they can be provisionally validated or "proven" and thereby in turn prove something about the power of the person to whom they are attributed. In the case of Swami Vivekananda appearing in visions such as Dr. Udupa's, the doctor's testimony itself functions as proof; in the case of Krishna giving a mathematics lecture for Swami Rama Tirtha, it is "proven" by Tirath Ram's (Swami Rama Tirtha's name prior to becoming a swami) signature on the college registers that day, and in the case of Swami Rama Tirtha's prediction that India would become independent within fifty years, that did indeed happen. In a sense, these recent miracles do provisionally fit into the Practical Vedanta framework insofar as they are presented as verifiable. It is likely that Swami Vivekananda and Swami Rama Tirtha would have emphasized that miracles (such as visions and affecting the outcome of future events) are proven when anyone who develops the requisite yogic prowess can replicate them; with the more recent miracle stories, however, the criterion of proof has shifted to supporting evidence that is presented as unassailable. Such miracle stories do not necessarily require that one have faith in a swami and his miraculous power, but that one accept the proof that the miracles occurred. Such proofs can be challenged, of course (for example, by noting the need to establish a direct causal connection between Swami Rama Tirtha's prediction and India's independence), but the proof stories themselves show how followers of Swami Vivekananda and Swami Rama Tirtha, at least, have made the eminently practical move of adapting Practical Vedanta and miracles to the needs of their own era.

Notes

1. In another context, Swami Rama Tirtha mentioned that his views on Jesus' post-crucifixion life were shaped by a book by Reverend Levy, *Life of Jesus Christ from the Cosmic Records*, which maintained that Jesus stayed in India for 17 years (Rama Tirtha 1978–90, 6:350).

2. For a detailed discussion of Swami Rama Tirtha's teachings and their Indian context, see Rinehart 1998.

References

Dhar, Sailendra Nath. 1975. *A Comprehensive Biography of Swami Vivekananda*. 2 vols. Madras: Vivekananda Prakashan Kendra.

Doyle, Sir Arthur Conan. 1926. *The History of Spiritualism*. 2 vols. London: Cassel.

Rama Tirtha, Swami. 1978–90. *In Woods of God-Realization*. 7 vols. Lucknow: Swami Rama Tirtha Pratishthan. Portions available online at http://www.ramatirtha.org/freebooks.htm.

Rinehart, Robin. 1998. "Swami Rama Tirtha's 'Practical Vedanta': A Message without an Audience." *International Journal of Hindu Studies*, 2, no. 2 (August):185–221.

———. 1999. *One Lifetime, Many Lives: The Experience of Modern Hindu Hagiography*. Atlanta: Scholars Press.

Vivekananda, Swami. 1964–68. *The Complete Works of Swami Vivekananda*. 8 vols. Calcutta: Advaita Ashram. Available online at www.ramakrishnavivekananda.info/vivekananda/complete_works.htm.

CHAPTER THREE

Miraculous Health and Medical Itineration among Satnamis and Christians in Late Colonial Chhattisgarh

CHAD M. BAUMAN

Introduction

The ever-present entanglement of modernity and tradition was revealed rather plainly to me when, during a period of fieldwork in Raipur, Chhattisgarh (one of India's newest states), I attended a conference on business communication at the invitation of an Indian friend. The conference was sponsored by Rai University and was held in the city's most impressive hotel, which was posh even by Mumbai's standards and paradisiacal by Raipur's. There, surrounded by the signs and symbols of luxury and modernity, two visiting Dartmouth professors presented papers on business communication skills. During the subsequent period of discussion, a rather wealthy, modern-looking Indian inquired of the professors whether their research had found "communication without technology or speech" to have been a useful business tool. After a great deal of *garbar* (confusion, agitation, bewilderment) it was determined that the questioner was asking the American professors about telepathy.

The easy dichotomization of tradition and modernity is undeniably spurious, as is the Whiggish assumption that societies travel on a direct and evolutionary path from the former to the latter. Yet the continued prevalence of such attitudes requires that the careful scholar constantly attempt to undermine them by drawing attention to what the Rudolphs long ago called the "modernity of tradition" (1967, 3–5) and what Saurabh Dube has more recently dubbed the "silent magic of modernities" (1998, vii). The need to highlight the constant entanglement of modernities and traditions is nowhere more necessary than in the study of colonial and evangelical interactions.

This chapter investigates one such interaction, and argues that while Satnami and Satnami-Christian Chhattisgarhis who came into contact with Western missionaries between 1868 and 1947 clearly rationalized their medical behavior as a result of the encounter, exchanging, in some ways, the miraculous for the mundane, they did not necessarily reject their traditional understanding of the causes, prevention, and treatment of disease. That is to say, they continued to accept supernatural explanations of etiology and cure. Moreover, this belief was explicitly encouraged by missionaries who—far from being thoroughly modern individuals—sincerely believed that the efficacy of allopathic (or Western) medicine was related to its association with Christianity. If modernity and modern science are typified by a privileging of rationality over religious belief, then it must be argued that in this context Christian missionaries were neither pure agents of modernity nor the purveyors of an adulterated modern form of medicine. Health and healing, for Satnamis, Satnami-Christians, *and* their evangelical interlocutors, were *miraculous*—that is, they involved supernatural elements above and beyond the mundane science of observable cause and effect.[1]

Historical Context

In the early nineteenth century, an illiterate Chamar (member of a leather-working caste) from Chhattisgarh, Guru Ghasidas, returned from a pilgrimage to the famous Jagannath temple at Puri with a message for his followers. Ghasidas's message was not unlike that of other Hindu reformers who had preceded him. He told his followers to reject the worship of divine images, to give up their meat-eating, and to avoid using Brahmans as religious functionaries. And rather than worship countless local and regional deities, as was their custom, Ghasidas instructed his followers to devote themselves solely to the one and only formless (*nirgun*) deity, whom he called "Satnam" (i.e., the True Name). Slowly, the guru gained a following, and by his death in 1850 a quarter of a million Chhattisgarhis, nearly all of them Chamars, had joined the Satnampanth and had begun calling themselves Satnamis.

Eighteen years after Ghasidas's death the first Western missionaries came to the region. The first group, sent by German Evangelicals living in the United States, arrived in Raipur in 1868 and later relocated to a tiger-infested swath of jungle north of the city, which they named Bishrampur (City of Rest). Two decades later they were joined by Disciples of Christ missionaries who concentrated on the areas around Bilaspur, which is now Chhattisgarh's second largest city.

Due to their work with the skins and bodies of dead animals, especially the sacred cow, the Chamars were considered among the lowest of the low castes of northern India. They were barred from entry to Hindu temples and were associated, in the popular imagination, with filth, treachery, and fetid odors. The reputation clung to Chhattisgarh's Chamars even after they had begun calling themselves Satnamis. (Today in Chhattisgarh, it is illegal to refer to Satnamis as Chamars.) Given their low social and economic status, the missionaries came to expect that the Satnami community would enthusiastically embrace Christianity. In fact, only a small number of Satnamis ever did convert, but the great majority of today's Christians in Chhattisgarh can trace their ancestry to the Satnampanth, and thus to the lowly Chamar caste.

Modernization and Medical Itineration

Before the arrival of allopathic medicine, there were three basic lines of defense for rural, village Chhattisgarhis in times of sickness. The first option, though they were not necessarily pursued in order, was to employ home remedies, some of them salubrious, others, as one can imagine, less so. The second option was to employ a *baid*, an ayurvedic practitioner versed in the restorative powers of certain roots, leaves, and other materials.[2] The third option was to consult a *baiga*, one of a class of tribal and lower-caste demipriests skilled in the diagnosis and healing of various sorts of diseases, especially those considered the work of disgruntled spirits, such as *bhut*s and *churail*s,[3] or of witches and ornery local deities.[4]

Some *baiga*s specialized in healing particular ailments, such as cholera, but most were employed as general practitioners. More often than not, *baiga*s worked with individual patients. They were experienced exorcists, and expelled entrenched spirits by a variety of methods, such as *jhar-phunk* (repeating charms and blowing—*phunkna*—in the ear), *tantra-mantra* (charms and incantations), and *jadu-tona* (magical arts). At times of collective suffering, however (e.g., of cholera epidemic, drought, or famine), *baiga*s were occasionally commissioned by an entire community to perform a ritual called "making the village" (*gav banana*), in which they propitiated local deities—frequently Thakur Dev, the protector of villages—in hopes of ameliorating the situation.[5] *Baiga*s also boasted other skills: they were called upon to foretell the future, to predict the gender of unborn children, to identify malignant witches and sorcerers, and to capture or chase away tigers (an activity that sometimes ended badly).

Villages also relied on *baiga*s to expose the nefarious deeds of *tonhi*s (witches). *Baiga*s used a number of ordeals in order to identify those responsible

for various misfortunes, especially inexplicable sicknesses. Sometimes the name
of each woman in a village was pronounced over a flame, a slight flicker indi-
cating the guilty party. In other circumstances, *baiga*s asked the women of a village to touch a pole that, it was believed, would wither or swell the hand of any
tonhi that touched it. After the ordeal, those showing symptoms were deemed
culpable. At other times, *baiga*s directed that women suspected of foul play be
tied in a sack and dunked in water. The guilty, it was understood, would float
while the innocent sank.[6] Unfortunately, this belief in the greater buoyancy of
guilty parties led occasionally to posthumous declarations of innocence. As early
as 1909, British records suggest that belief in *tonhi*s was beginning to fade, but
the practice of and belief in witchcraft continues even today in rural Chhattisgarh, as it does elsewhere in India.[7]

Those Satnamis who became Christian were rather quickly encouraged
to make use of the missions' allopathic medical facilities, and not surprisingly
the use of allopathic medicine became for Satnami-Christians one of the most
significant and salient symbols of communal self-identity. It was understood
by all Christians that "true" conversion entailed complete reliance on allopathic therapies and a considered and thorough rejection of the medico-spiritual care of *baiga*s. (*Baid*s occupied a somewhat more ambiguous position, to
be discussed below).

There is *some* evidence that in significant ways the reality matched the
perception. Those who became Christian did appreciably alter their medical
behavior. They accepted inoculations more readily, they attempted to live
more hygienically, they tried to used well water (rather than stagnant water
from the village tank, or *talab*), and they resorted earlier to allopathic medical
care. They also tended to avoid practices that were detrimental to their health.
They rejected, for example, the traditional practice of denying pregnant
women food after parturition. And they gave up, to some extent, practices
deleterious to the health of children. For example, Chhattisgarhi parents, like
parents in other parts of rural India, traditionally gave their children opium to
keep them docile and content while the parents worked in the fields. They also
frequently treated colicky babies with a hot iron applied to the stomach, and
they sometimes treated fevers with intentional dehydration. All of these practices were discouraged in the Satnami-Christian community, and as a result of
their altered behavior, members of the community began to live healthier and
longer lives, and to have relatively larger families.[8]

Due to an insufficient understanding of medical etiology, Euro-American medical methods were only marginally (if at all) more successful at treating "tropical diseases" than indigenous Indian methods until well into the
nineteenth century. By the end of the century, however, Western medical
advances (such as Robert Koch's discovery of the cholera bacillus) led to a
more sophisticated understanding of the causes and treatment of disease.

Not surprisingly, a concomitant sense of medical superiority emerged as part of the developing Western colonial identity. Medical improvement became part of the "civilizing mission" of British colonial figures (Arnold 2000, 57). For Western missionaries working in India (as for many colonial figures), the newly established superiority of Western medicine reflected not merely cultural differences, but religious differences as well. The scientific "rationality" of Christian missionaries and their colonial compatriots was contrasted with Hindu medical "superstition." Converts to Christianity in Chhattisgarh accepted the distinction. The shift in Satnami-Christian medical behavior was thus more than mindless mimicry—it symbolized the rejection of "heathen superstition" in favor of what was perceived to be a superior medical system, one that promised a longer and healthier life.

Satnami-Christians generally, therefore, rejected the use of *baiga*s, or at least kept up appearances of having done so. But becoming Christian did not entail the wholesale rejection of indigenous therapeutics. The medico-spiritual methods of *baiga*s may have been off-limits, but the ayurvedic medicine of *baid*s was not. Ayurvedic medicine, after all, relied on the healing properties of various florae, and no Christian could object to the use of God's creation for medical purposes.

One could argue that Satnami-Christians were in fact rationalizing their behavior, distinguishing the quasi-experimental methods of *baid*s from the more magical practices of *baiga*s.[9] The distinction received a modicum of support from missionaries, and Indian Christians could therefore consult ayurvedic practitioners without all the stealth and subterfuge required by a trip to the *baiga*. For some, in fact, conversion to Christianity was marked as much by a trip to a *baid* as by the use of missionary medical facilities. There is some evidence, in fact, that Satnamis who became Christian used *baid*s more frequently than they had before conversion. Satnami-Christians even occasionally trained themselves in ayurvedic medicine, and a few became known as skilled practitioners. Those living in remote areas frequently used ayurvedic medicine, which, according to informants, sometimes worked on occasions when allopathic medicine did not.

But the shift from *baiga* to *baid* may also reflect a shift in the social status of converts, perceived or otherwise. *Baid*s generally belonged to higher castes, whereas *baiga*s were usually members of the lowest castes and tribal groups. Given their low social status, Non-Christian Satnamis tended to favor *baiga*s, in part because they were often ill-treated (or not treated at all) by upper-caste *baid*s. Using ayurvedic medicine was thus a way for Satnami-Christians to assert a higher social status. Ayurvedic medicine therefore served three aims simultaneously for the Satnami-Christian community: it appeared more compatible with modern science, thus garnering the approval of missionaries; it asserted and promoted an elevated social status, and it provided an acceptable connection to the pre-Christian past.

Whatever the root causes of their altered medical behavior, conversion to Christianity clearly involved, for Satnamis, an element of modernized thinking and acting. As stated above, the perception of modernized medical behavior was among the most important symbols of Satnami-Christian communal identity. Yet the reality was not so simple. When asked about the medical habits of converts to Christianity, Chhattisgarhi informants initially spoke of a radical transformation—Christians, they asserted, took their medical problems directly to the mission's dispensaries and hospitals. But when pressed, these same informants often revealed a more complex reality. Frequently, Christian informants insisted that while they had always gone to the hospital, other Christians sometimes visited *baid*s and *baiga*s.

For example, Awadh, a seventy-seven-year-old Christian man who lived in Baitalpur, a small village along the Raipur-Bilaspur road, reported that during his childhood he and other members of his Christian family went directly to the mission dispensary for treatment of illnesses. But when asked again later whether people ever called upon *baid*s or *baiga*s, he said, "People from the village, [both Christians and non-Christians] . . . used to go first to the *baiga*. . . . When they were not cured by the *baiga*s, they would visit the local *baid*. And if [they still] were not cured, then they would go to the hospital to see the doctors."[10]

Priya, a ninety-year-old woman who was also from Baitalpur, echoed Vijay's sentiments:

> Q: In your childhood, when you fell ill, what did you do?
>
> A: We went to the hospital in Bishrampur.
>
> Q: Did anybody in the town ever visit a *baiga* or a *baid*?
>
> A: Yes, many people used to go to the *baiga*.
>
> Q: Christians also?
>
> A: [Yes,] Christians and Satnamis both went.[11]

In this context there was not, therefore, a direct, evolutionary path of development from reliance on *baiga*s and *baid*s to reliance on allopathic medical practitioners, but rather a history of medical itineration and therapeutic experimentation.

Many Satnami-Christians continued to consult *baiga*s, as a first line of defense against ill health, well into the twentieth century (though frequently at night, and with an abundance of discretion). Only later, if the prescribed therapy proved ineffective, or if the ailment progressed to a dangerous extent, would they resort to allopathic treatment. Certain diseases, especially those considered the work of irritable spirits or meddlesome deities, were in fact considered, even by some Christians, to be more properly the domain of *baiga*s. Some Christians believed, for example, that the *tantra-mantra* of *baiga*s was more effective than Western medicine in the treatment of snakebites, which they understood to be the work of the irascible snake godling, Nag Dev. And many Christians continued to pass along and use efficacious mantras, even if not directly consulting with *baiga*s.

Not surprisingly, Satnami-Christians living close to missionary medical facilities tended more quickly to place their trust in allopathic medicine than those living at a distance. But proximity to missionary medical facilities was no guarantee of reliance on allopathy. Christians undergoing long-term allopathic treatment, such as a course of antibiotics, were particularly likely to become impatient and seek out other alternatives, often consulting *baiga*s while still undergoing the allopathic therapy.

When one compares the behavior of Satnami-Christians with their non-Christian counterparts, however, it becomes clear that Christian claims to have transformed their medical mores and mien were more than mere delusion. Non-Christian Satnamis continued to seek out *baiga*s to combat disease and ill health even after hospitals and dispensaries became available in their region. But after a lag of five or ten years, fewer for those living closest to missionary medical facilities, non-Christian Satnami medical behavior came to resemble that of their Christian friends and relatives.

The lag may be partly explained by social pressure brought upon converts to conform to what was considered proper Christian medical behavior. Satnami-Christians were encouraged to make use of Christian medical facilities, and were occasionally offered incentives, such as reduced rates and the possibility of transportation to and from the hospital on a mission-owned bullock cart.

There were, in addition, a number of obstacles for Satnamis wishing to make use of Christian medical facilities. One was the perception, prevalent at the time, that mission hospitals were actually killing people, a perception arising from the fact that many resorted to hospital treatment only on the verge of death (Meyer ca. 1927). Satnamis also traditionally believed that evil spirits inhabited large, roomy, high-ceilinged rooms of the kind prevalent in missionary hospitals (McNeil 1901, 218). Another obstacle for Satnamis was the strength of tradition and the possibility of social ostracism for those who did use missionary medical facilities. A visit to a hospital required contact with members of other castes, some of whom (such as the sweepers) were considered untouchable by the Satnamis. Until the mid-1930s, Satnamis who sought treatment at hospitals risked being outcasted. Because of these and other obstacles, Satnamis who did not convert to Christianity continued to rely on *baiga*s until they had become convinced of the efficacy of *angrezi* (English) medicine, a process that required many years.

Richard Young has argued that among more educated and cosmopolitan Indians, Copernican scientific cosmology had become a "religiously neutral, culturally relative datum of mundane knowledge" by the end of the nineteenth century, and the evidence supports his claims.[12] In rural Chhattisgarh, however, medical science seems not to have attained this status until at least several decades later. Nevertheless, by the 1930s and 1940s, Satnamis had come to accept allopathic medical facilities as ritually neutral spheres, and henceforth visited them with greater ease and frequency.

And so it was that by the 1940s, most Christian *and* non-Christian Chhattisgarhis with access to hospitals or dispensaries turned first to allopathic care for medical treatment. Until that time, it was common for Satnamis and Satnami-Christians without access to allopathic medical facilities to turn first to *baiga*s, and then only out of desperation to allopathic medicine. But the itinerary began to reverse itself in the 1930s and 1940s, such that nearly all Chhattisgarhis for whom it was possible turned first to hospitals and dispensaries, and only out of impatience to *baiga*s.

The transformation of Satnami-Christian medical behavior must not be viewed, however, as a simple process of rationalization, or what Weber called "disenchantment." (And it should be remembered that the German term generally translated as "disenchantment," *Entzauberung*, could be more literally rendered as "de-magic-ation.") Chhattisgarhis had not simply chosen scientifically sound medicine over faulty local superstition. Rather, they continued to believe that health and healing involved the supernatural—health and healing remained, for Chhattisgarhis, *magical* and *miraculous*. And Christian missionaries contributed to this perception.

Unmodern Missionaries and Miraculous Medicine

Mission work in Chhattisgarh began at a time when medical work, or "clinical Christianity," had just begun to gain acceptance in the everyday practice of Protestant missionary societies.[13] From the beginning, Disciples of Christ and Evangelical missionaries in Chhattisgarh explicitly and implicitly linked Christianity to allopathic medical treatment. The first missionary in Chhattisgarh, the Evangelical Oscar Lohr, had been trained in medicine and was the son of a surgeon. But even missionaries with no medical training frequently dispensed medicines and treatment. Mission hospitals and dispensaries encouraged the perception that Christianity and allopathic medical treatment were related. Patients were sometimes required, as a prerequisite to treatment, to sit through evangelical sermons or worship services. Missionaries also made a practice of praying before working with their patients, implicitly suggesting, if healing ensued, that the prayer had been a contributing factor. In addition, peregrinating catechists and Bible women supplemented their evangelical message with one of disease prevention, sanitation, and hygiene.

The explicit linkage of allopathic medicine and Christian faith should not be understood, however, as a cynical evangelical gesture. Missionaries in Chhattisgarh believed that there *was* a connection between the power of (the Christian) God and the efficacy of Western medical treatments. After all, they reasoned, the Christian God had enabled Euro-American scientists to discover a more effective medicine. The general superiority of Western medicine was seen, therefore, as a mark of God's grace. Prayer was accordingly not just empty habit, but was, rather, believed to actually increase the efficacy of the treatment. For these missionaries, and many like them throughout India, Western medicine and faith in the Christian God were deeply enmeshed. Therefore, if "modernity" is to be identified by the prevalence of scientific rather than religious or "magical" thinking, then it must be asserted that missionaries were not simple harbingers of modernity.[14]

Missionaries understood themselves to be in possession of superior medical science, but actively sought to forge links between the superiority of allopathic medicine and the power of the Christian God. There is a curious paradox here, in that missionaries, in a sense, wanted it both ways. They desired, on the one hand, to undermine what they considered "heathen superstitions" with good, sound medical science. On the other hand, they wished at the same time to suggest that allopathy was *Christian* science, and that the ostensible superiority of allopathy was linked to the putative superiority of Christianity. Missionary interactions with sick Chhattisgarhis reflected this ambiguity. On an evangelizing tour, the Evangelical missionary Tillmanns said a prayer for a sick Teli and "promised to send some medicines instructing him at the same time that he should depend more upon God than medicine."[15]

Similarly, from the perspective of missionaries, there was a clear connection between the "flaws" of Indian religion and the "errors" of Indian medical practices. They reacted to both with a mixture of astonishment, revulsion, and sarcasm. Some sense of the missionary estimation of local Indian medical practices can be gained from a photograph that appeared in Miton Lang's 1932 *The Healing Touch in Missionary Lands*. The photograph captures the author and his wife standing on the veranda of the hospital, dressed in glowing white gowns. In front of them stands, as the caption puts it, a "native 'doctor,'" the quotation marks around "doctor" marking what Lang clearly considered the *baiga*'s inferior abilities (see figure 3.1). This view of Indian medical practices was shared by those Indians who worked with missionaries. One Evangelical Indian catechist reported in his journal that he had told a Hindu merchant: "If your science is true, contradict the English Science [*sic*] and ask any educated Hindu which one is true. If your Science is false then your religion is also false."[16] By opposing such beliefs, missionaries were playing a role long and deeply established in the imagination of Western Christians of the time. One missionary admitted that before coming to India he considered

FIGURE 3.1. Dr. and Mrs. Lang, Johann Compounder, and native "doctor." The "doctor's" drugs are on the verandah to the left. From Milton Lang, *The Healing Touch in Mission Lands* (1932), p. 59.

himself a thespian and had once enjoyed playing the role of an ungodly "village medicine man [opposed] to the egress [*sic*] of Christianity into his village" (Freund 1936).

Non-Christian Chhattisgarhis themselves accepted the notion that supernatural powers were involved in health and healing, and understood Christian medical efforts within this framework. For example, many Chhattisgarhis appear to have interpreted the Christian prayers that accompanied their medical treatment as mantras. By consistently prefacing their treatment with prayers, Christian doctors, both American and Indian, perpetuated this understanding. Non-Christian Satnami patients even occasionally *requested* that Christian doctors pray with them, believing there to be power in the spoken word of the attending physician.

Similarly, Chhattisgarhis interpreted the common Western medical practice of taking a patient's pulse within the traditional framework of *nari bhed*.

It was commonly believed by Chhattisgarhis that certain people, especially *baiga*s and *baid*s, had the ability to diagnose and determine the cause of a person's illness—and in some cases cure it—simply by feeling (*bhedna*) their pulse (*nari*). One Satnami-Christian who worked for many years at the Mungeli mission hospital run by Disciples of Christ missionaries was believed by both Christian and non-Christian Satnamis to be skilled in the art of *nari bhed*, and to be in possession of a miraculous "healing touch" (Gordon 1909, 98). A number of missionary doctors were regarded in the same way.

In an intriguing article in the *Annals of Science*, Irfan Habib and Dhruv Raina argue that the association of scientific empiricism with Christianity in the minds of many Indians may have prompted some to convert (1989, 601). While this may have been the case among the more educated Indians considered by Habib and Raina, for most village Chhattisgarhis the attraction of allopathic medicine was not its scientific basis, but rather the fact that it had proven effective.[17] Until the 1940s and 1950s, Christians in Chhattisgarh understood the greater perceived potency of Western medicine to derive from its association with the Christian God, not merely from its empirical foundations. Non-Christian Satnamis interpreted things similarly. One Satnami came to Christian doctors after his wife became pregnant. The man had lost six children with two different wives and was hoping the "protection of Jesus Christ" might help him achieve a happier end for the seventh (McGavran 1990, 102–3).

Rosemary Fitzgerald has argued that Indians seeking treatment at mission-run medical facilities "shrugged off" the religious aspects of the treatment and took the view of a Brahman patient who said, "The doctrine of the Christian is bad but their medicine is good" (2001, 129). Clearly, this would have been true for some Chhattisgarhis, particularly after 1930. Yet most seem to have accepted the efficacy of allopathic medicine as a function of its association with Christianity. Satnamis healed at Christian medical facilities would frequently offer mission doctors gifts of money, fruit, vegetables, eggs, or grain for the Christian god (Lang 1932, 66). The gifts were not payment, but were rather given by the Satnami patients in accordance with the traditional custom of presenting a thank offering to the deity (or representative of the deity) from whom one had requested and received healing.

Satnamis were therefore able to rather comfortably incorporate the medical power of the Christian god into their preexisting belief system. Corinne Dempsey claims that whereas scholars tend to portray religion as a system of belief, Christians in India, and adherents of other religions around the world, tend to understand it more as a "conduit of miraculous power" (2002, 134). For Chhattisgarhis, miraculous power did not need to be centralized in a single deity or religion, and was, in fact, generally quite diffuse. Because of this, the fact that a particular god proved especially skilled in healing did not obviate or vitiate the worship of one's own chosen deity (*ishtadevata*).

Some, however, did convert to Christianity, seeking in any way possible to improve their chances of recuperation. In the 1940s, a Satnami named Samunwa, who had consulted *baid*s and *baiga*s for help with his rheumatism, heard a Christian evangelist proclaim that "Jesus heals." Believing Jesus healed only those who had been baptized, Samunwa requested the rite from a Disciples missionary. After being baptized, he went to the mission hospital and was healed. Fearing harassment from his former caste fellows, he sold all his possessions in the remote village where he had lived, moved to Mungeli, where the mission was located, and took a job at the hospital. He reports having immediately lost his *viswas* (confidence, belief) in *baid*s and *baiga*s.[18]

Two articles in Robert Hefner's edited volume *Conversion to Christianity* suggest that the Chhattisgarhi understanding of missionary medicine was not unique. In one, William Merrill argues that some colonial Mexican Tarahumaras were induced to convert by the possibility of accessing the Jesuit priests' "supernatural" ability to cure Old World diseases. In another, Charles Keyes suggests that Christian missionaries working among the Thai came to be regarded as "men of prowess" because of their ability to heal the sick.[19] It seems to be the case that many Chhattisgarhis, both Satnami and Christian, interpreted missionary medicine not in terms of the triumph of Baconian empiricism but rather as a demonstration of miraculous power associated with the Christian god. Such an interpretation did not, for the most part, undermine preexisting medical or religious beliefs (as missionaries had hoped), but rather simply added to the perceived charisma of mission doctors and the prestige of the Christian deity.[20]

The new, as with the yet-to-come, can only be grasped according to what has already been, what is already "known." For example, in the 1920s, a Christian named Phagua was bitten by a *karait* (a poisonous black snake). Seeking help at the mission hospital in Mungeli, Phagua begged mission doctors to spare the serpent, convinced as he was that killing the serpent would anger Nag Dev and thereby endanger his own life. Not missing an opportunity to demonstrate their power (and the impotence of Hindu godlings), the missionaries had the snake killed. Phagua did suffer for some time, nearly proving himself correct. But he did finally recuperate fully, and declared that his Christian baptism had been the source of the recovery (Miller 1922). Note that Phagua did not reject an "enchanted" interpretation of the events in favor of a "disenchanted" one. Rather, he simply altered his interpretation of the event. Baptism, rather than the snake godling, came to be seen as the more significant causal factor.

The missionary literature, in this context and others, tends to suggest that "superstition" and medical ignorance obtained before the arrival of missionaries, and that these were eradicated thereafter. This great improvement, missionaries concluded, was the work of Christ. While some scholars would reject this conclusion, and others would wonder whether the eradication was worth the cultural effects of missionary "intrusion," most scholars dealing with evangelical encounters in the colonial context nevertheless tend to accept the notion that missionaries were agents of rationalization and modernity. They were, of course. But missionaries and Christianity cannot be *equated* with modernization. They promoted modernization, but neither the missionaries nor the medicine they practiced were purely modern. Missionaries did often assert, with one Disciples of Christ missionary, that "magic" was "the greatest enemy to human progress."[21] Yet at the same time, missionaries continued to believe that prayer and belief contributed—magically, one might say—to the efficacy of allopathic medical treatments. They therefore did little, whether in word or deed, to discourage the notion that the power of allopathic medicine lay in the Christian god.

Conclusion

There is no question that the encounter with Western missionaries contributed to the at least partial modernization of medical behavior among Satnamis and Satnami-Christians in Chhattisgarh. But the preceding discussion does suggest that one cannot simply observe what appears to be "modern" behavior and declare it so. Rather, the understanding of that behavior, from the actors' point of view, must be taken into account. It appears that many Chhattisgarhis continued to understand their "modern" behavior in quite "traditional" terms—to understand mundane science as miraculous power. The fact that the missionaries themselves were not fully modern individuals allowed and contributed to this understanding.

For the most part, missionaries of this time saw little or no distinction between Christianization and modernization. Christianity, and "Christian" medicine, they believed, would conquer irrational and "superstitious" thought. In 1932, for example, an Evangelical missionary wrote: "In medical missions we have a unique weapon against the belief in demons, evil spirits, and witchcraft. It is also a powerful means of attack on the heathen magician. The might of medical missions lies too in the demonstration, that by attacking disease at its source and [practicing] preventative medicine, belief in evil spirits, demons, malign gods and goddesses, and witchcraft must vanish" (Lang 1932, 25).

To the extent that modernity is marked by a tendency to value rationality over religious reasoning, missionary Christianity was indeed *relatively* more modern than the worldviews it encountered in Chhattisgarh. But the missionaries were not *purely* rational beings. They understood the efficacy of their modern science to be linked, at least in part, to the power of their Christian religion. They believed in the power of prayer to affect bodily healing. The Christian belief that God intervenes in mundane medical affairs is no less "enchanted" in quality than the Satnami belief in the spiritual nature of medical etiology and treatment. Likewise, Christian petitions to God for healing are no less "magical" than those of a *baiga* wishing to secure the protection of Thakur Dev.

It may be true, as Weber asserted long ago, that *Western* Christianity is comparatively one of the more rationalized (and rationalizing) religions of the world. But Weber's argument should not be taken to mean that the Christianization of a person or a community entails necessarily an equal degree of rationalization. In the nineteenth and twentieth centuries, for example, Christianity managed to merge comfortably with a variety worldviews throughout the non-Western world that were essentially pre-Enlightenment worldviews. And Christian scriptures, after all, reflect and provide justification for the continuation of a thoroughly premodern worldview.

Paradoxically, contemporary scholars, who are often quite skeptical about missionary aims and motivations, appear to have generally accepted the missionary conflation of Christianization and modernization. But the devil, as the proverb goes, is in the details. And in the context of Hindu-Christian encounter in Chhattisgarh, the details suggest that while Christianity did represent a *generally* rationalizing and modernizing force, it did at other times promote and perpetuate a premodern, "enchanted" view of the world, particularly with reference to medical cause and cure.

The complexity of the situation is reflected in—and even, perhaps, in some ways the manifestation of—a related linguistic ambiguity. Satnami and Satnami-Christian informants frequently spoke of a process whereby their *viswas* in *baiga*s was eroded as their *viswas* in allopathic treatment grew. But the semantic range of *viswas* covers everything from "trust" and "confidence" to "faith" and "belief," making it difficult to determine whether a person's stated *viswas* in certain forms of medicine (or lack thereof) was of an experiential kind or of a religious kind (and suggesting, as well, that the distinction did not exist in the minds of Chhattisgarhis). Did Chhattisgarhis therefore understand their modernized medical behavior as a response to better science, suggesting a process of rationalization? Or did Chhattisgarhis understand the changes in their behavior as a response to a more medically efficacious supernatural power? The evidence suggests that the dichotomy is a false one, and the answer must therefore be that Chhattisgarhis understood their behavior in both ways at one and the same time.

Notes

This article relies on archival sources as well as interviews conducted during a period of fieldwork in India in the first half of 2004. For more on this topic, and on the Satnamis and Satnami-Christians more generally, see Bauman, forthcoming.

1. There are a number of excellent texts pertaining to the interaction of Indians and colonial medical authorities, of which David Arnold's *Colonizing the Body* is perhaps the best known. There are surprisingly few investigations, however, of the reaction of Indians to missionary medicine. With few texts for comparison and contrast, it is therefore difficult to determine whether and to what extent my own assertions and conclusions could be generalized to other contexts. See Arnold 1993.

2. "*Baid*" is a regional variant of "*vaid.*"

3. *Bhut*s are male ghosts; *churail*s are the ghosts of women who die of complications related to pregnancy or childbirth.

4. For more on *baiga*s, see Babb 1975, 197ff.

5. To my knowledge, there are no published descriptions of this ritual as it is practiced in northern India. For ethnographic accounts of similar rituals performed in southern India, see Kumar 1986, 107–23; and Handelman 2006, 291–92.

6. For more on this topic, see Babb 1975, 205.

7. See Nelson 1909, 85. For a recent instance of alleged witchcraft in Raipur, see Indo-Asian News Service, "'Witches' Keep Dussehra Crowd in Thrall," *Times of India* (*Online Edition*), October 23, 2004; and Press Trust of India, "*SP* Gets Wife Killed for Practising Voodoo," 2003, available at http: //www.timesofindia.com.

8. Though the oral evidence suggests that Christians were living longer and healthier lives, the statistical evidence that can be garnered from census data is ambiguous. The 1911 census of the Central Provinces and Berar (which included information on Chhattisgarh) records infirmities by "selected castes, tribes or races." While .3 percent of Chamars in the region were suffering from blindness, only .16 percent of Christians had lost their sight (the regional average was .2 percent). However, a larger percentage of Christians suffered from all other infirmities listed, including insanity, deafness, and leprosy. This may suggest that Christianity did not appreciably improve the health of members of the community. But it more likely reflects the large number of people with disabilities who found care in Christian medical institutions and subsequently joined the community. This is especially likely to be true in the case of leprosy, where the discrepancy is the highest. India Census Commissioner 1911, 110.

9. Rabha converts made the same distinction; see Karlsson 2000, 183.

10. Awadh Lal (real name withheld), Baitalpur, Chhattisgarh, March 24, 2004, interview by author.

11. Priya Masih (real name withheld), Baitalpur, Chhattisgarh, March 24, 2004, interview by author.

12. See Young 2003, 184.

13. For an overview of the emergence and growth of "clinical Christianity" in British India, see Fitzgerald 2001.

14. Cf. Ranger 1993, 90.

15. The encounter is recorded in the diary of an unnamed Evangelical Indian catechist. Entry for September 4, 1908, found inside the journal of S. J. Scott,

Mahasamund catechist, Archives of the Evangelical Synod at Eden Theological Seminary, St. Louis, Missouri (hereafter AES).

16. Ibid., entry for June 13, 1908. Christian evangelists, Indian and American, were consciously or unconsciously imitating colonial officials such as the Scottish educator John Wilson, who took pride in pointing out the fallacy of scientific views associated with Hinduism. (Educated Hindus naturally reacted to Wilson's criticism by drawing attention to the Bible's scientific errors.) See Young 2003, 194.

17. Arun Jones argues, similarly, that the Igorot of the Philippines also evaluated the appeal of various medical methods according to the criteria of efficacy. Jones 2003, 229–29.

18. Samunwa (informant uses only one name), interview by author, Mungeli, CG, March 27, 2004.

19. See Keyes 1993 and Merrill 2003.

20. One mission doctor who was able to bring a sick woman back from a fever-induced coma was known far and wide to have the power to resurrect the dead. See Brown 1954, 136.

21. A quote from an unidentified book in M. P. Davis, "Indian Touring Notes, Parsabhader," ca. 1930, AES, 82–14 Qu2, Davis, M. P., Quarterly Reports, Articles, Newsletters, 1916–35.

References

Arnold, David. 1993. *Colonizing the Body: State Medicine and Epidemic Disease in Nineteenth-Century India.* Berkeley and Los Angeles: University of California Press.

———. 2000. *Science, Technology, and Medicine in India, 1760–1947.* New York: Cambridge University Press.

Babb, Lawrence A. 1975. *The Divine Hierarchy: Popular Hinduism in Central India.* New York: Columbia University Press.

Bauman, Chad M. Forthcoming. *Christian Identity and* Dalit *Religion in Hindu India, 1868–1947.* Grand Rapids, MI: Eerdmans Publishing Company.

Brown, Leta May. 1954. *Hira Lal of India: Diamond Precious.* St. Louis: Bethany Press.

Dempsey, Corinne. 2002. "Lessons in Miracles from Kerala, South India: Stories of Three 'Christian' Saints." In *Popular Christianity in India: Riting between the Lines,* edited by Selva Raj and Corinne Dempsey, 115–40. Albany: State University of New York Press.

Dube, Saurabh. 1998. *Untouchable Pasts: Religion, Identity, and Power among a Central Indian Community, 1780–1950.* Albany: State University of New York Press.

Fitzgerald, Rosemary. 2001. "'Clinical Christianity': The Emergence of Medical Work as a Missionary Strategy in Colonial India, 1800–1914." In *Health, Medicine and Empire: Perspectives on Colonial India,* 88–136 edited by Biswamoy Pati and Mark Harrison. Hyderabad, India: Orient Longman.

Freund, H. G. 1936. "The Indian Personal Attitude toward Illness," Archives of the Evangelical Synod at Eden Theological Seminary, St. Louis, Missouri.

Gordon, E. M. 1909. *Indian Folk Tales: Being Side-Lights on Village Life in Bilaspore, Central Provinces.* London: Elliot Stock.

Habib, Irfan, and Dhruv Raina. 1989. "The Introduction of Scientific Rationality into India: A Study of Master Ramchandra." *Annals of Science* 46:597–610.

Handelman, Don. 2006. "Guises of the Goddess and the Transformation of the Male: Gangamma's Visit to Tirupati and the Continuum of Gender." In *Syllables of the Sky*, edited by David Shulman, 283–335. Delhi: Oxford University Press.

India Census Commissioner. *Census of India, 1911.* Vol. 10 (Part 2, Statistics). Calcutta: Superintendent Government Printing.

Jones, Arun W. 2003. *Christian Missions in the American Empire: Episcopalians in Northern Luzon, the Philippines, 1902–1946.* New York: Peter Lang.

Karlsson, Bengt G. 2000. *Contested Belonging: An Indigenous People's Struggle for Forest and Identity in Sub-Himalayan Bengal.* Richmond: Curzon.

Keyes, Charles F. 1993. "Why the Thai Are Not Christians: Buddhist and Christian Conversion in Thailand." In *Conversion to Christianity: Historical and Anthropological Perspectives on a Great Transformation*, edited by Robert W. Hefner, 259–84. Berkeley and Los Angeles: University of California Press.

Kumar, P. Pratap. "The Sacred in Folk-Traditions of Rural Hindus." *Bangalore Theological Forum* 18, nos. 2–3:107–23.

Lang, Milton C. 1932. *The Healing Touch in Mission Lands.* St. Louis: Eden Publishing House.

McGavran, Donald A. 1990. *The Satnami Story: A Thrilling Drama of Religious Change.* Pasadena, CA: William Carey Library.

McNeil, Ada. 1901. "Bilaspur Medical Work." *Missionary Tidings*, November, 218.

Merrill, William L. 1993. "Conversion and Colonialism in Northern Mexico: The Tarahumara Response to the Jesuit Mission Program, 1601–1767." In *Conversion to Christianity: Historical and Anthropological Perspectives on a Great Transformation*, edited by Robert W. Hefner, 129–64. Berkeley and Los Angeles: University of California Press.

Meyer, Hulda. ca. 1927. "The Hospital—A Place to Be Feared, or Don't Ever Go Near the Hospital," Archives of the Evangelical Synod at Eden Theological Seminary, St. Louis, Missouri.

Miller, George E. 1922. "The Serpent That Failed." *World Call*, July, 28–30.

Nelson, A. E. 1909. *Central Provinces District Gazetteer: Raipur District.* Bombay: British India Press.

Ranger, Terence. 1993. "The Local and the Global in Southern African Religious History." In *Conversion to Christianity: Historical and Anthropological Perspectives on a Great Transformation*, edited by Robert W. Hefner, 65–98. Berkeley and Los Angeles: University of California Press.

Rudolph, Lloyd I., and Susanne Hoeber Rudolph. 1967. *The Modernity of Tradition: Political Development in India.* Chicago: University of Chicago Press.

Young, Richard Fox. 2003. "Receding from Antiquity: Hindu Responses to Science and Christianity on the Margins of Empire, 1800–1850." In *Christians and Missionaries in India: Cross-Cultural Communication since 1500*, edited by Robert Eric Frykenberg, 183–222. Grand Rapids, MI: William B. Eerdmans.

CHAPTER FOUR

Kataragama and the Tsunami

The Adbhuta, Ascarya, *and the* Pratiharya

SUNIL GOONASEKERA

Introduction

In this essay I examine mysteries and miracles in Sri Lanka with a special focus on Kataragama and the tsunami of 2004. Of particular interest to me are the conflicts between the modern and the traditional Sinhala Buddhist discourses on miracles. What do I mean by "modern" discourses? I take "modern" to mean "post-Enlightenment Western." "Modern discourse" refers to any discourse based on the scientific, objective, and systematic model of rationality and truth developed in Europe during the Enlightenment era. This model of rationality and truth considers public and universal verifiability or falsifiability of a proposition as the precondition for its validity.[1]

Technically, modern constructions of miracles attempt to explain what have hitherto been considered unusual, bewildering, or puzzling occurrences arising from supernatural interventions by establishing empirically and positively verifiable causal and functional relations among the phenomena of the world. As such, modern discourses have two basic functions: discovering truth and debunking all contrary notions (premodern as well as nonmodern) of reality. According to the modern weltanschauung, there are only natural phenomena and/or human inventions that await universalistic scientific explanations. The sociologist Max Weber employed the concept *demystification* to discuss the modern debunking of the premodern and nonmodern notions of truth on epistemological and ontological grounds.[2]

I take "modern" also to mean "contemporary." Here, the premodern and nonmodern European sensibilities and non-European discourses exist alongside their modern counterparts in our contemporary world. Considering the intellectual power of the modern worldview and the extent of its globalization during the past three hundred or so years, it is miraculous that the premodern and nonmodern perspectives still exist, rather robustly, even in the European civilization, and amazing that they continue to be the dominant perspectives in the non-European world. Here I focus on how contemporary Sinhala Buddhist cultural discourses defend the premodern and the nonmodern notions through modern constructions by employing various discursive subterfuges.

Native Notions

What are the native notions of the miraculous in Sri Lanka—or, for that matter, in the indigenous cultures of South Asia? Three concepts come to the forefront. They are *adbhuta*, *ascarya* and *pratiharya*. In discussions of the mysterious, *adbhuta* is a foundational concept. It translates easily as "mysterious." It means that something is inexplicable in terms of the possibilities in the everyday world as the everyday world is conceived in terms of the overarching worldview shared by all major indigenous South Asian cultures. The *adbhuta* events defy everyday logic and compel the witness to refer to phenomena beyond the everyday world for explanations.

Ascarya is not as easy to translate. It refers to a state of mind—the wonderment, bewilderment, or astonishment that arises when one encounters an *adbhuta* or mysterious occurrence. Therefore the *adbhuta* occurrences are also known as *ascaryajanaka* (*janaka*-engendering) events. Sometimes the concept *ascarya* is employed for the event itself and may be translated as "miracle." Ordinarily, an *ascarya* is a pleasant surprise. It could also be awe and respect for the phenomenon that produced this state of mind. The awe may arise because the occurrence brings about an enhancement of the awed person's existence and or a punishment meted out to another who had wronged him or her. It thereby shows supernatural support for his or her cause. It may also arise when one is the recipient of the negative impact of the mysterious happening. Here the mental state is beyond awe and trepidation. Rather, it is a shock, a fear, and a dread of more and worse occurrences to come, leading to remorse, sorrow, despair, and deep anguish. The affected individual experiences extreme *bhaya* (fear) and becomes *trasta* (terrified).

A *pratiharya* is a miraculous performance. Beings endowed with supernatural power perform *pratiharya* to convince an audience that they have such power, or that they are correct—particularly in an adversarial situation, or to teach lessons, to reward and help the good, and to punish wrongdoers. These beings are deities or humans endowed with divine capabilities.[3]

Native Doubts

It is important to note that even in the premodern era various South Asian schools of skeptics doubted the veracity of miracles. A well-known case in point is the Buddhist criticism and rejection of Brahmanical ritualism, theories of self-mortification and miracles associated with them, and beliefs in the existence of immortal souls. The Charvakas, also known as the Lokayatas, criticized even the Buddhist cosmological notions. Their perspectives come very close to modern theories of knowledge and truth. A brief discussion of their approach to reality is in order to show the extent of the early disputes regarding miracles, and the existence of doubts about the actuality of these phenomena even in contemporary South Asia.

The original compendia of Charvaka philosophy are lost. What we know about the Charvakas comes from secondary sources in which their opponents describe them only in order to refute them. Buddhist sources refer to Ajita Keshakambali, a contemporary of the Buddha, as a Lokayata. Brahmanical sources state that the founder of this paradigm was one Brhaspati.[4]

According to the Charvaka theory of knowledge the only way to know is through the five senses. Even the senses are unreliable, as they perceive unreal phenomena such as mirages and apparitions owing to mental infirmities. Inference is not a good source of knowledge, because it is merely a logical manipulation of what is known through sense perception, a manipulation that can lead to misconceptions. The Charvakas rejected all worldviews of their time, as these included mind as a source of knowledge, and rejected all notions of soul, supernatural beings and forces, karma, rebirth, afterlife, mysteries, and miracles. For them these were nonsensical notions that only created delusions. Thus, they rejected as nonsense the Vedas, all rituals, social distinctions such as caste based on the Vedas, and all religious epistemologies, ontologies, teleologies, and soteriologies. Their philosophy is often framed as a materialist individualistic hedonism, the latter term implying indifference to ethics and morality. However, the Charvaka philosophy did not reject morality and ethics. Charvakas condemned the religious professionals such as priests for perpetuating lies and deluding and exploiting ignorant people with their false pretenses. They did emphasize that the only pleasure one could obtain in life was through the satisfaction of bodily desires and that the only right thing a person could do was to take care of his or her own interests.

This far the philosophy of the Charvakas comes very close to European Enlightenment thought and philosophy of science. Where they differ is in their rejection of even inference as a valid way of knowing. Scientific empiricist positivism depends on experimentation and inference.

Charvaka thought is not dead. It exists today without that label as materialistic skepticism, but in watered-down forms. Many individuals in South

Asia reject all notions of the supernatural as inventions by the ignorant, because of their stupidity and gullibility, and by crafty rascals who use such notions and practices to exploit the deluded fools around them. However, they neither know about Charvakas nor claim that they are Charvakas. These contemporary materialists are not necessarily philosophically trained people, although many individuals with modern education profess this perspective. And they do not go as far as the Charvakas and reject even inferences as dubious propositions. The distinguishing characteristic of the contemporary materialists is their skeptical attitude toward supernaturalistic explanations of the phenomena of the world. Thus, as far as South Asian cultures are concerned, the local materialists, in whatever form they exist, challenge miracles and attempt to give materialist, naturalistic explanations for such phenomena. This is to say that the people of South Asia have never been unanimous about miracles. They were intellectually contested phenomena.

The impact of modern thought appears to enhance these local doubts. On the one hand, modern education reoriented the worldview of some local people compelling them to reject traditional ideas about miracles. On the other hand, some traditional doubters with modern education buttress their convictions with modern notions coming from the natural sciences or Marxist materialism or both. Here, the nonmodern and the modern materialisms blend to some degree to produce antitheses to the traditional notions of mysteries and miracles.[5]

Contexts

Before I present two contexts in which the nonmodern, premodern, and modern constructions of miracles abound in Sri Lanka, let me give a brief introduction to the religious communities on the island. Sri Lanka hosts four major religions of the world—Buddhism, Hinduism, Islam and Christianity—and the religion of the Vadda tribe. Nearly 70 percent of Sri Lankans are Buddhists. About 17 percent are of Hindu faith. The remaining 13 percent or so are Muslims and Christians in roughly equal numbers. The Vaddas are a historically, socially, and culturally significant but demographically insignificant group whose principal religion may be anthropologically defined as ancestor worship. Most Buddhists and many Christians adhere to various Hindu beliefs that lay at the foundation of the indigenous South Asian civilization. Aspects of Vadda ancestor worship and other local microreligions such as spirit possession and performances of rituals to harness the presumed powers of the world, currently classified as magic, also permeate the religious beliefs and practices of the Buddhists, Christians, and Hindus. Interestingly, some Sri Lankan Muslims also participate in these native premodern constructions about the world. The two contexts are Kataragama and the tsunami that pounded Sri Lankan coastal regions in 2004.

Kataragama is perhaps the best-known place in Sri Lanka for mysterious occurrences, some of which are believed to be miracles. The maker of these phenomena is the god of the village, the Kataragama Deiyo, also known as Kanda Kumara, Skanda, Kandasamy, Subramaniam, Arumugam and Muruga, and many more names. Kataragama Deiyo is believed to be the lord of the Ruhuna—the southern and southeastern parts of the island—and one of the four guardian deities of Sri Lanka. Hindus and Buddhists visit Kataragama in large numbers, particularly during the festive season of Asala that falls between mid-July and mid-August in the Roman calendar.[6] A few hundred pilgrims visit Kataragama even on a nonfestive day. The Sufi Muslims who believe that Allah is the only god also believe that Kataragama Deiyo is a *nabi*, a messenger of Allah. They visit Kataragama and engage in the festivities from a Sufi Muslim perspective. Some Catholics participate in the Hindu/Buddhist cult of the goddess Pattini/Kannagiamman by identifying her as St. Mary.[7] Some Christians believe in Kataragama Deiyo and worship him in much the same way the Hindus and Buddhists do.

The tsunami left traces of inexplicable occurrences. I have come across instances where the miracles of Kataragama blend with those of the tsunami, and hence my choice of these two contexts for the exposition of such phenomena in Sri Lankan cultural life. The examples I present are contemporary and therefore, in the second sense I elucidated above, modern. They present opportunities to understand how modern Sri Lankans conceive of the amazing occurances in Kataragama and the tsunami, and the intellectual dilemmas they encounter in the formulation of these notions.

Miracles of Kataragama

All pilgrims of Kataragama, arriving from all different paths in life, hope to witness a miraculous event that would render their pilgrimage an unconditional success. Some mysterious events are signs of the god's blessings and benevolence, and the others are signs of the god's wrath and punishment. Either way, the *adbhuta* event reaffirms the existence and the power of the god. In Kataragama, every miraculous event is a *pratiharya* (miracle) directly performed by the god and indirectly through his devotees.

The most regularly witnessed miracles are the ascetic performances by certain deeply devoted individuals who also function as nontraditional priests. Such individuals are known as *sami*s. There is no gender preference, although the majority of the *sami*s are male.[8] The *sami*s in Kataragama and elsewhere display their special relationship with the god by performing various acts that are *ascaryajanaka* (capable of producing pleasant awe and astonishment in the minds of the onlookers). These spectacular acts are, from the onlookers' point of view, expositions of the *adbhuta* (mysterious) power of the god as well as of the performer. The popular belief is that ordinary people are incapable of such performances.

There are many types of miracle performances. The best known among them are fire-walking, body piercing, hook-hanging, and *emuvaikkavadi* (wearing nailed sandals). These are performed during the festive season mentioned above.[9] It is important to note that these activities originated in South India and are not confined to Kataragama. But in Sri Lanka, the Kataragama festival is the occasion on which one notices the highest incidence of these practices.[10]

The Sufi Muslim practices in Kataragama add to the sense of the miraculous in Kataragama. At least from the eighteenth century, Sufi pilgrims from the subcontinent, the Middle East, and Central Asia have visited Kataragama and performed various kinds of ascetic feats that express the mysterious nature of the presence of Allah and his messengers known as *nabi*s. Like the Hindu devotees, the Sufis have begun to practice body piercing of various kinds, and these practices are of early twentieth-century origin.[11]

These activities, seen from the local perspectives, invoke the sense of the miraculous attributed to the god of Kataragama, the boon giver and protector who is at the highest level in the effective pantheon of deities. He is invoked whenever disasters occur, and he is pleaded to for help. In Kataragama, his power is recalled whenever people perceive some occurrence as extraordinary. Another aspect of these miracles in Kataragama is that these were only recently introduced to Kataragama through interventions of modernity.

Modern Introduction of Nonmodern Constructions

The performances mentioned above originated in the nonmodern, non-Sanskritic native cultures of Tamil Nadu. The British colonial regime that existed in Sri Lanka from the late eighteenth to mid-twentieth centuries introduced these cultural practices to Sri Lanka through their importation of the practitioners as laborers to work on the coffee, rubber, coconut, and tea plantations. Modern European business management required such imported labor, as native labor was unavailable and unsuitable. Thus, through modern business and political practices nonmodern religious practices entered the contemporary Sri Lankan religious culture.[12]

To this day, the vast majority of Sri Lankan Buddhists and Hindus view and understand these practices through traditional lenses. The native concepts, outlined above, set the standards and canons for the understanding and interpretation of the miracles, although *these* events in Kataragama were only recently introduced into the contemporary culture, which is a mixture of traditional and modern cultures and premodern European cultural strains. Although the events are contemporary, introduced by modern means, their constructions—the logics of these thoughts, principles, and practices—are not modern. Each of the three religions that converge in Kataragama has its own sense of the miraculous phenomena, and all have developed conceptual systems and practices to discourse on them. The concepts and the logics of these discourses are derived from the respective premodern cosmologies. In other words, modern European culture caused the diffusion of nonmodern ideas and practices into Kataragama through colonial enterprises ranging from plantation economics to educational and administrative systems.

The result was the generation of a new dynamic, even confusion, in the colonized cultures. The new cultural elements also engendered local critics. The miracles described above are socially restricted to low castes, mostly to untouchables, and lower classes. The high-caste Hindus of Sri Lanka reject these performances as unholy. The Brahmanical asceticism that they value does not involve this sort of public display. They never permitted these practices in their *agamic* (orthodox) or Sanskritic temples, as these, from their perspective, were the aspects of the religion of the *mleccha* groups and *tribal* peoples who are also *mleccha* (indigenous peoples) because they are not a part of the imagined Vedic community. These practices, from the orthodox perspectives, are inherently polluting and devoid of any soteriological value.[13]

Buddhists have mixed attitudes toward these practices. They express both awe and disgust. The Buddhists are amazed and shocked by the Hindu and Sufi practices and view them with wonderment and respect for the courage of the practitioners to indulge in them. They also respect the religious virtuosity signified by such performances. Yet Buddhist soteriological theory considers these bodily mortifications as worthless practices of the ignorant. They find physical torment repulsive.[14]

But the orthodox Hindu and Buddhist rejections are founded upon nonmodern conceptions of the natural, supernatural, and soteriological phenomena. Their skepticism, however, is distinguishable from the Charvaka skepticism mentioned above. Orthodox Hindus and Buddhists do believe in miracles. They only reject the kind of activities found in Kataragama and other comparable places in the subcontinent.[15] Even regarding Kataragama, they believe in miracles of different kinds, such as mysterious divine interventions in human affairs outlined above. They reject the physical and emotional expressions of devotion and spectacular exhibitions as spiritually unwholesome involvements with the unholy and trickery by charlatans.

The majority of Sunni Muslims in Sri Lanka reject Sufism and never visit Kataragama, reject the institution of tomb worship, object to the performances of the Sufi *pakir*s, and condemn them as abominations and heretical beliefs and practices. Nonetheless, among the Sunnis of Sri Lanka, there is general tolerance and indifference toward Sufi performances. However, recently, there have been attacks on and even murder of Sufi practitioners by extremist orthodox Sunnis influenced by Wahabis who blame Sufis for adulterating Islam with beliefs and practices of unbelievers.[16]

Modern Deconstructions of Nonmodern Constructions

From the late nineteenth century onward, these recently introduced nonmodern cultural events and institutions came under the gaze of modernity, at first that of the European intellectuals and later that of their local protégés. The modern intellectuals reject the miraculous in principle, as David Hume did. They consider miracles as myths and fantasies, symbol systems invented by creative minds to address phenomena of the natural world indirectly.

One of the first to discuss the miracles of Kataragama from a modern perspective was R. L. Spittle, an allopathic physician, in his accounts of the body piercing that he witnessed in the 1930s. There he uses standard modern vocabulary, conceptual schemas, and attitudes to describe, evaluate, and reconstruct the mysteries of body piercing. For Spittle, modern medical science was incapable of explaining these acts of faith. Nevertheless, Spittle does not say that they are unexplainable by modern concepts. These concepts had to come from some area of specialization in science other than medicine. But his contemporary British administrators with modern mentalities were not so open-minded. They saw these acts as primitive and bizarre products of superstitious minds.[17]

Modern Sri Lankan critics vigorously discount the occurences in Kataragama. Body piercing is naturalistically explained as the driving of hooks and other metal spikes through the epithelium of the skin, which is devoid of blood vessels and major nerves. For them the miracle worker is a trickster who deludes the ignorant peasants with inadequate intellectual training. Fire-walking is also similarly dismissed as a naturalistically explainable phenomenon. Socially, the performers are urban working-class people who walk barefoot. This lifestyle thickens the epithelium of their soles. Thick skin insulates the sensitive interior from heat. Besides, the duration of actual contact is very small. In the late 1960s, Carlo Fonseka, a well-known professor of medicine, set forth to debunk the superstition that fire-walking could be done only with a god's blessing and proclaimed that anyone could do it. He gathered a group of similarly materialist thinkers and demonstrated his theory at a local fire-walking ritual. They indulged in polluting activities prior to the fire-walk, and walked on the embers while blaspheming the gods. He and his cohort escaped without any injuries.[18] The point that Professor Fonseka endeavored to establish was that the notion of supernatural help was not necessary to explain firewalking and other such activities, and that naturalistic conceptual schemes were available to provide satisfactory explanations.

Around the same period, another scientific materialist thinker named Abraham Kovoor challenged all the local sorcerers, witchdoctors, swamis, *samis*, and every other performer of magical acts to create miracles, or even to perform black magic to kill or maim him. He, too, based his arguments on scientific empiricism. As far as he was concerned, there was nothing called the supernatural and there was nothing beyond what the senses could perceive directly or indirectly.[19] Later on, anthropological studies based on psychoanalytic theory explored the mentalities of the performers and constructed models of the social contexts and mind-sets involved in miracle performances. However, the anthropological studies did not attempt to debunk the nonmodern constructions.[20]

In any case, the local thinking about the *adbhuta*, *ascarya*, and *pratiharya* fell into two tracks. The society at large steadfastly retained the nonmodern constructions, while a few—a relatively negligible population no bigger than the population of miracle performers—subscribed to the modern constructions. Even among them, the majority vacillated between premodern and modern constructions.

The faithful defended the miracles and the performers. Some leveled ad hominem attacks on the fire-walking professor and his cohort, claiming that they were Christians and/or Marxists trying to destroy the local religions. Some others said the fires that they trampled were so small anyone could do it. A third rebuttal was that the materialists applied a chemical on their soles to insulate them from heat. There was also the tongue-in-cheek claim that there was no difference between the miracle makers and their opponents, as both sides were motivated to do the same thing before an eager public. After all, they did the same thing and expected from the public the same thing. Only their rhetoric was different. The modern materialists eventually gave up publicly contesting the nonmodern culture. Nonetheless, as we shall discuss later on, Fonseka and Kovoor did make a dent in the native discourses on these beliefs and activities, at least among those who were exposed to modern education, by providing them with an alternative explanatory idiom. Perhaps, they buttressed the traditional skepticism with modernist ideas.

Tsunami of 2004 as Legendary and Unprecedented

The Sri Lankan community, until the tsunami of 2004, had only a mystical sense of the sea flooding the land. Empirical understandings of the ocean included concepts of high tide and low tide caused by the phases of the moon, tides that only temporarily changed the geography of the island to a negligible extent, but such understandings did not allow for the possibility of a wave encroaching the land to the magnitude of the tsunami of 2004.

Nonetheless, the sixth-century Sinhala chronicle *Mahavansa* records a story of a great tidal wave. The story of the wave is linked to the story of King Dutthagamani, who ruled in the first century before the Common Era. Dutthagamani's mother, a princess in the kingdom of Magama, was sacrificed to the deep seas to appease the angry gods who had sent the sea inland, causing great destruction. But, rather than drowning, the princess's boat floated in the ocean. The gods directed the vessel to the port of Magama, and the ruler of Magama, finding that she was from a royal household, married her. Dutthagamani was their first son.[21] Dutthagamani became the great king who defended the Sinhala suzerainty on the island and the Buddhist religious establishment from Tamil invasions from South India. His birth itself was a miracle that occurred just when the Buddhists needed a defender. The miracle of his birth was preceded by the miracle of his mother's survival; that, too, was preceded by the miraculous oceanic invasion.

The tsunami of 2004 was immediately followed by a tsunami of information about tsunamis in general and this tsunami in particular, leaving no time to develop local models of what and how it happened. While the water was receding, a huge stock of ideas grew out of the information disseminated by the media, particularly the radio and the television. Live images showed the extent of the disaster, and an international exchange of information provided the scientific basis to understand what happened. It soon became common knowledge that the tsunami was caused by a massive geological plate movement in the ocean floor, very near the island of Sumatra. The resultant oceanic turbulence pushed a forty-foot swell of water at five hundred miles per hour. This incredible force thrust the water in the Bay of Bengal eastward, demolishing many small islands and parts of Sumatra, and spread all the way to Thailand and Taiwan. Westward, the forty-foot swell took three hours to cross the Bay and hit the coast of Tamil Nadu and the eastern and southern and southwestern seaboards of Sri Lanka. This image of what really happened was available within the hour to all Sri Lankans on television, in newspaper pictures, and in all the spoken languages.

All the while, the TV newscasters were looking for an appropriate local word to call the disaster. Tsunami is a Japanese term. What is the local term? Some proposed *dala rala pela*—line of rough waves. It was quickly rejected for being ridiculously poetic. Then came the term *udam rala*—swollen or inflated wave. That term was just mentioned and forgotten: too poetic and too contrived. For the lack of a neat term, the reporters called the entire incident *muhuda goda gelima*, a phrase derived from the story of Dutthagamani—ocean flowing into the land. Within a few days, the media adopted and assimilated the Japanese term *tsunami* and settled on the *muhuda goda gelima* as an acceptable local term in Sinhala.[22]

Within a few days, the local interpretations were in circulation. At first these interpretations fell into at least two large categories: interpretations of local events and interpretations of the tsunami as a whole. The local events were the local discoveries of signs of mysterious powers and their miraculous manifestations. These included religious objects as well as the satellite images of the tsunami itself.

Mysterious Images

The satellite image that drew the attention of a Muslim was the tsunami near Kalutara, a tourist resort on the southwestern seaboard. He found Allah in Arabic inscribed with foam on the sea swell.

A small statue of the Virgin Mary that was stuck in the sand on the beach in the southern town of Matara drew the attention of local Catholics. The statue was in the shrine on the premises of St. Mary's convent—a nunnery and Catholic girls' school—situated on the seashore, right in the path of the tsunami. The Catholics who noticed the statue drew the conclusion that the statue remained on the beach while the receding wave carried away much heavier objects into the ocean because of the mysterious power of Our Lady. She performed a miracle by staying on the beach, braving the force of the wave that retreated with even greater momentum than when it flowed inland. She refused to leave her flock.

Another religious image was the statue of the Buddha that stayed on the beach near Moratuwa, on the southwestern coast, while everything else—the buildings and parapets made of cement and bricks and large trees—fell apart. All those who had access to a television set saw many times the images of the tsunami in Galle town near Matara. While large busses that carried seats for sixty passengers floated about like tin cans, the rush of seawater swirled around a small shrine with a Buddha statue that stood firm under a *bo* tree[23] but failed to cause any harm to it. In another area near Galle, the devastation of the older buildings was severe. But a large statue of the Buddha stood firm. Many interpreted all these as the miraculous expressions of the Buddha's power. Soon, a theory was constructed to show the mysterious properties of the architecture of the statues of the seated Buddha. Water moving at hundreds of miles per hour could not damage the statues, as its architecture provided for excellent resistive capacities, comparable to the aerodynamic properties of modern buildings, airplanes, motor vehicles and ships, allowing the water to quietly flow away by the sides of the statues. In other words, whoever designed the statues already mysteriously knew about such properties without ever conducting wind-tunnel experiments as modern engineers do. Such is the miraculous power of the Buddha.

Tsunami and Kataragama

Several individuals connected their personal experiences of the tsunami with Kataragama. I find truly modern constructions of the miracles of Kataragama and the tsunami in these accounts. These constructions are significant because they reveal something larger than Kataragama, the tsunami, and the miraculous. They present Sri Lanka's postcolonial intellectual dilemmas. Perhaps, structurally, these dilemmas are not unique but are shared by many other societies where nonmodern cultural elements coexist with their modern counterparts. The basic premise here is that the god protected his devotees from the tsunami. The theoretically important aspect of this premise is how the modern devotees articulated it and how this articulation differed from the earlier modern articulations of the miracles of Kataragama from the scientific naturalistic perspectives.

Mr. Jayawickrema's Account

Mr. Jayawickrema is a devout Buddhist who is also thoroughly educated in both traditional and modern knowledge systems. He is well versed in traditional South Asian epistemology, ontology, and teleology, and in Buddhist and Hindu philosophy. He holds a doctorate in linguistics from a major British university. Apart from linguistics, Jayawickrema is knowledgeable about folklore, mythology, comparative religion, and Western philosophy, including the philosophy of science. He may not be an expert in these areas of knowledge, but the Western knowledge systems have significantly influenced his thinking.

Jayawickrema's daughter recently married a young artist who is a devout Buddhist and a devotee of the god of Kataragama. Three months after the marriage, the new couple and Jayawickrema's family visited Kataragama to pay respects to the god. They carried out all the ritual procedures, worshipped the major Buddhist stupa in Kataragama, and left the religious town early on the morning of December 26, 2004. Twelve miles south of Kataragama, there is a Buddhist stupa more famous and holier than the one in Kataragama. This is the great stupa in Tissamaharama. The son-in-law had suddenly developed a strong desire to worship it. His enthusiasm was infectious. Soon everybody wanted to worship the stupa. They spent about half an hour to forty-five minutes worshipping and admiring the stupa and then drove southwest on the coastal road with excellent vistas of the ocean.

When they reached the coastal town of Hambantota, the pilgrims noticed an unusual commotion and traffic congestion on this normally calm road. As the van crawled ahead, people came rushing to it and told them that the ocean was flooding the land. Jayawickrema did not take this warning seriously, as there was nothing unusual about the high tide occasionally encroaching on the land. But then he noticed, about half a mile further down the straight road, water crashing on the road and demolishing the houses on the seaside. He saw several passenger busses being tossed around by this massive onrush of the sea. What to do now? The traffic ahead of and behind him clogged the road. There was no question of going ahead, but he could not turn back, either. He swung the van to his right, out of the road, turned back and drove away in frenzy, through the coconut trees, and came across a cart-road that ran inland. But he could proceed only a few yards, as that road also was clogged with vehicles. Jayawickrema was speechless and trembling.

Suddenly, a middle-aged man came to the passenger side, opened the door, and entered the vehicle completely uninvited. He commanded Jayawickrema to drive according to his instructions. Jayawickrema meekly followed the stranger's imposing and powerful commands, constantly wondering how this man could find his meandering way through an impossible traffic situation. He seemed to have in his mind a blueprint of the space around him. Jayawickrema steered the van this way and that way as the man commanded and wound up near a cluster of houses in an open space on higher ground. The stranger got out and said that the Jayawickremas were safe, and they would find all the necessary assistance from the families around. Then he said that he had to leave them immediately to help others. Jayawickrema wanted to thank him and walk with him. But the stranger had already gone; he had simply disappeared. The very thought of that moment still sends a chill up his spine. Who was that man? From where did he come? Where did he go? What a character!

Of Men and Crocodiles

My next example comes from an essay published in a local newspaper. I call the author Jayantha Rajapaksha to protect his privacy. Mr. Rajapaksha's account appeared in the Features section of the *Sunday Island* newspaper of February 23, 2005. I have edited Rajapaksha's essay for the purposes of this research. I include a segment of the original editor's comments that introduce the author.

EDITOR'S INTRODUCTION

Mr. J. L. A. Rajapaksha is a prominent citizen of Matara. The story presented here is about a near-death experience which he had when the tsunami washed away his entire house including all his furniture and personal effects. He attributes his almost miraculous survival to the swimming and life-saving lessons he had while a student at Richmond College in Galle, but more immediately according to him, an almost personal relationship which he had cultivated with a crocodile![24]

MR. RAJAPAKSHA'S ACCOUNT

The croc which saved his friend from the jaws of death.

The Sunday of 26th December 2005 was like any other Sunday at *Land's End*. My sister Gayani was teaching some forty pre-teenage girls and boys. When the class fell silent, I left my desk to investigate. I found them with Gayani at the bay-window, gazing at the river, fascinated by the water which as never before was rippling as if music was playing in the background. As I moved my eyes upriver, I saw a monster block of brown tide about ten feet high zooming up river towards our home. I shouted to the children to rush into the hall. As they did so, the tide came into the house throwing them into confusion, pushing them into the hall. In a flash, the receding tide which by now had risen to my neck level, swept me off my feet, taking me at speed toward the estuary.

A grey fog covered my sight. An eerie silence blanketed the scene. The long boats at anchor, moved up and down, lost their moorings and soon went to pieces. I could barely see the coconut palm fronds bending over to reach the water which was not now identifiable as river or sea. To my surprise, I was gripping a wooden chair in my left hand and a substantial twin layered stool in my right. The furniture gave me buoyancy in the raging water. I was floating face upwards and doing well so far.

The incoming tide drops me into a deep trough, one high-end I see as a swirling cliff. It takes me up in a swing and hurls me back into the trough to fall face upwards with the furniture in a firm grip in my hands.

By now, I had time to take stock and learn the rules for survival. I found that the tide arrives in three movements, the first one heavier than the last. Between them there is a gap of about four minutes, I could not correctly assess. The first rule to discipline my mind, avoid panic. To stay afloat and to conserve energy. Concentrate on deep breathing whenever possible. Recollections flash through my memory. . . .

Floating face upwards, I can see what I believe is the gray sky. Getting buffeted by the angry water, my sight does not go far. I realize that it is impossible to swim in the raging swirling water which changes its character within minutes. A deep trough bowls me over and flings me down like a broken doll. I have the chair in a firm grip. In my right hand the stool which has two panels. I learn to turn it the right way as an ineffective disc brake. When I swing the stool in a circular movement around my shoulder, I think I have achieved some movement. In minutes all my efforts are set at naught. I see that my legs are ten feet long. I can retract them at my will.

Then comes a massive mountain of water which sweeps me upstream from my place at the estuary. On its return, it takes me out to sea. I am being buffeted over the rocks of Galgodiyana. I am dashed against one which I see as a mountain. As the water surges on, I lift my chair hand and move my left leg as a crab will do to climb the rock. The next thing I know is that a huge monster has thrown me off the rock and is taking me back towards the estuary which is a kilometer away. The chair has gone out of my hand. I am floating head above water, breathing well using my energy with reserve though twisted and twirled like a puppet out of control. Without the chair I cannot maintain my balance. In spite of all my efforts, I turn over many times and take some water. I paddle with my long legs. I try the stool as a rudder. I am in the same place. There is nothing to show where I am or how much time has passed. The usual flights of sea gulls are not to be seen. I realize that in my village and in Thotamuna which lies across the river all are not in the land of the living. I am on my own. There is no point crying for help.

It was around 9.30 a.m. when the sea in its fury dragged me towards the estuary. I could have been six to seven hours at the whim and fancy of the sea. Without the balance and buoyancy of the chair I was in no position to keep control. The tide is high and unpredictable. There is no boat or person to hear, see or come to my help up to at least a kilometer up river. Rescue is out of the question . . . without any forethought these words escaped from me "*Kataragama Divya Rajothamayan wahansa! mata mayka wenna denna epa!*" (Oh! Your Majesty, the Great and Exalted God-king of Kataragama, please do not let this happen to me!) He soon went out of my mind. I return to the task of staying alive.

I am looking for the good fortune of a floating door, table or a log which should come my way. I could keep my balance with a hold on my left hand. In the churning waters which circumscribed my view I did not know whether I was in the river or out at sea. Even with the strongest will to survive. I realize that unless I keep my balance the end is not far. Again hazy thoughts are dredged from memories of the past. . . . The tide comes, overpowering me, furling me head to foot in rope, net and flotsam.

What is this I see some distance away? The surging water cuts me off from time to time. The other debris I had encountered moved in a different manner, without any set pattern. My attempts to reach this object are fruitless. They are at risk to the stability of mind and body which is maintained so far. It looks like a log moving slowly towards me. I am face up and my movements are restricted. Surely it is a log, black, shining and moving slowly towards me.

As I watched with impatience, the log came alongside me. Nobody had to tell me to quickly put my left arm in a grip as with the chair across its bulk. As I did so, I see odd protuberances in this log. My under arm feels awkward. A quick glance. Bloody hell! It is a crocodile. In fear of my life at the hands of a crocodile that will hide me in a swamp until I am done enough for his dinner, I black-out. My head falls into the water on the side where the stool is in my hand. I come and the crocodile gives me a sharp nudge with his belly on my hip, taking off like a jet with me holding fast to him and the stool. He is taking me upstream, the spray flies across my body and we are speeding upstream.

I believe that I blacked out at least five times. My arm was firm on the crocodile so was my right hand with the stool. My head would have been near his neck. My left arm is just below his right leg where it is narrow and widens at his belly. I only knew that the crocodile was sprinting upstream with me in tow somehow I know not how, holding on.

I only knew that the crocodile was racing upstream at a burst of speed I could not assess. I was in great fear and the few black-outs helped me to keep my head. I found myself in shallow water on the river bank resting on the debris that had come with the tide. I had a flash view of the bridge. Only my head was above water. I heard human voices. I raised my left hand. *"Yako! Marila nay! Adhapan! Adhapan!"* some one shouted. The black-out clears for the moment for me to see a man standing on my stomach pumping out my water ruining my birthday suit. Some one said *"Oka atha-harinna!"* and I let go of my magic stool. I hear them identify me by name. I am laid out on a door.

Around 10.30 that night, I regain consciousness to the cries of my sister. She had looked for me everywhere in the overloaded hospital finally in the mortuary. The people of my village had seen me being taken away by the sea. My sister with forty children and fifteen others were saved by the initiative and leadership displayed by my sister who enlisted the support of those others who were in danger themselves.

[Mr. Rajapaksha was airlifted to an elite hospital in Colombo where he recovered from various injuries.]

"Lands End" has been my home since my retirement in 1994. I lived alone and I was glad to see my sister arriving from Colombo to spend the weekend. When the evenings are fine, a friend might visit me. More often than not I was alone but not lonely. I would take a chair on the lawn and watch the sunset blaze in all its glory. My dogs would be playing at the river's edge. Over the ripples of the river, many species of bird life arrive in flights of color to roost on the island until the break of dawn.

Three young crocodiles who infest the river see my dogs as prime delicacies for their dinner. In course of time, I found that one of them would approach me, swimming only with his tail to stop yards away from me to emerge only with his red goggle eyes showing in a focused gaze.

It became my practice to call out to him. "Ado! You son of a bitch! Have you come for my dog? If you take my Patow I will come after you and shoot you through you know where." The next time, I would speak in terms of endearment. "Just see man! No one has come to see me. No friend. No girl friend. I am alone as you are." When my watcher arrives at seven in the morning he is sun bathing on the river's edge.

During the seven hours of my ordeal my mind was clear. There was no possibility of rescue by human resource. The rescue parties were at the bridge some 1 1/2 kms away. How the crocodile knew the fact is beyond my understanding. It amazes me how the crocodile can be motivated even in the background of our rapport to rescue me. While celebrating my, life, my sentiments reach out to all those bereaved by the tsunami.

Those who have heard the fantastic story of my rescue by a crocodile might be incredulous, they being unfamiliar with crocodiles, the river and of course as we all are the Tsunami. More so, those who do not know me might find the story hard to digest.

Moving out of hospital and while convalescing, I thought I will conduct an experiment which if nothing else will demonstrate that the crocodile had established a rapport with me. A relationship which was strong enough to make him seek me out in the turbulence and to come to my rescue.

I intended to restore the house. When I was back at home I will, at sunset take a seat on the lawn at the river's edge and await my usual visitor. The area of the river where our meetings took place was in deep water, fronting the uninhabited island. Across our garden, on the other side, the river is shallow with mud at two feet. The crocodile never approaches from the shallow river.

On Saturday 22nd morning I visited Land's End to survey the damage inflicted by the tsunami. I took a seat at the shallow edge of the river, facing the house. With me were eight members of my family, a few friends and some young men from the village. After about half an hour, the crocodile was seen gliding towards me in the same old manner, swimming with the end of his tail. He stopped just fifteen feet away from me and the river's edge. Only the knot of his forehead could be seen but he opened his goggle eyes and focused his gaze on me. He kept his place for some fifteen minutes and disappeared into the river.

The experience convinces me that my Saturday visitor is the same crocodile who rescued me. He would have caught my scent and come from across the river to establish contact with me. He seemed not to take any notice of the throng around me. I was the only person who was seated and his gaze was focused on me.

I said to him "You, my friend, saved my life. By that merit may you be released from this existence and be born as a human being."

Going back to the time when I was being tossed about in the water, having lost the chair from my left hand and being left with the stool in my right, losing my balance, nearly being drowned, I was wondering why the log was taking so much time to get to me. I would think that the crocodile approached me slowly so that he would not alarm me into a panic. I would then lose my upright position. He would not have been able to take me to the bridge unless he held me in his jaws.[25]

Discursive Strategies

These two accounts illustrate how Sri Lankans with modern education float between two mutually exclusive worldviews. The intelligentsia in Sri Lanka are burdened with the need to live with these mutually exclusive ways of imaging not only the unusual events but also the usual everyday events. As the formal education in European scientific rationalism and the informal education in domestic models of the world clash and from the nineteenth century onward the former achieved a socially and intellectually superior status, intellectuals must present the socially acceptable European scientific model when communicating with their peers in order to sustain intellectual rigor and credibility. This became more so since the late 1960s as Fonseka and Kovoor openly problematized and challenged the hitherto unchallenged native discoursing on miracles that became, at least in formal intellectual discourses, outmoded and unacceptable. The power of scientific naturalistic discourse, established by the theory of proof and illustrated and substantiated by technology, smothered the premodern concepts and worldview. But when in intimate company and there are no intellectual politics, they use the domestic model. Which model is deployed depends on the microsociological context.

In both these examples, the Western-educated devotees of the god socially did not commit themselves to any one model. Jayawickrema merely presented his experience and ended his conversation with questions and gestures. "What caused the sudden irresistible motivation to worship the stupa and spend time there? Why? Who was that man? From where did he appear? Think about how he forced himself into the van. How could he do that? It is very unusual for strangers to do that. It was as if he had some kind of irresistible power in him. Where did he go afterwards? What happened to him? The whole thing surprises me! If not for him all of us would have been killed in the Tsunami!" Jayawickrema did not commit himself to either of the two models available to him. Instead he leaves the "facts" in suspended animation for his audience to deal with them. Yet he does leave a few clues to his unexpressed conviction. The questions, the silent knowing nods, the raising of eyebrows, the shrugs accompanied by the puckering of lips, and the grimaces communicated the sense of mystery. The *adbhuta* character of the events, the *pratiharya* performance by the stranger, and the *ascarya* that he still experiences tilt him toward the premodern model, yet he does not commit himself to it, as it is socially unacceptable in his intellectual milieu. He does not take the materialist model either, for he does not want to insult or damage in any way the wonder and poetry he feels about his experience. One using the empiricist model would construct a different explanation. When the travelers were in danger, many people went forward to help the needy. It could well be that the stranger was a local volunteer who knew his way around and possessed a fine intelligence to sort his way out of difficult situations. He helped them and went away to help others. It is not unusual for volunteers to be rather pushy and assertive when the beneficiaries face dangerous circumstances. There is nothing *adbhuta* about that.

However, Jayawickrema's stance reveals another fact of his world. Encountering someone like this man is nothing less than a miracle, because good people who would not exploit another's adversity are in short supply. If mutual respect, support, and confidence were everyday experiences in his community, Jayawickrema would have no grounds to find anything mysterious and miraculous in this encounter. Jayawickrema cherishes the moment of discovery that good people do exist precisely because they are very rare, at least in contemporary Sri Lanka. Everybody seems to wait for the slightest opportunity to exploit the victims of unfortunate circumstances. He explains his rare experience by slyly invoking divine intervention.

I detect a language game in his sly expressions.[26] People in tight situations employ this discursive strategy as a face-saving device. This linguistic operation involves all available modes of signification appropriate for a given context to express contradictory views. My friend Jayawickrema employed these tactics to save face as a modern educated person who continues to uphold nonmodern views because they are existentially meaningful.

Mr. Rajapaksha admits that under dire need he prayed to the god of Kataragama, but he immediately states that he forgot all about the god. Then he saw the mysterious log coming toward him. The log became a crocodile that carried him to safety. That in itself is, as the editor of the paper remarked, miraculous, for crocodiles are man-eaters and no one, in Sri Lankan experience, has ever taken a ride in a crocodile's mouth and lived to tell the story.[27] Even in zoos the world over, the keepers, despite their knowledge of crocodile conduct, keep the crocodiles that they daily encounter at more than arm's length.

It is interesting how Mr. Rajapaksha connects his experience with the god of Kataragama—merely by mentioning his prayer to the god. Thereafter he never associates his experience with the god. Another person using nonmodern logic would have associated the impossible rescue as the work of the god. But Rajapaksha is a modern man. He would not stoop to peasant thought. He represses all thoughts about the god immediately after his prayer. Attribution of his rescue to the god is what the peasants do. He has a modern explanation. What follows from here has to do with the possibilities of the rationally knowable and demonstrable empirical facts. He managed to stay afloat with the training in swimming that he received at Richmond College, Galle, founded by European missionaries and renowned for the fine European-style education that it disseminated. Then he came across the crocodile that carried him in his mouth to safety. The crocodile would not even cause any excitement, as that would jeopardize its rescue effort. How do you explain that? Crocodiles are man-eaters. This crocodile saved his life by carrying him to safety between its jaws. How can one address this aporetic experience? Mr. Rajapaksha suggests that daily encounters between him and the crocodile somehow produced this sort of endearment. Notice that many weeks later, when he was on Land's End with his relatives, the crocodile reappeared. Mr. Rajapaksha is sure that the crocodile was looking squarely at him: "He seemed not to take any notice of the throng around me. I was the only person who was seated and his gaze was focused on me."

Although Mr. Rajapaksha opts to forget about the god, he leaves a clue to a possible nonmodern explanation of the miraculous rescue by detailing how he prayed to the god. He does not have to mention that he prayed to the god, but he did. Then he vigorously denies any involvement with the god: "[W]ithout any forethought these words escaped from me '*Kataragama Divya Rajothamayan wahansa! mata mayka wenna denna epa!*' (Oh! Your Majesty, the Great and Exalted God-king of Kataragama, please do not let this happen to me!) He soon went out of my mind. I return to the task of staying alive."

Having left that traditional door open, he chooses to crawl through the modern windows that are socially and intellectually more respectable. His statements have an empiricist color. They are testable as statements about observable crocodile behavior, even crocodile emotions—if the researcher feels that there is a psychology to all this. Mr. Rajapaksha implies a psychology, the kind of romantic emotions that, quite literally, bring about crocodile tears.

This seems like a perfect opportunity to conduct a controlled experiment in true scientific spirit. Technically, this is what the researcher needs to do. He should associate with a crocodile for a period of time, talking to it the way Mr. Rajapaksha did and one day, when he is confident that the relationship is strong enough, approach the crocodile and hold it the way Mr. Rajapaksha did. Theoretically, although somewhat slippery, these are the steps he must take, and they are practicable, as crocodiles are not mythical beings. But I have a few misgivings. Who is to say that this would not be our researcher's last tango?

That is where the rub is. One can make perfectly objective, seemingly testable propositions that are, in fact, experimentally impracticable. Such statements have the color of scientific rigor without being scientific. This is where the mystery is. Mr. Rajapaksha's experience is seemingly repeatable but unique, and one must take the risk of his life in order to verify it. He is a very clever man, this Mr. Rajapaksha, for he created a modern aporia to hide his commitment to the god of Kataragama, which he is embarrassed about. His language game involves aporetic statements with conceptual schemes that are as slippery as the moss and the mud on crocodile skins.

The discursive strategies employed by the modern devotees of Kataragama do not make direct expressions. Rather, they make indirect expressions of complex characteristics. Perhaps, since these occurrences are products of South Asian communicative practices, it is appropriate to invoke a model that the Sanskrit linguist, grammarian, and poet Anandavardhana constructed. Anandavardhana, judging by his contemporary practices—which seem to survive and thrive in all South Asian cultures to this day—employed the term *vyanjana* to denote the construction of expressive signs of a special class. *Vyanjana* means "mixed," "blended," "set together," "to form a composite expression."[28] Such expressions produce *dhvani* or echoes of meaning that are not directly expressed but slyly suggested. The surface meaning may be misleading, for the sign user intends not the direct meaning that anyone can readily grasp but the indirect meanings that only a *sahrda*—one of equal heart—can discern.[29] There is a play of meaning in the communicative act between the speaker and the listener, the writer and the reader, the performer and the audience. To invoke Ludwig Wittgenstein, this play is a language game. The challenge is to catch the meanings intended by the speaker/writer/performer as best as the listener/reader/audience can. In the modern constructions of mysteries and miracles, these language games are frequent occurrences. Here the meanings are echoed by means of strategic uses of discursive elements that function as *vyanjana* expressions with *dhvani*, so that the speaker/writer/performer can mean two or more things—nonmodern/premodern/modern/religious/scientific—simultaneously in one composite expression. All this shrugging, nodding, and puckering of lips while making seemingly factual statements, or a tango with a crocodile, are elements of the same strategy of surreptitiously invoking the nonmodern while openly engaging in modern empiricist discoursing. It is a different kind of discursive tango, not so deadly but just as slippery, almost like an anthropologist's entanglements with religious phenomena.

Notes

1. I use the term "modern" in a truncated sense to deal with data specific to this research. Lyotard 1979, Habermas 1985, and Best and Kellner 1991 provide extensive discussions of the concept. By "European" I refer to all European as well as American, Canadian, Australian, and New Zealand societies and cultures that descend from Europe. "False" in this context means failure to establish scientific veracity and to be conclusively disproved through experimentation, in the sense Karl Popper used the term "falsification."

2. Weber 1958 and Weber 1922.

3. See Monier-Williams [1899] 1979 and Rhys-Davids and Steed 1921, 1979 (1993, first Indian edition) for Sanskrit and Pali references.

4. Cowell and Gough 1914 and Radhakrishnan and Moore 1957, 227–49 are among the best sources on the Charvakas.

5. For interesting contemporary discussions log on to http://www.mukto-mona.org . Also see n. 27 below.

6. See Wirz 1966, Obeyesekere 1978, 1981, Rasaiah 1982, Fernando 1985, Gombrich and Obeyesekere 1988, and Saparamadu 2004 for the annual festivities in Kataragama.

7. See Obeyesekere 1984 for details of the cult of the goddess Pattini.

8. Singular: *sami*. This male-female *sami* ratio may be changing. During the past couple of decades, females outnumbered males in religious performances in Kataragama. See references in n. 6 above for detailed discussions of phenomena surrounding the *sami*.

9. See references in n. 6 for details of these performances.

10. However, since the ethnic conflicts began in the 1950s and exploded as an ethnic war in 1983, many Tamil *sami*s withdrew from Kataragama and now perform their feats at temple festivals in the northern and eastern provinces where they predominate and in the plantations in the central province.

11. For Sufi practices in Kataragama, see Spittle 1933. None of the nineteenth-century colonial administrative reports mention these practices in Kataragama. However, they existed elsewhere. Cordiner witnessed hook-hanging in Colombo in 1799.

12. See Wesumperuma 1986 and Daniel 1997 on the plantation laborers and their culture.

13. See Pfaffenberger 1979 on high-caste Tamil attitudes toward these practices.

14. Awe and disgust are not mutually exclusive, at least in Kataragama. They are extremes in a continuum of attitudes. The majority of the Buddhists entertain a synthesis of respect and disapproval, amazement and revulsion.

15. These practices are found in Malaysia and Fiji as well, because Tamils of these classes and castes migrated to those countries and established their religions.

16. See Balachandran 2004.

17. Steele 1872 is a good case in point.

18. Fonseka's theses on the nature of fire-walking appear in Fonseka 1971. There is a complex body of modern scientific literature on the nature of fire-walking in general. See Mailis 1995.

19. Regarding Kovoor, log on to http://www.uni-giessen.de/~gk1415/kovoor.htm. Kovoor published several books on materialist themes. The best known among them is Kovoor 1976.

20. For anthropological studies of Kataragama performances, see n. 6 above.

21. See the *Mahavansa* for earthquakes and tidal waves in early Buddhist experience.

22. I am only reporting on the Sinhala reactions to the tsunami. Tamil Sri Lankans faced similar linguistic problems and adopted the Japanese term.

23. *Ficus religiosa.*

24. Mr. Rajapaksha uses the Sri Lankan version of British English. Although ungrammatical and nonidiomatic in several instances, I choose to leave Mr. Rajapaksha in his own words, as the usages show on their own the nature of local adoptions of foreign paradigms of and for construction and expression of notions and the confusions inherent in such practices. These are, perhaps, structurally parallel to the confusions involved in the adoption of modern models of and for reasoning in nonmodern or only superficially modern societies.

25. Goonasekera 2006.

26. I borrow the concept from Ludwig Wittgenstein 1953.

27. Mr. Rajapaksha initially states that the crocodile carried him on its back and that he clung to it with all his strength. But he later rationalizes, as in the last sentence in the quotation, that it could have been impossible for the crocodile to carry him to safety unless it held him in his jaws. With this last observation, Rajapaksha enhances the miraculous nature of his improbable rescue.

28. In Sinhala, *vyanjana* also means a curry prepared by mixing a variety of spices and other ingredients.

29. For Anandawardhana's work, see Senanayake 1969, Kunjunni Raja 1963, and Todorov 1978.

References

Balachandran, P. K. 2004. "Lankan Muslim Sect Attacked for Spreading 'Hindu' Ideas." November 6. http://www.HindustanTimes.com/.

Best, Steven, and Douglas Kellner. 1991. *Postmodern Theory: Critical Interrogations.* New York: Guilford Press.

Daniel, Valentine. 1997. *Chapters in an Anthropology of Violence: Sri Lankans, Sinhalas, and Tamils.* Delhi: Oxford University Press.

Fausbøll, Viggo, ed. 1875–97. *Jataka Nidanakatha in Jataka, Together with Its Commentary, Being Tales of the Anterior Births of Gotama Buddha.* London: Pali Text Society.

Fernando, W. Lionel. 1985. *Kataragama and its Festivals* (1819–1939). Colombo: Ananda Press.

Fonseka, Carlo. 1971. "Fire-walking: A Scientific Investigation." *Ceylon Medical Journal*, June, 104–9.

Geertz, Clifford. 1973. *The Interpretation of Cultures.* New York: Basic Books.

Geiger, Wilhelm, trans. 1912. *Mahavamsa: The Great Chronicle of Ceylon.* Assisted by Mabel H. Bode. Colombo: Ceylon Government Information Department.

Gombrich, Richard, and Gananath Obeyesekere. 1988. *Buddhism Transformed.* Princeton, NJ: Princeton University Press.

Goonasekera, Sunil. 2006. "Bara: Buddhist vows in Kataragama." In *Dealing with Deities: The Ritual Vow in South Asia*, edited by Selva Raj and William Harman, 107–28. Albany: State University of New York Press.

Habermas, Jürgen. 1985. *The Philosophical Discourse of Modernity.* Translated by Frederick Lawrence. Cambridge, MA: MIT Press.

Hassen, M. C. A. 1968. *Kataragama Mosque and Shrine.* Colombo: S. A. M. Thauoos.

Kovoor, Abraham. 1976. *Begone Godmen.* Bombay: Jaico Publishing House.

Kunjunni Raja. 1963. *Indian Theories of Meaning.* Madras: Adyar Library and Research Centre.

Lyotard, Jean-Françoise. 1979. *The Postmodern Condition: A Report on Knowledge.* Translated by Geoff Bennington and Brian Massumi. Minneapolis: University of Minnesota Press.

Madhava. 1914. *Sarva-Darsana-Samgraha.* 1914. Translated by. E. B. Cowell and A. E. Gough. 4th ed. London: Kegan Paul, Trench, Trübner & Co.

Mailis, Angela. 1995. "Mind, Body, and Pain: Are There Any Borders?" *Humane Medicine Health Care* 11:4.

Matilal, Bimal Krisha. 1987. "Carvaka." *The Encyclopedia of Religion*, ed. Mircea Eliade. New York: Macmillan Publishing Company.

Monier-Williams, Monier. [1899] 1979. *A Sanskrit-English Dictionary.* Oxford: Clarendon Press.

Obeyesekere, Gananath. 1978. "The Firewalkers of Kataragama: The Rise of Bhakti Religiosity in Buddhist Sri Lanka." *Journal of Asian Studies* 37, no. 3:457–76.

———. 1981. *Medusa's Hair: An Essay on Personal Symbols and Religious Experience.* Chicago: University of Chicago Press.

———. 1984. *The Cult of the Goddess Pattini.* Delhi, Motilal Banarsidas.

Pfaffenberger, Brian. 1979. "The Kataragama Pilgrimage: Hindu-Buddhist Interaction and Its Significance in Sri Lanka's Polyethnic Social System." *Journal of Asian Studies* 38, no. 2:253–81.

Pieris, Paul E. 1950. Appendix AA, "Kataragama Deviyo and the Ritual of Worship." In *Sinhale and the Patriots, 1815–1818*, 696–701. New Delhi: Navrang.

Radhakrishnan, Sarvapalli, and Charles Moore. 1957. *Source Book in Indian Religion.* Princeton, NJ: Princeton University Press.

Rasaiah, Arumugam. 1982. *Kataragama: Divine Power of Kathirkamam and Methods of Realization.* Colombo: Frewin & Co.

Rhys-Davids, T. W., and William Steed. 1993. *Pali-English Dictionary.* London: Pali Text Society. Originally published in Delhi by Motilal Banarsidas, 1921.

Saparamadu, S. D. 2004. *Kataragama: The Esala Festivals from the Government Agents' Diaries.* Dehiwala: Tisara Prakasakayo.

Senanayake, G. S. B. 1969. *Dhvanyaloka Vivaranaya.* Colombo: M. D. Gunasena & Co.

Spittle, R. L. 1933. *Far-off Things.* Sooriya edition. Colombo: Sooriya Publishers.

Todorov, Tzvetan. 1978. *Symbolism and Interpretation.* Translated by Catherine Porter. Ithaca, NY: Cornell University Press.

Weber, Max. 1922. *The Sociology of Religion.* Translated by Ephraim Fischoff. Boston: Beacon Press.

———. 1958. *The Protestant Ethic and the Spirit of Capitalism.* Translated by Talcott Parsons. New York, Scribner's.

Wesumperuma, Dharmapriya. 1986. *Indian Immigrant Plantation Workers in Sri Lanka: A Historical Perspective, 1880–1910.* Colombo: Vidyalankara University Press.

Wijeyewardene, Gehan. 1979. "Firewalking and the Skepticism of Varro." *Canberra Anthropology* 12, no. 1:114–33.

Wirz, Paul. 1966. *Kataragama, the Holiest Place in Ceylon.* Translated by Doris Berta Pralle. Colombo: Lake House Investments.

Wittgenstein, Ludwig. 1953. *Philosophical Investigations.* Translated by G. E. M.Anscombe. Oxford: Blackwell Publishers.

———. 2003. *Tractatus Logico-Philosophicus.* New York, Barnes and Noble.

Zebian, Maureen. 2005. "Sri Lankan Buddha Statues Survive Tsunami." January 15. www.en.epochtimes.com.

PART II

Making and Breaking Shrine Reputations

CHAPTER FIVE

Showing Miracles in Rajasthan

Proof and Grace

ANN GRODZINS GOLD

The language of miracle tales encountered at regional shrines in rural Rajasthan tells of deities who "show" miracles to human beings, rather than enacting or performing these deeds of blatant power. Although the phrase *chamatkar dikhana*—literally, "to show a miracle"—is a convention of speech, it seems to be a meaningful one. Miracles in these stories, often denoted with the synonymous term "proof" (*parchya*), are not simply manifestations but explicitly communications to human audiences or witnesses. Some miracle stories carry clear didactic messages to mortals, suggesting they reform offensive behaviors. Others testify powerfully to a divine grace that may reward for unstinting devotion persons otherwise stigmatized by illegal occupations.

In the central and substantial portion of this essay I present five brief miracle narratives associated with pilgrimage to Rajasthani deities. In addition, in order to place the distinctive qualities of shrine miracles in a broader context of devotional understanding, I contrast these five examples with a woman's worship tale from the same folklore community. As a genre, worship stories portray miraculous intervention in a fashion somewhat different from shrine narratives. Existing in a timeless realm of divine immanence, they assume the miraculous, and speak of grace but not of proofs.

The stories I assemble here constitute both substance and argument. Most serve to deliver lessons or morals that are right on the surface, requiring little subtle analysis. My aims are simply to use these narratives to enhance our comprehension of rural religiosity in north India. In closing I muse on miracles and wonders in the broader context of this volume's conundrum theme.

Aditya Malik has recently argued in his important study of the Rajasthani hero-god Devnarayan's epic that "divine testimony" structures this oral narrative and that this testimony "is the most central theme . . . on which perhaps all other meanings hinge" (2005, 9). Malik views the entire epic as a process establishing Devnarayan's worship, arguing that this is never taken for granted. Testimony is so crucial and central, Malik observes, because Devnarayan, "even while being God," is not always recognized, and throughout the tale "must 'prove' who he is" (170). Moreover, providing a direct link to this volume's central focus, Malik observes that the battles Devnarayan wins "are not won forcefully but 'miraculously.'" These victories are indeed "testimony" to his divinity, and thus the means by which Devnarayan "'enrolls' his devotees and establishes his cult" (137). Malik's observations on the working of miracles internal to the Devnarayan epic narrative seem entirely congruent with the impact of the miracle tales associated with Rajasthani regional shrines that I wish to consider here. The difference is only that shrine tales are persuasive in ongoing fashion in real time, versus epic time.

There is of course clear mythological and theological continuity between the types of short miracle narrative that flourish in the context of healing shrines and the stunning divine deeds embedded in the plotlines of Rajasthan's regional oral epic traditions. Devnarayan as well as Ramdevji, of whose miracles we shall also hear, are both hero-gods celebrated in these epics. They are equally the reigning deities of two shrines that figure in several pilgrims' stories discussed in this chapter.[1] Both hero-gods have biographies punctuated by miracles; their epics may indeed be organized by the bards who perform them according to episodes involving a numbered series of miracles or "proofs." However, three of the five tales considered are about goddess shrines, and the goddess has many forms and many stories but no epic establishing her worship. Nonetheless, her pilgrimage miracle tales are very much in the same mode of proof or testimony as are Devnarayan's and Ramdevji's. Shrine miracles clearly do not depend on an elaborated epic backdrop. It does seem to me, however, that all shrine stories participate in continuities with the worlds of meaning known to Rajasthanis through these larger regional tales.

In all cases, shrine deities prove who they are by repeatedly showing miracles to pilgrims and others. If the proofs slow down or cease, so does the flow of pilgrims. There is an interesting theological tension between the deep eternal and ineffable truth of God and the scrappy, contentious, and even quarrelsome mode by which invisible existence is proven through displays and exploits of power. This tension is apparent in regional epics as well as in shrine lore where deities present sometimes violent proof of who they are to notoriously dense humanity with its clouded vision and stubborn temperaments. In gentler modes, they may protect their devotees and flummox others.

Real-Time Miracles

The five place stories I shall relate are translated from interviews recorded during two different fieldwork spells in Rajasthan, north India. Various speakers in various contexts describe actual, witnessed miraculous events. I would not want to say that I have selected "typical" stories. I chose these from a far larger pool of similar tales in hopes that they would pique readers' interests and seize their attention. More precisely, I have selected the five tales on two criteria: for drama and for vivid messages—whether about society, divinity, or both. I would nonetheless claim that these stories do exemplify a genre of oral narrative performance in the area where I have been doing research since 1979: the *chamatkari ghatna* (miraculous event) story. Sometimes seen by the teller, sometimes reported to the teller by a witness, miraculous event narratives would be comparable in some ways to urban legends in American folklore. That is, like urban legends, they are recounted as actual occurrences that happened either to the narrator or to a close acquaintance or ancestor of the narrator.[2] Thus rather than removed to remote "once-upon-a-time," their assured veracity exists in—to use the language of computer communications—real time: these stories are indeed a kind of "instant message."

Of course, this analogy to urban legends has not to do with content but with the key quality of veracity, critical for both urban legend and miraculous event tales. For both genres, the witness element—unmediated knowledge— is a crucial factor. As noted earlier, Rajasthani deities are said not to "do" miracles but to "show" them, thus by definition requiring viewers. One of our interviewees repeatedly punctuated his miracle narrative with the word *sakshat* (witnessed). Although this case was, significantly, a courtroom miracle, *sakshat* does have broad semantic implications in the world of popular religion that go well beyond legal matters. In my own ethnographic experience, I heard various persons use the adjective conversationally to refer to powerful waking visions of deities that they explicitly distinguished from dreams. That is, although a message from a deity who appears in a dream may be readily accepted as a true divine manifestation, to see or "witness" a deity's divine form while awake—referred to as *sakshat darshan*—is a more intense and transporting experience.

I gathered four of five event tales during preliminary research on regional shrine origin stories in January–February 2003, accompanied as ever by Bhoju Ram Gujar, who has worked with me as research collaborator and coauthor for over twenty years.[3] All the shrines I visited that winter were served by male hereditary non-Brahmin priests (*bhopa*). While some of these men were artisans such as potters and carpenters, most belonged either to the Mina or Gujar communities. These are both numerically strong communities in the region, and are associated with agriculture and herding. While each has a distinctive history, Minas and Gujars together stand apart from other farming communities in sharing an identity as fierce and skillful fighters—sometimes co-opted by ruling landholders as guards, and sometimes opposing rulers to take on the identity of outlaws or bandits.[4] Today Minas and Gujars often find routes to wage-earning prosperity in government service, especially the police and the military. At Rajasthani shrines dedicated to regional forms of the Goddess, Minas were most often in attendance as worship-priests, although in one case the hereditary priest we interviewed was a Khati or carpenter. At shrines of the epic hero-god Devnarayan we usually spoke with Gujars—the group most strongly identified with Devnarayan's epic worship.

Although particular shrines are indeed associated with and managed by particular castes or even lineages within caste communities, pilgrims from diverse backgrounds freely come to worship and request boons from regional divinities who are thought to deliver many kinds of grace to all who sincerely seek it. Pilgrims may range from Brahmin, Merchant, Rajput castes—the so-called twice-born—to disadvantaged leather workers. However, the demographically preponderant farming and herding communities often form the majority of worshippers. Power apparent in human hierarchies and power expressed in shrine miracles may conflict and sometimes displays radical fissures. For example, class conflict seems right on the surface of meanings in the telling of the "Stupid Landlord's" tale, and caste discrimination is roundly critiqued in the "Twice-blind Carpenter" story.[5] This last I recorded in 1980 during my first fieldwork, when my subject was pilgrimage. Because it was recorded from a member of the formerly "untouchable" Regars or leather workers, it adds another social strata to the performance contexts, and perhaps reveals the clearest didactic intentionality.

Narrative Density on the Ground

Schattschneider writes about a sacred mountain in Japan, a very different religious and cultural context, that "[n]arrating miraculous visions and revelatory knowledge of the mountainscape is one of the most important responsibilities of the senior members of the shrine. . . . There is . . . a deeply accretive quality to the paths. . . . One walks along a path . . . suffused with the collectively held remembrances of the shrine community . . ." (Schattschneider 2003, 153). In Rajasthan also sacred places have this "accretive quality"; accumulated layers of stories produce a kind of narrative density. The more miraculous events associated with a place, the more power it evidently possesses. This accumulation of miracle tales as collective memories operates as a magnetic field, drawing needy mortals afflicted by all kinds of troubles.

The intersection of healing, miracle narratives, and natural beauty at Rajasthan's regional shrines offers a compelling religious complex. Elsewhere I have focused on tree-protection miracles and the ways that robust ecological health, most especially when it contrasts with desiccated surrounding landscapes, is not only a sign of divine power but also a promise of efficacy for human well-being (Gujar and Gold 2006; Gold forthcoming). Although the stories I have chosen to present in this essay include motifs of healing and divine tree-protection, my focus here is upon constructions of power. In a sense, manifestations of power are primary; they provide the context in which healing occurs and natural beauty flourishes. However, these causalities also display circularity. To use Malik's terms, testimony acknowledges power that is already there, but it also attracts pilgrims whose experiences add to that testimony, and in some ways establish that power. A damaged environment is countertestimony, and pilgrims may stop attending a deforested or polluted shrine.

Two of the tales below—"The Goddess, the Thief and the X-ray" and "The Stupid Landlord"—involved straightforward punishments. Two involve rescues, in both cases of criminal devotees who were in dire danger of punishment from human authorities. Hence, in "The Opium Seller's Story" and "The Outlaw's Plunge" listeners must fathom how grace is bestowed in unlikely places. Finally, "The Twice-blind Carpenter" has a double move from boon to punishment. Taken together, these stories reveal that the capacity to punish and to grant grace are fully merged conceptually.

Punishment tales deliver useful moral lessons that appeal to our outsider interests in the social workings of religious narratives. Deities frequently correct human folly by inflicting direct and painful reminders of truth. Many tales of boons, by contrast, are less dramatic: an afflicted person appeals for help and gets it. However, in two cases I have chosen to present here, boons arouse our curiosity because they seem morally arbitrary or even counterintuitive. These tales, by evaluating devotional fervor above behavioral codes, remind us not always to seek earthly morals in divine lessons. The gods respond to those who ardently worship them—no matter what those worshippers' motives or misdeeds. This motif goes right back to ancient mythology.[6]

It is also easy to observe in some tales recounted here vivid demonstrations of public, social, and even subversive messages of the type anthropologists cherish. Nonetheless, if we leave out the apprehension of inexplicable power at their center and the surplus of grace created by devotion, I believe we fail fully to comprehend even their mundane impacts and implications.

The first two narratives were gathered in one day at the same shrine. One is of punishment and one is of rescue.

The Goddess, the Thief and the X-ray

At the shrine of Ghanta Rani, outside the town of Jahazpur in Bhilwara District, Rajasthan, pilgrims often attach pieces of cloth and clothing to trees belonging to this powerful form of the mother goddess. These operate as channels between the ailing body of a sick person and the divine, grace-giving body of the Mother, touchable through her protected trees. The same practice takes place at countless other regional shrines. In January 2003 at Ghanta Rani's place, along with the usual variegated strips of cloth, we also saw dangling from

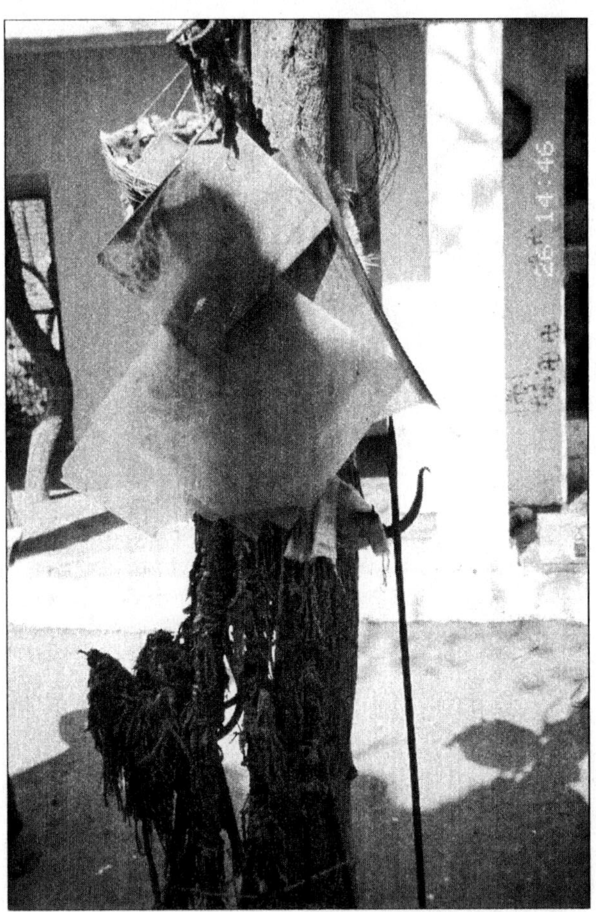

FIGURE 5.1. X-rays on display at the shrine of Ghanta Rami, 2003. Photo by Ann Grodzins Gold.

a branch what appeared to be two sheets of murky-gray translucent plastic (see figure 5.1). Bhoju identified these as X-rays and asked the priest about them: "Whose X-ray sheets are those? Where did they come from?"

The priest replied, in storytelling mode:

> There was a man who broke the lock of the donation box, and took the money from inside of it. Later he became sick. He went to deities' places, and to the hospital, but he couldn't be cured. Then in the Jahazpur hospital, Dr. Rathor took an X-ray of him. When the doctor looked at the X-ray, he saw [inside the man] images of the donation box, the lock, and the Mother [her icon].
>
> So then that man came straight here, he grabbed Mataji's feet and legs [that is, he metaphorically threw himself on her mercy, because the actual icon has no feet or legs] and then he offered five thousand to six thousand rupees. And after coming here, he didn't become completely well, but he became well enough to walk around. He was a Mina from the village of Beyi, a Mina.

Bhoju, my companion in research who is quite willing to believe the extraordinary, is at the same time always determined to examine logical flaws in any tale. He inquired, "Can we still see those things on the X-ray sheet?"

"No," the priest answered, "they have faded in the sun and the rain; but when he brought them here you could see the whole thing."

THE OPIUM SELLER'S STORY

Later that day, at Ghanta Rani, we met a man with long black hair sitting by the "renouncer's fireplace" (*dhuni*). These hearths, which serve as subsidiary shrines, are found at many Rajasthani pilgrimage places. They have been installed specifically to honor world renouncers. Often, itinerant holy persons stop at such places for a few days to rest and bless passing pilgrims. We took this man at first, then, to be a renouncer himself. Bhoju asked him if he knew of any miraculous events associated with Ghanta Rani. He replied immediately that he himself had experienced a miracle, and then he gave us this brief and startling account:

> I used to do "number-two labor" [slang for dealing in opium]. The police grabbed my goods and after they got my goods, they put me in jail. But while in jail I had great faith in her [Ghanta Rani, the goddess], so—in witnessed form (*sakshat*) she had my case dismissed on the grounds of insufficient evidence.

This was my own miracle, and so I accept her. All things I saw myself with my own eyes, and this is why I have faith that this is Mother, in witnessed form (*sakshat*).

When we listened to this tape, Bhoju commented that the man had spoken about the Goddess as if she had been his actual lawyer, causing his case to be dismissed.

Bhoju asked the man if he had given up his former criminal livelihood after this miracle, and he replied ambiguously. First he said, laughingly, "What? Does one give up one's work? I do it with faith in her." Then he amended, "Even so, I don't do it. It's the truth, now I don't do it." Perhaps he was putting us on, first joking, and then serious; or perhaps it was the other way around.

The Outlaw's Plunge

In 2003 we recorded another story about a goddess saving a criminal, elicited from the shrine-priest Bhavar Lal Khati at a major goddess shrine called Joganiya Mataji—the largest and best-known site we visited that year. The story is set in pre-Independence India, over half a century ago, and has the ring of a legend, but the priest, who was an old man, claimed it was something he had seen with his own eyes.

There was an outlaw named Nanda Mina, from the village of Bhat Kheri. At that time it was the state period [that is, the location was governed by the princely state of Mewar]. So Nanda offered a feast here at Joganiya Mata. To try to catch him the police came here. And at that time he was in the temple prostrating himself to Mother [that is, to the Goddess]. He had with him a twelve-bore gun, double barrel.

One of his companions was ready to turn witness for the police, and was conspiring to get him captured; this man was a *banjhara* [a community of peddlers, often untrustworthy in folklore], but he was connected with the police. So Nanda had set down his twelve-bore gun in order to prostrate himself. And right at that moment, the *banjhara* took the gun.

Then Nanda realized he was surrounded by police, and he said to Mother [that is, to the Goddess], "Hey, Old Lady, I've come to you, so do you want to have me killed? You are the object of my devotion, so I have to come here. But now they will kill me!"

That is all he said, and then he jumped from the wall—right where those monkeys are sitting—into the ravine [this is a huge drop]. Crying "Victory to Joganiya Mother!" he jumped into the ravine!

And there were police on both sides of the ravine, on one side from Indore, and on the other side from Mewar, and they fired eighty times at him. Later they counted the empty shells [and there were eighty], but not even one bullet touched him. And after the shooting was over he got straight out of the ravine and escaped with his life.

This is a miracle that I have seen with my own eyes.

As if the rest flowed naturally from this extraordinary event, the priest continued, "If someone has a disease, like paralysis, they become well. Sometimes pilgrims come here and witches or ghosts are in somebody's body, but still they become well. Sometimes they stay two or three days, but they become well." Although to conserve space and avoid repetition I have not cited such codas in every instance, it is striking how often a refrain of healing follows a dramatic miracle story.

THE STUPID LANDLORD (*THAKUR*)

Banjari ka Devji is the Devnarayan to whom Bhoju Ram's parents credit his birth and survival, after many babies had perished in infancy; he is also the divinity to whom Bhoju and his wife, Bali, credit the birth of their first son.

FIGURE 5.2. Telling miracles at Banjari ka Devi shrine, 2003. Photo by Ann Grodzins Gold.

Here we spoke with a Gujar priest named Bhairu, on February 8, 2003. Because of our ongoing interest in tree protection, Bhoju pursued this topic especially, asking the priest if anyone were allowed to cut wood in the shrine's territory.[7] The priest replied that no one but he and his family—hereditary shrine attendants who live on the grounds—are allowed to use this wood. He added, "[N]obody cuts, because they are afraid of Devji."

Bhoju then asked, "Was there any event where he showed a miracle?"

The priest immediately responded in the affirmative and launched the following narrative:

> There was a big landlord, whose name was Madho Singh. (He lived near Abhaypur; his lineage was that of Dhul Singh.)
>
> In those days, in Bhairuji's *bani* [protected grove] there were huge *dhokara* trees.
>
> [This is a Devnarayan shrine, but Bhairu is always understood to be Devnarayan's agent in the world—literally, the "one who goes ahead of him." This story of divine intervention, then, is by definition a story of Bhairuji.]
>
> So, this landlord cut down a tree and having cut it, he took it to the place where he was building a two-story house. He wanted to use the tree for a roof beam. So having cut it, he made it his roof beam.
>
> When his house was complete, then the landlord came back to Devji, and at that time my great grandfather, my forefather, was a medium, and he was possessed by the deity.[8]
>
> "Oh Madho Singh!" [the possessed priest—that is, the deity—calls]
>
> "Yes, Grain-Giver!"
>
> "How is your two-story house?"
>
> The stupid landlord . . . he replied, "Lord, it is so nice, it is just like a place where deities would roam."
>
> Then he [the deity speaking through the medium] replied, "I will cause *akaro* trees [inauspicious, poisonous plants that grow in desolate places] to grow there and dogs to roam there. And then you will understand that I am Bhairuji."
>
> So later he showed him miracles, and little by little destruction happened to the whole house. [No details are given here, but the sense is that one thing after another breaks or goes wrong in this household.] Finally the landlord himself tore down the rest of it and took the roof beam, he took it back to Bhairuji, and that very piece of wood is still there, in front of Bhairuji's shrine—where the spears are. That is the beam that the landlord returned. This happened about 125 years ago.

Bhoju asked about the current condition of the Madho Singh's estate, and the priest answered with some satisfaction, "It is now so spoiled, that people go there to shit; there is nothing left but a wall, and people do their latrine work behind it."

This story of wealthy arrogance brought low certainly reflects Rajasthan's socioeconomic hierarchies and their inherent tensions and resentments. These have been handed down through generations into a present when many of the former rulers have indeed been sorely reduced by secular processes of democratization and land redistribution. Yet the twenty-first-century telling loses none of its gleeful punch; the crumbled grandeur of former nobility is attributed to genuine sins and viewed as just deserts.

THE TWICE-BLIND CARPENTER

This tale was narrated to Bhoju and me together in 1980 by Bardu Regar, an untouchable leatherworker. Bardu had recently traveled to Ramdevra in Western Rajasthan—the site of a major pilgrimage center. The deity there, Ramdevji, is a Rajasthani hero-god who is especially connected with untouchable groups, although he may be worshipped by members of the higher castes—especially when they are seeking relief from affliction. Ramdevji himself was born into the Rajput caste, but an untouchable friend/devotee plays an important role in his legend.

Ramdevji's legend asserts in a number of ways that he is a god who disapproves strongly of such discriminations as are encapsulated in the term—*chhutachhut*—used for matters of touchable and untouchable. He also is known for giving immediate "proofs" to devotees—either of favor or displeasure.

In the course of our discussion with Bardu of his experiences on a recent journey to Ramdevra, and of devotion to Ramdevji in general, Bardu had been talking about the curative power of bathing at the tanks near Ramdevji and associated temples, especially for blindness. He then moved without any prompting into a more elaborated miracle narrative.

> Before, on a previous pilgrimage, there were ten or twenty farmers with us. [By farmers he means higher caste nonuntouchables]. Among them were Narayan Khati [Carpenter] and Bhura Khati [his wife]. Narayan Khati was blind. We sat him on a stone seat, put all our stuff with him, and went to look around—at the place of Mandor Bhairu.
>
> When we came back, Narayan Khati said, "Now I can see."
>
> People asked him, "What things do you see?"
>
> So he said, "There are horses," and he counted them. He said, "Over here is the gate."
>
> So everyone thought, it is very good if a miracle happens to one of our villagers. Everyone will praise Ramdevji. So everyone called "Victory."

I told him he should touch the feet of all the company. But he didn't do it. Perhaps there was hypocrisy in his heart.

In this company were Regar, Chamar, Khati, Mali [two leatherworker untouchable and two clean castes], all together. When he saw all the peoples' things mixed together, including food, he said to Bhura, "Hey, why are all the things put together?"

At that very spot, he became blind again. [Bardu concludes:] On this road, the road to Ramdevji, untouchability should not be and should not be spoken.

Bardu Regar toward the end of this interview brought out some of Ramdevji's *prasad* and gave it to us to eat. I thought nothing of it, as the sharing of *prasad* is a major meritorious act enjoined upon returned pilgrims. Bhoju also casually swallowed the *prasad*.

Later Bhoju told me that for him to consume anything in a leatherworker's house was a major violation of his own caste's dharma, and that he never would have done it except for fear of Ramdevji's anger. Some miracles, then, retain their force back home. Perhaps Bardu deliberately tested the effect of his story by offering Bhoju *prasad*. This last narrative, perhaps more vividly than all the rest, reveals a performative breakthrough after the fact: of miraculous lessons into ordinary social interactions, changing them in this case to extraordinary ones.

Stone Truth

Vernacular devotion explores the gap between the inanimate nature of stone and a capacity to deliver grace and miracles, between the always questionable nature of a stone god and the always truthful but ineffable reality that may be crystallized in icons. If there are gaps, there are usually bridges. A popular truism, "Greater than God is the devotee!" offers one such bridge. A mysterious expression, it takes stories to unfold. This one I recorded from a Rajput woman named Shobhag Kanvar during the ten-day worship of Dasa Mata (a form of Lakshmi) in 1980.[9] Here the paradox of an omnipresent divinity embodied in a lifeless stone statue is played upon both for humor and for religious impact. Absurdity becomes high truth.

As do the stories of the bandit and the opium dealer, this tale prizes inner devotion above all other attributes. Yet there is also a striking difference between this worship story and the event stories just related. Here miracles happen—not to prove anything, but as part of the way things are. In other words, if there are teachings embedded in these stories, they are implicit. Worship tales transmit an ongoing knowledge about the nature of reality, rather than a sudden implosion of miraculous meanings into human worlds.

Because this is a lengthy tale, I give only the first portion in direct translation and then summarize the rest in paraphrase.

GANESHJI AND THE MERCHANT'S SERVANT

There was once a shopkeeper who had a stone statue of the elephant-headed god, Lord Ganeshji. He habitually worshipped Ganeshji every day. Before he ate his food he would always recite prayers to Ganeshji, and bathe the statue. One day, as he was a busy man, he decided to hire a servant. He hired a young boy, about twelve years old. He told his new servant boy, "You take care of this statue of Lord Ganeshji. Bathe it and give it a walk around the garden. If you do this work every day, then I will give you two pieces of bread every day." Now the shopkeeper was something of a miser, and it hurt his soul to give bread. This is why he would only allow the boy two pieces. The servant boy was an orphan and came from a class of very poor farmers. In the house where he lived with some distant relations there was total poverty.

Every day in the morning the merchant gave him his bread. Then the boy bathed Ganeshji and decorated him with pieces of sparkling colored foil. After this he took the statue in his arms and carried it around the garden. The boy would put Ganeshji down by the well in the garden and take out the bread in order to eat it. Then a very surprising thing would happen. Slowly, moving forward step by step [try to imagine the ponderous and awkward gait of a fat stone elephant] Ganeshji would come and take one whole piece of the boy's bread for himself, snatching it with his trunk, and eat it up. So the boy had only one left for his meal. He began to get very weak from lack of food.

That poor fatherless boy was actually dying of hunger, and could not do his work. The shopkeeper told him, "Do this! Do that!" but he was not able to work. Finally he went to the shopkeeper and said, "Master, I am dying of hunger. These two pieces of bread do not satisfy me."

"How can that be?" the shopkeeper replied in surprise.

"Ganeshji eats up one piece of bread so I have only one left for myself. What will become of me?"

The shopkeeper laughed. He said, "It is a statue made of stone and no stone statue eats bread. Why are you lying?"

The boy answered, "It's up to you if you don't want to believe it, but I don't eat two pieces of bread. Ganeshji eats up one of them and I eat only one. I'm weak in the knees and dying of hunger. Why don't you see for yourself?"

Then the shopkeeper thought, "Ho ho, a lot has happened if a stone statue eats bread."

What happens next is that the merchant suggests a feast and hides himself in the garden. Ganesh tells the boy to meditate on his "father," meaning the merchant, and thus foreshadows the happy ending. Ganesh himself promises to meditate on his divine progenitor, Lord Shiva. Both paternal figures appear as the feast is laid out, and the poor boy is downcast, fearing he will once again go hungry. Miraculously, there is plenty of food to go around, and the tale ends with the merchant touching the boy's feet and promising to treat him as his true son for ever after and bequeath him half his property.

The hypocrisy of the rich and the blessedness of the simple are perhaps familiar—even universal—themes here. Like the story of the stupid landlord, this tale comments on social hierarchy, but it does so in a somewhat different register. The poor orphan is better than the rich merchant because—even though he thinks of his own needs—he is without guile, and his faith is not in any way contrived. It is not even named as faith. He treats Ganesh as present, and so the god responds to him. The boy's hunger is acute, and rural listeners may well be familiar with those pangs. The storyteller uses voice and gestures to evoke the improbable gait of a lumbering statue. Moving stone captures the imagination as comical, yet it is also a miraculous vision; better yet, it leads to hunger's satiation. To the poor boy, filling his belly is what matters, not consorting with deities. Yet it is just this simple-hearted quality that renders him worthy of seeing God.

Such stories, told in contexts of domestic worship, play around the truth and impossibility of spirited stones. They are, by definition, performative nature tales told in order to worship the gods. That is, worship stories are part of what is offered rather than accounts of what has been received, as the shrine tales are. In this Ganesh story, deities reward the poor and innocent-hearted devotee through miraculous visions and material bounty. Thus, the Ganesh worship story has continuities with the located event stories related in the preceding section, in that it shows miracles infusing everyday life and comments critically on class and caste, rewarding true hearts above all.

Worship tales also differ from shrine tales because they are not witnessed events involving real persons and places. Strongly distinguishing the two genres is that the deity here, Ganesh, is not an enshrined Ganesh present in a particular locality. Similarly, the characters are not Nanda Mina or Bardu Regar but types: a Rich Merchant and a Poor Orphan. Worship stories are always set in a once-upon-a-time world. That world, nonetheless, strongly resembles the familiar world except for its being a place where good people are ultimately rewarded.

Musing on Miracles

This volume's editors, Corinne Dempsey and Selva Raj, describe miracles and the miraculous as "foundational" in South Asian religions. Yet, when we compare these topics with ritual, myth, or mysticism, miracles have received relatively scant attention from scholars. Is this neglect due to an inescapable contradiction between academic analyses and popular faith? This could seem like a double bind: we ignore a vital and pervasive phenomenon if we ignore miracles. At the same time, if we try to talk about miracles we inevitably engage in reductive or demystifying practices and fail to do them justice. And if we attempt to avoid such practices, we risk sounding gullible or, worse crime still, unscholarly.

Dempsey and Raj highlight conundrum as a key trope in the study of miracles on several levels. Miracles may be vexing puzzles for academics, whether phenomenologists or ethnographers, who aspire to apprehend fully and portray fluidly an alien cosmos. For devotees, as well, miracles display divine "play" (*lila*) that resists human understanding. But it seems to me that miracles present worshipers not so much riddles to be solved but glimpses of causalities beyond the visible; they present potentialities of grace not open to calculable manipulation but nonetheless capriciously available. Narratives such as those I have presented here helpfully display proofs in action to devotees and equally offer scholars assistance by allowing insider voices to transmit key meanings.

Surveying a few scholarly discussions of miracles, especially those that focus on miracle tellings, reveals suggestive intersections among the comments of those who work on Christian and on Hindu traditions. Mullin, whose interest is "modern religious imagination" in Euro-American contexts, defines miracles as having a "public character" (1996, 6). Bull's study of miracle narratives surrounding a Marian shrine in medieval France also stresses that these tales present the miraculous as having "the potential to have social consequences and to shape exchanges between different people and groups" (1999, 37). Richard Davis affirms that for India, "miracles are social acts in several senses" (1998, 4). And Korte writes in introducing a cross-cultural collection on "women and miracle stories" that "[i]t is the act of telling [a social exchange] which constructs the miracle as such" (2001, 13). In all these works scholars come to terms with miracles not by acknowledging or even confronting a mysterious or inexplicable core, but rather by stressing their social nature.[10]

The examples I have presented here of event stories also run very strongly in the direction of miracles at work in the world. And it seems to me that this is because the people who narrated the stories to us were equally interested in this very angle; what is most compelling is the impact. The stress in the telling is less on the amazingness of divine intervention in human affairs and more on the results: whether afflictions or boons, they are results that others may wish to avoid or to obtain. In all cases they seem to mesh well with Malik's notion of divine testimony. The woman's worship story, by contrast, proves nothing. Ganesh exists, and his gifts to faithful worshipers—those faithful in their hearts, that is—are not so much wondrous as mundane.

I would argue nonetheless that the social emphases observable in miracle tellings do not displace divine intervention from the heart of action and interpretation. This brings the two genres I have carefully contrasted in this essay quite a bit closer together, although further away from an outsider analysis that embraces transparency too happily. In all six stories the absolute power of deities is a given, a no-brainer, the premise of all else that transpires. If in that sense miraculous power remains opaque to scholarly gazes, its narrative flowering consistently offers a variety of attractions to would-be interpreters.

In presenting these Rajasthani miracle stories my aim has been to allow the tales themselves to demonstrate a few crucial aspects of their own nature. Some miracle narratives are quite transparently teaching stories with easily recognized morals: "Don't steal from the Mother" or "Don't violate the protected trees or consider yourself equal to Lord Devnarayan" or "Don't discriminate against the low-born, at least not when you're on a pilgrimage to Ramdevji." Moreover, the satisfaction of knowing that the former arrogant landlord's estate has become a place for defecation is clearly a view from the bottom of the social hierarchy, as is the leatherworker's narrative of the carpenter's comeuppance. These tales vividly demonstrate public, social, didactic, and even subversive functions of the miraculous. We could add the Ganesh worship tale to this list as well, with a message similar to that of the Gospels about how difficult it is for a rich man to enter heaven; or a message about the futility of ritual worship without a heart to match, which resonates strongly with the well-known teachings of devotional poet-saints such as Kabir.

In the three punishment stories—about the thief, the landlord, and the twice-blind pilgrim—miracles come as shocks to persons who have broken well-known rules, persons who deliberately refuse to acknowledge deities' power over human lives. The two rescue tales usefully offer wonders that evade at least the most obvious levels of functional analysis. In the rescue story involving the bandit's plunge, again there is shock value: the power of devotion is greater than bullets and law. It is even greater than common codes for conduct assumed to be the basis of law. Here we could get morally worried, for the story gives us no indication as to whether this bandit is a Robin Hood type with redeeming virtues or is a plain scoundrel. The point is only that whatever else he is, he worships Joganiya Ma.

In the firsthand miracle experience related by the possibly reformed opium dealer, we may be shocked by the Goddess granting her grace to such a person, but we also could see a more harmonious alignment. The Mother has saved him and he has grown his hair and seated himself at her place, perhaps deliberately taking on the appearance of a holy person. There he readily tells her story, which is also his story, to inquiring strangers. Yet in our interview his deliberate, even teasing, ambiguity about whether or not he had forsaken his life of crime left us somewhat bemused and unsettled—the story lacked closure, or, we could say, lacked a moral.

Bynum in writing on "wonder" attempts to distinguish wonder from miracles in Western thought by suggesting that miracle accounts can often be dull but wonders are always surprising; and that miracles may be incorporated but wonders are "nonappropriative." She writes, "Thus we wonder at what we cannot in any sense incorporate or consume, or encompass in our mental categories; we wonder at mystery, at paradox . . ." (1997, 12).

Now if you look up Hindi *chamatkar* in the Hindi-English dictionary, you find first "miracle" and then "wonder." Does this term confound Bynum's distinctions? In some respects I would say it does. One of the implications carried by "to show *chamatkar*," as we have seen, is definitely to startle, shock, shake up, and thus cause wonder at the permanently inexplicable. Nonetheless, Rajasthani miraculous event stories in large doses might indeed seem dull, because patterns repeat. Yet to most listeners and tellers, in the performative moment they are not dull but gripping. What makes them gripping is not the repetitive plotted schemes of rules violated/punishment suffered or devotion rendered/grace received. Rather, the compelling nature of testimony lies in its ability to shift realities for a receptive audience.

Dempsey's ethnography of a Hindu goddess temple in upstate New York comments on the way that, for priest as well as participants in the temple's miracle-saturated ambiance, "events that once seemed extraordinary can become routine" (2006, 62). But they do not on that account become dull; or rather, the flip side of dullness is burnishment, luster. An unspoken assumption of radical divine agency renders routinized miracles equally wonders. That such an assumption might be shared by nonliterate farmers in rural north India and educated upper-middle-class urban devotees in the United States is worth pondering, conundrum or not. In Ganesh's worship tale, statues walk and eat and talk, but the message is that this surprises only those whose devotional sensibilities are limited. In this view, wonder could be a sign of spiritual obtuseness: the merchant is wonder struck, but the simple-hearted child accepts the manifestations of gods in his life as something not at all out of the ordinary.

Notes

1. For Ramdevji see Gold 1988, 147–49; Khan 1997. Besides Malik's work, see Miller 1994 for a comprehensive study of the Devnarayan epic.

2. The original classic on urban legends, which spawned a whole series of collections, is Brunvand 1981.

3. See Gold and Gujar 2002, 30–52 for a description of our collaborative research practices.

4. For Gujars and Minas in the region of our story collecting, see Gold and Gujar 2002, 31–33, 59–64.

5. See Gold 1998, which focuses on the ways vernacular myths deconstruct caste and gender hierarchies.

6. See O'Flaherty 1976. Stuart Blackburn has called attention to moral lessons in Tamil folktales, writing that "the marvelous is less significant than the moral" (2001, 19). However, devotional Hinduism or bhakti has historically favored fervor over rule-bound behavior (see, for one example, Hiltebeitel 1989 on demon devotees). The stories treated in this chapter are all in a bhakti mode.

7. For many more tree-protection miracle stories, see Gold forthcoming.

8. The phrase used was *chauki ana*, a common idiom referring to possession of a shrine priest specifically when he is giving advice to pilgrims.

9. For more about the storyteller and the ritual context in which she performs, see Gold 1995.

10. Dempsey 2006 manages a wondrously more complicated account in her discussion of modern miracles at a Hindu temple in upstate New York.

References

Blackburn, Stuart. 2001. *Moral Fictions: Tamil Folktales in Oral Tradition*. Vol. 278, FF Communications. Helsinki, Finland: Suomalainen Tiedeakatemia.

Brunvand, Jan Harold. 1981. *The Vanishing Hitchhiker: American Urban Legends and Their Meanings*. New York: W. W. Norton.

Bull, Marcus. 1999. *The Miracles of Our Lady of Rocamadour: Analysis and Translation*. Woodbridge, UK: Boydell Press.

Bynum, Caroline Walker. 1997. "Wonder." *American Historical Review* 102, no. 1:1–26.

Davis, Richard. 1998. "Miracles as Social Acts." In *Images, Miracles, and Authority in Asian Religious Traditions*, edited by Richard H. Davis, 1–22. Boulder, CO: Westview Press.

Dempsey, Corinne. 2006. *The Goddess Lives in Upstate New York: Breaking Convention and Making Home at a North American Hindu Temple*. New York: Oxford University Press.

Gold, Ann Grodzins. 1988. *Fruitful Journeys: The Ways of Rajasthani Pilgrims*. Berkeley and Los Angeles: University of California Press.

———. 1995. "Mother Ten's Stories." In *Religions of India in Practice*, edited by Donald S. Lopez, Jr., 434–48. Princeton, NJ: Princeton University Press.

———. 1998. "Grains of Truth: Shifting Hierarchies of Food and Grace in Three Rajasthani Tales." *History of Religions* 38, no. 2:150–71.

———. Forthcoming. "Why Sacred Groves Matter: Post-Romantic Claims." In *Do Villages Matter?* edited by Diane Mines and Nicolas Yazgi.

Gold, Ann Grodzins, and Bhoju Ram Gujar. 2002. *In the Time of Trees and Sorrows: Nature, Power, and Memory in Rajasthan.* Durham, NC: Duke University Press.

Gujar, Bhoju Ram, and Ann Grodzins Gold. 2006. "Malaji's Hill: Divine Sanction, Community Action." *Context: Built, Living and Natural (Journal of DRONAH, Development and Research Organisation for Nature, Arts and Heritage, Haryana, India)* 3, no. 1:33–42.

Hiltebeitel, Alf, ed. 1989. *Criminal Gods and Demon Devotees: Essays on the Guardians of Popular Hinduism.* Albany: State University of New York Press.

Khan, Dominique-Sila. 1997. *Conversions and Shifting Identities: Ramdev Pir and the Ismailis in Rajasthan.* New Delhi: Manohar.

Korte, Anne-Marie, ed. 2001. *Women and Miracle Stories: A Multidisciplinary Exploration.* Leiden: Brill.

Malik, Aditya. 2005. *Nectar Gaze and Poison Breath: An Analysis and Translation of the Rajasthani Oral Narrative of Devnarayan.* New York: Oxford University Press.

Miller, Joseph. 1994. "The Twenty-Four Brothers and Lord Devnarayan: The Story and Performance of a Folk Epic of Rajasthan, India." PhD diss., University of Pennsylvania.

Mullin, Robert Bruce. 1996. *Miracles and the Modern Religious Imagination.* New Haven, CT: Yale University Press.

O'Flaherty, Wendy Doniger. 1976. *The Origins of Evil in Hindu Mythology.* Berkeley and Los Angeles: University of California Press.

Schattschneider, Ellen. 2003. *Immortal Wishes: Labor and Transcendence on a Japanese Sacred Mountain.*

CHAPTER SIX

A Miracle (or Two) in Tiruchirapalli

WILLIAM P. HARMAN

> The height of folly is to place reliance on miracles; the depth of
> wisdom is to know that miracles take place.
>
> —Neusner and Neusner

The modest Anandaswami Temple lies on less than an acre of land in a suburb named "Kamala Nagar," a short bus ride north of the city of Tiruchirapalli
in the central region of the state of Tamilnadu. The suburb is a planned neighborhood: it was designed about forty years ago, and is one of the newest and
most systematically laid out on the north side of the city. It is relatively pros-
perous, with large, modern two- and three-story reinforced concrete homes. It
is populated primarily by upper-middle-class families and their servants.
Many of the suburb's residents are associated with managerial and administrative positions either in the nearby hospital or in a local industrial complex
that exports textiles. I resided in this neighborhood off and on for several
months. Compared with earlier experiences of suburban living in the towns of
Madurai and Chennai, this occasion struck me as quite different. Neighbors
not only knew about each other; they knew each other. A sense of egalitarian
neighborliness seemed to prevail, despite the fact that people were not kin.[1]
The place in which they tended almost always to meet and to socialize was a
community temple, a relatively new one constructed in 1981. Fascinated with
this dynamic, I decided to find out more about the temple and the human
interactions that were constantly taking place there.

The vast majority of families in this suburb are observant Hindus, and
many with whom I spoke about the new Anandaswami Temple in their

community expressed a sense of worshipful gratitude that the relatively recent construction of the temple brought—and continues to bring—a double blessing to people living there. First, it grants a cosmic legitimacy to Kamala Nagar: no community with a sense of identity and self-awareness should be without a temple, I was told. One Tamil proverb says it clearly, "How could anyone live in a town that has no temple?" (Lazarus 1894, 310, no. 354).[2] More than simply providing a social focus for a community, a temple sanctifies and legitimizes a locale, orienting its residents and their residences in relation to supernatural and spiritual perspectives. That the story of the temple's, and therefore the community's, sanctity emerges from what locals perceive as a miracle is icing on the cake: "No ordinary suburb is this and no ordinary community are we" might well be the implied declaration. Talk about the temple's miraculous beginnings becomes in this sense a witness to the extraordinary sanctity of the building, the place, and the people who inhabit the place.

Second, this perceived cosmic role for the temple has its functional advantages as well: the temple's shared sanctity serves to create community cohesion. This miraculous sanctity becomes the spatial and spiritual common denominator to which those willing to acknowledge it can appeal as a source of community. And so it works that way: it is a place where groups tend to meet to hear talks, to sing devotional songs, and to offer occasional classes in the evening to adults interested in some of the classic religious texts of Tamil Shaivism.

A full-time resident Brahmin priest and his family also lend a sense of credibility and legitimacy. They ensure that daily *puja*s (worship) will be conducted, and respond to individual needs for specially requested and financed ceremonies. This priestly family has taken an interest in educating the community in matters religious, as well. For example, the priest's son posts each day on a blackboard near the temple entrance brief sayings from Tamil religious literature. He will often engage in conversation with children passing by on the way to school as he encourages them to memorize the passages. At the end of the week, students who can repeat any one of those sayings by memory are offered a tempting sweet for a snack.

The temple also makes it possible for those concerned about regular temple activity to participate in individual worship (*puja*) without having to take a bus ride into town to visit a shrine there. The temple is a convenience and a blessing for Shaiva worshippers living in Kamalanagar.

As with so many sacred places in India, sanctity and spiritual efficacy can almost always be traced to divine origins. The rule seems to be that genuine spiritual authenticity must be traceable to transcendent etiologies.[3] The Anandaswami Temple meets this criterion, and doubly so. There are two miraculous versions of the story depicting the origins of this temple. They are not really mutually exclusive: one deals in broad outlines and the other is "modern." The first is engraved on a slab of granite embedded in one of the prominent temple pillars near the entrance. This engraved version, in literary Tamil, states clearly that it is the official version of the temple's history, and so claims the generic sacred literary status of the *sthalapuranam*, the holy temple's "place history." Every temple of respectable repute will have a "place history," though the histories vary in length, sophistication, and form. The more modest and more recent will be brief and appear as inscriptions or in pamphlet form. Others will be extensive, multivolumed literary, poetic works of some sophistication.

In some instances, the local temple *sthalapuranam* remains in strictly oral form. The second version of the Anandaswami Temple history was oral when I first encountered it, but now has been committed to a written version in English.[4] This second version has been rather aggressively advertised as the "modern version," intended for the degenerate Kali epoch in which we now live. Both versions present the temple as a miracle. That is, they suggest that the existence of the temple bears witness to the miraculous power that it houses. The "modern" version is more deliberate with its depictions of miracles, but still, both stories envelop the temple's origins in wondrous powers discovered on that spot. I turn now to these two temple "histories."

Here is my translation of the earlier, engraved version. It would be accurate to call this one the "official version." It reflects a relatively sophisticated Tamil literary influence, and seems especially concerned with expressing the eternally venerable presence of a sacred power christened by Tamil literary sophistication.

THE TEMPLE HISTORY OF THE
ANANDASWAMI HOLY TEMPLE, KAMALA NAGAR

When this sacred land was a forest many thousands of years ago, people settled nearby, establishing a city.

In seeing this self-born lingam, people were attracted to it in the same way that Kannappar was attracted to [the] Kalakasti Natar [lingam].[5]

Grace abounded as the people experienced God's gracious love.

They bestowed [on the lingam] the sacred name of Anandaswami, conducted daily worship, and on June 21, 1981, they built this temple, the shrines of Shri Komathi Ampal, Shri Vinayakar, and others with the sacred donations of Shri Muthukumaraswami, our patron, who conducted the anointing ceremony [*kumpapishekam*].

A Multitude of the Faithful

21-6-98

An anonymous gift to the temple covered the costs of having this brief history engraved on the temple edifice. No one with whom I spoke was able to tell me the origins of the story. It seems, simply, to have appeared. Still, when I asked people about the temple's origins, it was never this particular story they chose to narrate. Rather, there was a far more popular and current oral version about how the temple became established, and one in which we see miracle more directly. This second story is certainly more entertaining, and it abounds in imagery invoking the miraculous. The man who first told this story to me is, in some ways, one of the heroes of the narrative. He has good reason to propogate the story actively. Still, despite his vested interests in the account, I am convinced that he fervently and devoutly believes this story and promotes it in something of an evangelical style.

Here is the story he told me, and which I heard with only slight variations from other neighborhood devotees.

The Oral Version

The suburbs to the north of Tiruchirapalli have, for decades, been experiencing unusual growth, with a marked number of large, well-appointed middle-class houses. One of these houses, and much of the bordering land around it, belongs to Mr. Shanmugam Pillai, a wealthy, now-retired manager for the British-owned textile plant nearby. Since his eldest child and only daughter was born, he has wanted to build a house for her and her new husband on the plot of land he owns just next door. It would make a splendid dowry. But there were serious concerns that posed possible problems for this project. Six years before Shanmugam's daughter achieved the appropriate age for her marriage to a suitable boy, Shanmugam began having a recurrent and disturbing dream.[6] The deity Shiva would appear to him and insist that the land next to his house not be given away with his daughter's dowry. Rather, because of a special sacred presence there, it should be consecrated as the site of the suburb's only temple.

Shanmugam resisted the suggestions of his dream and, when the time for arranging his daughter's marriage arrived, he resolved to proceed with plans to build a new house on that land, and to give it as a part of the dowry. Construction workers began clearing the land but found themselves facing the task of somehow removing a large protruding granite outcropping, the tip of which barely appeared above the surface of the ground. The depth of its base was impossible to determine. The bulldozing machinery broke down in an attempt to dislodge the stone, and so the foreman of the crew decided to return the next day with explosives. That night, however, both the foreman and Mr. Shanmugam had the same dream: Shiva appeared and said that the protruding rock was in fact a *svayambhu lingam,* a miraculously self-born lingam, the symbol par excellence of the Lord Shiva, and that it was on this spot that a temple should be built. The foreman resigned from the work, claiming he did not want to dynamite a lingam. Shanmugam called a halt to the land clearing at his wife's urging. Discussions about the wedding and the dowry were postponed.

A month later, one of Shanmugam's business-related friends by the name of Shri Muthukumaraswami [the name appears above in the engraved temple history as the temple's patron] visited him for a holiday from Kashmir. The first night he slept in Shanmugam's house, he also had a dream in which Shiva appeared to him and asked him to finance the construction of a temple next door. The next morning, he told Shanmugam about the experience and offered to donate an enormous amount of money for the temple.

Shanmugam decided he had no choice, and so took the money and commissioned the construction of the temple, with the featured central shrine, that same rough hewn, unlodgeable lingam, protruding through the temple floor. That granite lingam, local devotees testify, grows several millimeters each year. It is the sacred centerpiece of the temple today.

I heard this story several times during the period I lived adjacent to the temple. People in the neighborhood were ready to recount it any time I mentioned the temple. I was rather surprised by the consistency of the recited details. I took notes on several occasions when I could elicit such recitations, and eventually assembled this composite English account presented above, approved by Shanmugam and, after my departure from India, privately published and distributed in pamphlet form on the temple premises as the temple's *sthalapuranam.* No mention of the compiler was made, and so posterity will simply have to take my word for it that I am the author of a divinely inspired, eternal, and in principle authorless Sthala Puranam, presumably channeled from Shiva and through me.

It would not be difficult to argue that this second story, and its publication, served as something of a power play by Mr. Shanmugam and his associates. It is a story that directly heralds him as the key player in this divine drama, and my talks with him persuaded me that he aspired to be the central character in the divine drama this second miracle story portrays. Though quite well off, he ranks in an intermediate position in the caste hierarchy. His role in governing the temple, however, was unequivocally prominent, and he clearly wished it to remain so even after the arrival of a Brahmin priest and his family. The publication appeared to be privately printed, though it had no indication as to its date, place, or publisher. When I asked, people told me the obvious: it was distributed in the temple and therefore published by the temple. This seems to lead back to Shanmugam, since little was done in the temple without his sponsorship or direct approval. The second story focuses on the land *he* donated, on the dreams *he* had, on the money *he* found to begin temple construction. He is a man around whom miracles happen, just as the temple is the location around which they occur. The more recently revealed sacred story provided him with significant social and ritual status in the community, status that he seemed to cherish and to nurture at every opportunity.

We note, then, that in this second story, miracles are reflected and suggested by dreams that occur simultaneously to different people but with the same content. Here miracles imply interior events, though they have significant reference to the everyday world. In the older and shorter account, the miracle is the discovery of the lingam; it is the recognition that something normally considered ordinary is, indeed, supernatural. The miracle is constituted by the experience of something sacred or numinous. It begins with the experience and proceeds to incorporate realia, the object of worship, into the supernatural context defined by a wondrous experience. This suggests a line of argument I have found sustained, at least in the Indian context. The argument is pretty much straightforward: a miracle is not an event. Rather, it is an experience. This is not to say that miracles do not refer to events, or that they have nothing to do with events in the world "out there." Indeed, most miracles are claims about events in the exterior, objective, observable world. Even so, they are first and foremost experiences, perceptions, and interpretations of events. Let me illustrate what I mean by considering the vocabulary Tamil speakers use in speaking of miracles.

If I am to speak about miracles in the context of Tamil culture, it might make some sense to probe the meaning of the word "miracle" in Tamil. I consulted three English-Tamil dictionaries (Fabricius [1897] 1972; Lipko 1966; Winslow et al. 1986) three Tamil-Tamil dictionaries (*Tamil Lexicon* 1956; *Kriyavin Tarkalat* 1999; Kathiraiven Pillai 1981), a French-Tamil dictionary (Mousset and Dupuis [1911] 1984), a Tamil-French dictionary (Mousset and Dupuis 1984) and a Dravidian etymological dictionary (Burrow and Emeneau 1961). The clear consensus is that the preferred Tamil terms for the word "miracle" are *arputam* and *putumai*, in that order.[7] These reference works listed several other terms as well, along with occasional glosses. Most of the terms for "miracle" are glossed in all the dictionaries, as well as in the *Tamil Lexicon*, as, essentially, an experience, a feeling, an emotion: in short, a subjective response (*Tamil Lexicon* 1956). Anything is an *arputam* that is accompanied by the sentiment of intense wonder, marvel, or admiration. Something is a *putumai* when it is accompanied by the distinctly surprising, even overwhelming, sense of newness, novelty, and freshness.

Taking the line that a miracle is a subjective event might well suggest a wholesale capitulation to subjectivity in discussions of miracles. In the Western context we are likely to recoil from thoroughgoing subjectivity, because it excludes the possibility of a shared verifiability. Subjectivity seems to exclude independent confirmation of an event or third-person verification. Strictly speaking, perhaps so, but the experience of miracles in relation to this temple was definitely shared by scores of people who clearly understood the miracles of the temple to be based in objectively verifiable contexts.

There was something very powerful at work as people spoke about the miracles associated with the temple. Simply recounting the stories permitted them to enter back into the experiences of wonder and remarkable novelty. And while many of the neighbors had no direct experience of the miracles, it seemed as if the experience was reproduced and relived in their retelling. Entering into that world of wonder was no more difficult for them than was opening themselves up to a good story. And it seemed the more I heard the story the more believable it became. The power in this recounting had much to do with the willful, intentional creation of a reality that people wanted to inhabit. In this case the reality was the existence of a faith community that, as a group, bought into the miraculous protocol the temple represents. And just as the repetition of a dream for several people was taken to be a miracle, so, too, the repetitive account by different devotees of the miraculous events was considered to be a confirmation of miraculous truth.

It might be accurate to say that these dual dreams—and others, for that matter—emerge from a consciousness of open expectation and from a willingness to allow into a devotee's life the experience of enchantment, wonder, and marvel. Margaret Case's study of the miraculous appearance of Krishna in the form of a black bee tends to come to this conclusion. She writes in her epilogue,

> This book began with the appearance of the black bee, which was accepted by Maharaj-ji [an honorific title for a religious leader] and his devotees as a manifestation of Krishna. I was often asked whether I believed that this was, in fact, Krishna. My answer: within the context, yes—and the context is everything. The quest to see divinity and the question of whether what was seen *was* divinity can only be addressed within context. The seer is a seeker, not passive, but with an active role to play. What is seen, though profoundly personal, is not idiosyncratic, but understood by a community to be a manifestation of divinity. And the experience is supported by a narrative—by stories that are traditional, living in memory, and re-created at each telling or reenactment. (Case 2000, 151)

What I found especially interesting in talking with the neighbors about their new community temple was the airtight logic that provided a contextual support for miraculous thinking. The temple, they explained, was obviously sacred because it was the result of so many miraculous events: the discovery of the lingam and then the appearance by Siva in the dual dreams of the key players. But if a person is tempted to doubt that the events that led to the establishment of this wonderful temple must be miracles, there is obvious proof of their supernatural inspirations. The holy temple's very existence and the community's newly acquired self-consciousness as a faith community are an obvious witness to and proof of the powerful and miraculous events that brought the temple and its community into being. The temple testifies to the power of the miracles and the miracles testify to the wondrous nature of the temple. The logic may seem circular, but it is airtight in the eyes of the devoted beholders. In this sense, the miracle, for those who are open to its occurrence, is undeniable.

Mark Corner's perspective on miracles emphasizes the sometimes surprising fact that reported miracles are, remarkably, an everyday phenomenon in the modern world, much as they were thousands of years ago. People in the United States are among the world's more enthusiastic endorsers of miraculous events (2000, 57). The issue seems to be whether faithful people are willing to make the choice to live "as if" miracles occur.

> There is nothing observable in an event itself—however striking it may be—that compels us to call it a miracle. It certainly doesn't have to be called that. In some cases it can be called a coincidence, in others, the working of an as yet undiscovered law. Moreover, as Hume reminds us, we may question the honesty or accuracy of witnesses to an event. . . . But just as there is nothing in the event itself to demand that it be explained as a miracle, so also there is nothing in the nature of any event which can stop it from being a miracle. It doesn't have to be something in the "microworld" where cause and effect do not apply, or something which the laws of nature cannot explain. It can neither be said that a miracle "cannot happen" nor that a particular event "can only be" a miracle. (Corner 2005, 200)

It would be tempting to deal with probing discussions about miracles as simple arguments in which no one can present definitive proof regarding a miracle's occurrence. The exchange could be considered just another "He said, she said" verbal jousting match with no proof or verification possibly able to settle the question. But for those who perceive that miracles take place, who have decided to live "as if" miracles occur, arguments and proofs against the credibility of miracles are superfluous. It would be like trying to convince an ardent, dedicated football fan that football is really a silly, useless phenomenon that makes no ultimate sense.[8] Passionate football fans (fanatics) have decided, however, to live "as if" football were extremely important. And as they live out that decision, as they invest their time, energy, money, and egos, football begins to assume an enormous importance. The choice to live "as if" becomes an indisputable, self-confirming commitment.[9]

Seen without the passion, without sympathy for this "as if" decision, and for the discipline its commitment imposes, football becomes a silly waste of time and effort—people watching grown men endanger themselves fighting for a few yards of turf in an arbitrarily contrived game centered on a relatively small ball of negligible value and invented as an ultimately nonproductive pastime. From the perspective of the committed fan, however, football becomes an absorbing and compelling activity. Some regard football as a spiritual template for living, a guide for decision-making, and a model for understanding the way the world works: particularly in the competitive male world of power wielders, it is not unusual to hear people talking about their work or their personal lives from the perspective of such football metaphors as "end runs," throwing the "Hail Mary pass," "punting," insisting that "the best defense is a good offense," or "running a reverse." It is, I think, no coincidence that in talking about the worldview of the football devotee we should not be surprised to hear discussions of miracles in football. The newspapers are cluttered with them, in fact.[10] When we deal with a conceptual world such as that of the life of a Hindu focused on a temple or that of a football fan focused on a team, we find that the self-authenticating nature of the experiences in that world encourage an openness to positive and unexpected events that lend themselves to being perceived as miraculous. As a person or a community actively constructs a reality, it makes sense to construct that reality so that wondrous, surprising, and miraculous events are built into the system. Indeed, the joy of such communities often derives from the luxury people allow themselves to be optimistic about the possibility of miracles, whether in prospect or in retrospect.

A miraculous experience can involve not simply what might happen prospectively. It can mean seeing the past in a whole new way, and in so doing, it involves discovering the miraculous in what has already happened, perhaps long ago. In this sense the miracle comes to be understood not simply as that which defies expectation, but also as that which defies the temporal and the historical.

When it comes to miracles, there is another neatly self-authenticating, congruent mechanism at work, as well, one that confirms that the miracle of the temple is consistent retrospectively, from the perspective of history. This mechanism reconciles the Indian notion that, on the one hand, only what is ancient is sacredly authentic and, on the other, the relatively common perception that what is modern is more relevant, more accessible.

In the context of India's revered traditions, truth is eternal. It has always existed since it is coextensive with divine reality, with the way the cosmos "is." The Vedas, for example, are eternal texts, understood to reflect and bear truths unconditioned by the vagaries and accidents of history. They are *shruti*, preexisting, revealed truth heard by the great seers. *Smrti* refers to truth that humans play some active part in recovering: these are the "remembered" texts." Human beings may hear or remember aspects of that truth from time to time, but they never are its inventors, original authors, or creators. They are simply its transmitters, much as I became not the author of the temple's sacred text (and therefore deserved no mention as author), but simply the one who "channeled" it, who received it from transcendent sources.[11] The engraved temple history indicates that while the construction of the temple began in 1981, the history of the temple dates to the beginnings of time, when the land was virgin, unsettled, and entirely forested. That was the point, it seems, when the preexisting lingam stone image was discovered for the first time. That was the early, ancient, authenticating miracle, by implication. The more modern story assures us that the sacrality of the spot is confirmed now—in modern times—through simultaneous dreams of people who still live today in the community. There is a vagueness about what it was that actually happened at the sacred site, since its discovery presumably thousands of years ago. But that vagueness is also an assurance that there is a long history of continuity of the miraculous sacrality people sense today.

Temporally and logically, what we see here is how a shared conviction enables a community to tap into and to disseminate a perception about the miraculous. And if the miraculous is, indeed, all about perception and context, then the miracles in question stand and fall with the experience of the people. I have mentioned earlier that as people recounted the temple's miraculous stories, they sometimes seemed to enter back into the experiences of wonder and novelty associated with the miracles. We are accustomed to describe what is reliably true as that which we can experience repeatedly, and in varying conditions. In that sense, peoples' experiences of the temple's wondrous miracles are repeatable and replicable. And it is not simply the hard-core true believers who have access to this perspective.

The community, in fact, implicitly invites others to join voluntarily in a perspective that discovers a charm, an attraction, and a simple explanation for reported events not otherwise or easily comprehensible. In this sense, miracles simplify rather than complicate experience. They encourage us to accept divine intervention rather than to attempt to explain events as the product of unpredictably complicated and often guileful human activities and motives. Indeed, in my discussions with many of the faithful, I myself experienced a subtle temptation to be drawn into the community ethos that presupposes miracles, a temptation to assent to the direction and flow of miraculous interpretations, and to indulge in the joy and innocence to which the faithful were so clearly enthusiastic witnesses. That I should have become—quite unintentionally—the redactor of a small-time temple *sthalapuranam* has, from my rather limited perspective, become the most significant of the miracles I associate with the Anandaswami Temple.

And I conclude, much as Margaret Case has concluded, that the reality of miracles is bound up in a community's perception. Cultures and communities trace valued institutions and ideals to miracles as one way of understanding the unknown or the unknowable. But then those miracles create a perception and an awareness that valorizes cultural forms with which they are associated. In this sense, miracles function much like the vocabulary of a language: discovered or created by a community, language begins to take on a life of its own, and, over time, it becomes associated with meanings and experiences that sustain new communities. So it happens that miracles at the Anandaswami Temple are a part of the language of the faithful: not to be taken literally, necessarily, but to be taken seriously as testament to the sanctity of origins and to the possibility of new futures.

Notes

I am appreciative for the instructive advice and comments of my colleague, Professor Dileepan Parthasarathy, who responded to portions of this paper in its early phase. I have also benefited much from the suggestions of Corinne Dempsey and Selva J. Raj. I have changed several of the proper names both of locations and of persons in order to preserve the privacy of those involved.

1. It is tempting to speculate about this "neighborliness," since it did cross caste lines. People generally did not visit each other in their homes; when they gathered, it was in the surroundings of the temple, which seemed to provide neutral ground and a "purified" ritual context in which differences were temporarily "disabled." Just the same, one of the key indications of egalitarian sensibility, the sharing of food, was never something I witnessed in the temple.

2. My thanks to Daniel Jeyaraj for this reference.

3. The most comprehensive scholarly demonstration of this principle is perhaps the work of David Dean Shulman, who demonstrates how an unusually large collection of lore and history is embodied in the hundreds, possibly thousands, of sacred histories of various temples in Tamilnadu. His comparative analysis makes it clear that these histories (known as *talapuranams*) present themselves as the miraculous recountings of the relationships between supernatural and human actors in the context of a particularly sacred religious site that eventually becomes a great temple.

4. It may seem strange that the version would first appear in English rather than Tamil. The reason for this will be explained in due course

5. The reference here is to a famous Tamil bhakti devotee who discovered the sacred image of Kalakasti Natar (Shiva) in a forest, and instituted worship there for that deity. A "self-born lingam" is a stone image that contains the essence of the deity Shiva and that appears spontaneously out of the ground. It gives birth to itself.

6. It is not at all unusual for devotees to report messages from deities delivered in dreams. In my interviews with devotees of the village goddesses, I was struck by how

often people reported taking vows as a result of being so instructed in dreams by various goddesses. This same phenomenon is reported by McDaniel in West Bengal (2004, 29–32, 199–204).

7. *The Dravidian Etymological Dictionary* did not list the term "miracle." Nor did it list the term *arputam*. It did list the word *putumai* as "wonder" and "intense experience." See Burrow and Emeneau 1961, 3511.

8. A perspective humorously represented in the famous 1953 live recorded monologue that launched the comedy career of Andy Griffith, entitled "What It Was, Was Football."

9. Though my discussion of football is primarily informed by the style played in North America, much of what I say can easily be transferred to European football, or soccer. It should be noted that enthusiasm and commitment to a miraculous event are much more specific than enthusiasm and commitment to football. Nevertheless, commitment to football as an activity that merits attention and time is much like commitment to a religious world in which miracles merit attention, time, and credibility. It is a matter of deciding (or in some cases being born into a decision) to live "as if" the narrative of the miracle or the spectacle of the football drama have verifiably ultimate significance. These observations are based, in part, on the works of Percy and Taylor (1997), Edge (2002), and Schumer (1996).

10. See, for example, the article by Mike Corwin (1998, 14) about the "miracle" of Yale's winning football team. A commercial videotape about the final "miraculous" coaching season of Lavell Edwards at Brigham Young University was entitled "Last Miracle for Lavell." See Mitchell 2000.

11. Indeed, to have named me as the author would have been to diminish the power of the text. It would be to say that I created it myself, rather than that I received it from transcendent sources. Whether the sources through whom it came to me were transcendent or wholly human could be a matter of dispute, of course. But there is precedent for taking a religious perspective: it is said that often Shiva takes human form in order to reveal divine plans or intentions. Indeed, certain of those forms can be astoundingly humble, such as several we see in the temple history of the great Madurai Meenatci Temple, where Shiva becomes, among other earthly forms, a mother pig (vol. 2, chapter 45), a wage-earning low-caste laborer (vol. 3, chapter 61), a vindictive swordsman (vol. 2, chapter 27), and a poet (vol. 3, chapter 54). See *Tiruvilaiyatarpuranam of Parancotimunivar* 1927.

References

Annamalai, E., P. R. Subramanian, S. Ramakrishnan, K. Narayanan, P. Sankaralingam, eds. *Kriyavin Tarkalat Tamil Akarathi*. 1999. Chennai, India: Kriya Patippu.

Burrow, T., and M. B. Emeneau. 1961. *A Dravidian Etymological Dictionary*. Oxford: Clarendon Press.

Case, Margaret. 2000. *Seeing Krishna: The Religious World of a Brahman Family in Vrindaban*. New York: Oxford University Press.

Corner, Mark. 2005. *Signs of God: Miracles and Their Interpretaion.* Burlington, VT: Ashgate Publishing.

Corwin, Mike. 1998. "Football's Miracle of '98: Worth the Wait." *Yale Daily News,* December 3.

Edge, Alan. 2002. *Faith of Our Fathers: Football as a Religion.* London: Mainstream Publishing Co.

Fabricius, J. P. [1897] 1972. *Tamil and English Dictionary.* Tranquebar, India: Lutheran Mission Publishing House.

Kathiraiven Pillai, N. 1981. *Tamil Moli Akarati.* 6th ed. New Delhi: Asian Educational Services.

Lazarus, John. 1894. *A Dictionary of Tamil Proverbs.* Madras: Abington Press.

Lipko Tamil-Tamil-English Akarati. 1966. Cennai, India: Ti Littil Palvar.

McDaniel, June. 2004. *Offering Flowers, Feeding Skulls: Popular Goddess Worship in West Bengal.* New York: Oxford University Press.

Mitchell, Kevin, producer. 2000. "Last Miracle for Lavell." Salt Lake City: Brigham Young University Productions.

Mousset, M. M., and J. Dupuis. [1911] 1984. *Dictionnaire Français-Tamoul.* Pondicherry: Imprimerie de la Mission.

———. 1984. *Tamilprancakarati.* 2 vols. New Delhi: Asian Educational Services.

Neusner, Jacob, and Noam Neusner. 1996. *The Book of Jewish Wisdom: The Talmud of the Well-Considered Life.* New York: Continuum.

Percy, Martyn, and Rogan Taylor. 1997. "'Something for the Weekend, Sir?' Leisure, Ecstasy and Identity in Football and Contemporary Religion." *Leisure Studies* 16, no. 1 (January 1): 37–49

Schulman, David Dean. 1980. *Tamil Temple Myths: Sacrifice and Divine Marriage in the South Indian Saiva Tradition.* Princeton: Princeton University Press.

Schumer, Dirk. 1996. *Gott Ist Rund: Die Kultur des Fussballs.* Berlin: Berlin Verlag.

Tamil Lexicon. 1956. 6 vols. Madras: Prasad Press.

Venkatacami Hattar, Na. Mu., editor and commentator. 1927. *Tiruvilaiyatarpuranam of Parancotimunivar.* 3 vols. Cennai, India: Tenintiya Caiva Cittanta Nurpatippu Kalakam.

Winslow, M., J. Knight, S. Hutchings, and L. Spalding. [1852] 1986. *Winslow's English-Tamil Dictionary.* New Delhi: Asian Educational Service.

Woodward, Kenneth L. 2000. "What Miracles Mean: Woven into the History of the World's Religions, Miracles Are More about Faith Than Fact." *Newsweek,* May 1, 56–60.

CHAPTER SEVEN

The Science of the Miraculous at an Upstate New York Temple

CORINNE G. DEMPSEY

Aiya, the head priest at the Shri Rajarajeshwari Temple in Rush, New York, has a story for nearly every occasion. One of his better-known autobiographical tales chronicles a dramatic shift from one vantage point to another; one set of possibilities are exchanged for a radically different one. As Aiya describes it, the event transplanted him to a new mode of perception from which there was no return. As such, the story often serves, as Aiya phrases it, as a "testimonial" recounting his conversion as a young adult. For the purposes of this chapter it also serves as a template from which to think about the abundant yet elusive category of the miraculous within the Rush temple setting.

Aiya was born and raised in Sri Lanka, and trained to be a good Hindu by his devout mother. By the time he was a teenager, however, he had become, as he describes it, a cynical, rambunctious young man. When he was twenty years old, in 1964, his passion was playing cricket and singing in nightclubs. His mother worried about his choice of friends and would suggest he sing devotional hymns instead of film songs. But he would resist, touting the well-worn Marxist philosophy he shared with his friends. He would quip that her God seemed in need of spectacles, since he obviously could not see the world's problems. Otherwise God would, as a good God should, tend to them. Aiya furthermore suggested that his mother first round up God so he could get some explanations about the world's injustices. Only then would he sing God's praises.

Eventually, the glamour of nightclubs began to wear thin for Aiya. As he describes it, singing before a half-drunk audience was losing its appeal, as were the songs themselves. At that time, he was associate editor for his college magazine, *Young Idea*, and had begun composing poetry. Always in search of quiet places to write, he rode his bicycle one evening to the nearby village, Araly, and found a spot to sit in a secluded paddy field. Engrossed in his compositions, he did not take much note of an old goddess temple a short distance away. As dusk descended, he looked up from his notepad and saw a small group of people inside the lighted temple, preparing for an evening festival. From where he sat he could also see into the inner sanctum where the temple image, or *murti*, of the goddess, tall as a full-grown woman, stood in her festival finery.

Without thinking, Aiya walked his bike to the temple, parked it near the entrance, and entered. As he had done in his childhood, he started walking clockwise around the inside of the temple. When he reached the point directly behind the sanctum he suddenly remembered the temple's reputation for being powerful and dangerous, particularly at twilight and for people between the ages of seventeen and twenty-four. Trembling with fear, he scrambled toward the main entrance, where he was surprised to find a Dalit (Untouchable) woman, a basket balanced on her head, standing near the ceremonial flagstaff. She asked him in colloquial Tamil, "Why are you afraid and where are you running?" Intent upon getting out of the temple, Aiya mumbled a nonsensical reply and fled.

As he reached his parked bicycle, Aiya saw the temple *pujari* walking toward him from across the road and decided to tell him about his odd encounter with a woman who would have been barred from the temple in those days. The priest responded with surprise, "You have seen her too?" and nudged Aiya back into the temple, where the woman was nowhere to be found. Left where she had been standing were two flat mounds of vibhuti ash in the shape of footprints. At Aiya's insistence, the priest swept the ash of the left footprint onto a piece of paper, folded it up, and gave it to him.

As Aiya describes it, the moment the priest handed him the vibhuti, he felt transformed: "I was aware of a shift in focus inside of me and the feeling of being separated from myself. This reorientation process continued throughout the bicycle trip home. By the time I reached home I became aware of a complete change within me and without me. It was an eerie feeling that some strange phenomenon was unfolding within the confines of my perception."[1] Once home, he recounted the story to his mother and, overcome by his tremendous love for her yet not wanting to make a spectacle, he went to his room and let his tears flow. When he had calmed down, he took a bath, smeared some of the vibhuti onto his forehead, and went to the family shrine room to pray, sing, and cry some more. After that, Aiya spent most of his spare time in the family's *puja* room meditating and loudly singing devotional songs. He stopped performing in nightclubs and quickly gained a reputation for singing devotional hymns at nearby temples.[2]

As pivotal and powerful as this 1964 event was for Aiya, I have never heard him refer to it as a miracle. Perhaps this is because, over the past three decades, Aiya describes visions of the goddess in her various forms, particularly that of a little girl, as somewhat routine and, according to his Sri Vidya tantric tradition, to be expected.[3] Perhaps he does not apply the term "miracle" to the story since its point is not so much about the apparition itself but about personal transformation. For the purposes of this chapter, I nonetheless label this event as miraculous since, within the Rush temple context, I find the category more often associated with worldview shifts than with particular experiences themselves. The fact that Aiya describes this event as instigating a "reorientation" of his perception, one from which he gladly has never recovered, makes it a perfect fit for the category of the miraculous I am proposing.

The fact that miracles, in this context, are defined subjectively is not to rule out the possibility for various types of religious experiences. Put another way, according to the Rush temple's Sri Vidya tradition, seemingly supernatural experiences are not only desirable but are often fully anticipated and, as such, are not necessarily miraculous. Furthermore, in many cases, ritual power and mystical experiences come with scientific explanations. In the end, miracles—defined here as dramatic, unanticipated encounters with divine power—are ultimately in the eyes and mind of the beholder: among the spectrum of temple participants, one person's miracle will be another's explicable, routine experience. Over time, a temple practitioner's framework becomes altered through education and experience to such an extent that, ideally, nothing and everything is miraculous. Conventional categories of mundane and miraculous become—in accordance with Sri Vidya theology—impossible to extricate and isolate.

The Science and Power of Ritual

The Rush temple in upstate New York, it so happens, has built somewhat of a reputation for itself. It has become well known among diaspora and domestic Hindus as a place where non-Brahmins, non-South Asians, and non-males (that is, women) are trained and encouraged, against convention, to publicly lead Vedic temple rituals. While this often distinguishes Rush from other temples, it is not its biggest draw. The largest group of regular participants by far, members of the Sri Lankan Tamil community from the Toronto area, are not dedicated initiates who perform priestly functions. They make the three-hour journey to Rush in spite of a number of well-established Sri Lankan Tamil temples in their vicinity, not simply because the Rush temple is Sri Lankan Tamil in style, but because of the residing goddess Rajarajeshwari's reputation for miracle-generating power.

For temple insiders, the power of the Rush goddess is directly related to the temple's elaborate ritual practices (see figure 7.1). The tantric Sri Vidya tradition has historically focused on harnessing divine power through ritual, and Rush is no exception. As stated by Douglas Brooks in his extensive study of Sri Vidya, "Divinity is nothing other than power that can be contained,

FIGURE 7.1. Aiya offers a camphor flame to the goddess Rajarajeshwari during a ritual in 2002. Photo by Aparna Hasling.

appropriated, and even controlled through the mechanisms of ritual" (1992, 152). Contributing to the sense that divine power is an anticipated and reasonable by-product of temple activity is Aiya's use of language brimming with terms and concepts borrowed from physics, geology, and physiology to describe the cause and effect of ritual and meditative practices. His scientific bent aims at appeasing the cynics in his midst who, like his teenage premiracle self, find God needing explanation. In some ways Aiya's technical discourses encapsulate ritual power within the safe cocoon of science, securing it as nonthreatening if not nonmiraculous.

As described by Aiya and according to the Sri Vidya tradition, ritual efficacy hinges on the power of the *shri chakra* yantra, a sacred geometrical design consisting of forty interlocking triangles, four central triangles facing upward representing the male principle and five facing downward representing the female principle. Sri Vidya adepts understand the *shri chakra* yantra to be the source of all yantras and the model for the universe as divine embodiment. The *shri chakra* yantra becomes activated—and thus acts as a means for accessing divine presence and power—through the chanting of sacred mantras (see

Brooks 1992, 117–18). Aiya likens the yantra to a motor that keeps the temple charged with sacred energy. Following traditional south Indian protocol, yantras at the Rush temple lie beneath each of the main temple deities. They are understood to emit sacred energy into the temple *murti*s, or deity statues, that, in turn, release the sacred energy into the atmosphere. Ideally, temple yantras are charged prior to their installation below the *murti*s. At Rush, one particularly dedicated devotee prepared the temple yantras by reciting Sri Vidya's main fifteen-syllable mantra two and a half million times in their presence. The task took him three years to complete, with recitation lasting up to eight hours at a stretch. Ever since, regular ritual three times a day keeps the yantra motor running and maintains the temple's flow of sacred energy.

During an informal conversation one summer morning in 1998, barely one month after the Rush temple consecration, Aiya described to me in basic terms the cause and effect of temple energy: "The moment that [yantra] goes in there—and it's enhanced by the addition of other things like the nine gem stones: fine metal, mercury, and all these things [also placed below the *murti*s]—that energy is beginning to escape out into the ether. To maintain that level of energy is why the ritual is done every day—the chanting, and all that is going on—because [the *murti*] is absorbing and it is placing it there. And people will come, the devotees come, and they will experience that shower of grace." Aiya, according to convention, associates temple energy with a divinity who showers grace upon those who enter. He speaks freely and often about the goddess's grace, particularly potent in a temple where so much ritual work has been done.

Yet Aiya is just as likely to explain temple energy in scientific terms. The grace of the goddess and electromagnetic energy, it turns out, need not be mutually exclusive. The following excerpt from a December 1998 *puja* workshop, held at a small house on the temple property, offers a scientific angle. Here Aiya described how proper hygiene—along with chanting—enhances temple energy that, in turn, he associates with static electricity. In attendance at the workshop were devotees mostly of South Asian heritage in their late teens and twenties from various regions of the United States. As Aiya held forth at the front of the room, he occasionally expounded on points by sketching diagrams onto his flip chart:

When you do *puja*, what you're doing is you're creating a field of static charges around your body. So I get up, I bathe, I take a towel and I dry. All the little hairs that are like this will stand up. [Aiya shows with his pinky finger how they stand up]. OK? And at the end of those follicles is a static electric charge. The shastras tell you to wear at least two pieces of freshly washed clothes. Not things that you've worn before. Why must you not wear things that you've worn? Because oils are there in that too. And they also tell you not to wear tight clothing. Smart people! What happens when you wear loose clothes? I'll tell you. You know the shawl that I keep throwing [Aiya comically pantomimes the motion he constantly makes, flipping back an imaginary shawl] over my shoulder? What's happening is that thing is loosely rubbing against my skin and it's charging those hair follicles.

A female college student interjects at this point and asks Aiya, "Doesn't the *puja* itself do that?"

Aiya responds, "Oh yes, also. But this enhances it, when you're chanting the mantras. Now you understand why I have the drone playing in the temple. I'm chanting at that pitch and you hear the *whole* room is vibrating. *All* the atmospheric molecules are around me, the molecules of air around me are hitting against each other and my sound is coming out and they're charging. And there is a field of electricity created around me."

The student interjects again, for clarification, "So when you bathe and everything, you go in already charged."

Aiya goes on to explain,

Yeah, you're going in with the basic charge already present in your system. The ancient rishis probably didn't call it static electricity and all that but they knew there was something going on here—they knew that. Now I'll tell you. When you come out of the bathroom, the telephone rings, don't sit here [Aiya sits with legs crossed answering an imaginary phone while people chuckle], "Hello?" You've lost it. You've already lost that charge that you've created. Don't touch anybody; don't touch anything. Sometimes it's impossible to avoid this. Someone sees you, they've come from after six months from far, far, away and they come and want to touch your feet. Can I tell them, "Don't touch me, I'm . . . I'm charged!"? [Laughter erupts.] But if you have this basic knowledge you'll know not to approach.

At this point, a few of the Tamil-speaking people in the room recalled an admonition they sometimes heard in a ritual context, "Don't touch, he's pure." Aiya suggested that people use this wording since they are familiar with issues of purity and pollution and not electromagnetic forces—although concern for priestly hygiene is not, as he sees it, primarily about purity.[4] The fact that Aiya's response, "I'm charged," elicited laughter from the room demonstrates how temple science is not only unfamiliar to the average devotee but can be comically so. Although science can, for some, offer legitimacy to ritual power, the mix can also, at times, seem oxymoronic.

Temple practitioners more commonly associate religion and science when describing the physiological effects of meditation, also essential to the Sri Vidya tradition. Although ritual is crucial to Sri Vidya practice, it is not an end in itself—as it would be for more traditional Vedic ritualists—but is a means to enhance internal yogic practices. This yogic component draws from the philosophically oriented Vedantic branch of Hinduism that traditionally rejects the importance of ritual and promotes, instead, renunciation to fuel meditational experiences (see Brooks 1992, 171–73). Sri Vidya thus distinguishes itself for its combined emphasis on external rituals and internal practices, yet it ultimately gives higher priority to the latter. Once a practitioner advances far enough in the tradition, he or she is understood as no longer requiring external ritual devotion. As conceived by Sri Vidya, an internal bodily yantra, generating divine energy within, has begun working, replacing the need for the temple yantra.

In the meantime and for most practitioners, external devotion augments internal yogic practices. One way of viewing this interrelationship is through the power of mantras, understood to fuel the temple yantra and thus the energy emitted into the temple yet also understood as funneling divine energy into human participants. Just as Aiya describes the external effects of mantras in religious and scientific terms—associated with divine grace as well as electromagnetic energy—he explains their internal benefits, manifest most explicitly through mystical experiences, using the language of religion as well as physiology.

The following excerpt is from a December 1999 Sunday gathering of about thirty parishioners from a Catholic church in Syracuse. Constituting all ages and featuring a number of teenagers from that year's confirmation class, the group came for morning *puja* and a visit with Aiya. Aiya energetically held forth on an array of subjects, one of which was the physiological and mystical effects of mantras. He opened the subject by reciting a particularly lengthy mantra that devotees ideally chant in one breath, dramatically inhaling at the end of the passage. As people around the room laughed, Aiya continued, noting the connection between ritual prescription and yogic breathing practices: "So the tradition is that you don't have to teach the guys to breathe in a separate lesson. These things are structured in such a way that when they tell you to learn to do this in one breath, the breathing exercises are planned." He then described how an increase in breathing capacity eventually alters lung capacity, gradually affecting the flow and constitution of blood vessels. He further explained,

> When you're breathing in, the metabolic rate is so beautifully set, the heart is already pumping from the right ventricle, being carried into the lungs through the pulmonary vein enclosed there. And it is richly supplied; this transfer of gasses [referred to a moment earlier] is taking place there. So, from the blood corpuscle, the red blood corpuscle, the hemoglobin will release the carbon dioxide, the carbonic base into the lungs—into the air sac—and absorb the oxygen and become oxygenated blood. Then it will go back to the heart and the heart will pump it and it will go up here into the

artery and go into the brain and go through the rest of the body. OK. But when that carbon dioxide gets into your lung area, the air, the moisture that is there, profusely supplied with water vapor, the water vapor will attach itself to the carbon dioxide molecule and it will become carbonic acid. H2CO3.

At this point, Dan, a middle-aged parishioner and physicist, interjected that he thought Aiya said his guru was a nuclear physicist—which he is—and asked how Aiya learned so much about biology. Aiya responded that he didn't learn this from his guru; it came to him as part of his spiritual practice, from the Mother. Suzanne, a church cantor, concerned that Aiya's new tangent would take us offtrack, raised her hand and quietly suggested, "Would you finish?" to which Aiya responded, "Yes! I will tell you! You people are really good!" He then went on to describe how carbonic acid will get hydrogenized and will ultimately affect the PH value of the blood plasma. From here Aiya moved on to a discussion of all-important pineal stalk located in the brain just above the central palate.

> That pineal stalk, if you can keep the PH value within certain optimum range, for each person—depending on the person's emotional stability, their upbringing, their ability to stay calm under duress and distress, not to lose their temper, not to be fluctuating in their emotions and things like that—then every single layer of the pineal stalk will begin to produce what are called endorphins. These are neuropeptides. That means they are brain chemicals.
>
> Now, suddenly over the last few years you will find—do you ever go to the supermarket, you stand in the line, and you look at the counter? You see the *Globe* and the *Star* and the *National Enquirer* and all that? You don't have to buy them to read them; all you have to do is look at them [Aiya makes a funny sideways glance like he's reading the headlines]. You will find "Melatonin Has Been Discovered!" "Seratonin Has Been Discovered!" This is very old. Melatonin and seratonin, these are chemicals that are formed in the interior layer of the brain.
>
> Why do you think the young ones go and roll these things, get this good Colombian stuff and go [Aiya pretends he is taking a toke; the group chuckles]? Why do you think they do it? Because it produces this effect inside. But you don't have to ever use any chemical. Let us say that you choose one beautiful stanza of anything—take the Twenty-third Psalm— and keep chanting it over and over again, or chant the Lord's Prayer over and over again. You will have it. These endorphins will be released into your system. You will feel a spiritual high. You will experience ecstasy.
>
> Now look at the source of this thing. The breathing is the source. Slowly, slowly, slowly. It won't happen overnight. Don't think you can go

home and sit down and go [Aiya does exaggerated breathing exercises through one nostril and then the other] or, say, hold your breath until you're blue in the face. Don't think it will happen. There are 6.4 billion cells in this system. Different tissue systems are there, and once these endorphins are released into the brain cavity they will get into the spinal fluid which continues right up into the base of the spine.

From here, Aiya described the system of energy points, or chakras, located at different places along one's spine, activated by kundalini energy rising within the spinal column, spurred on by chanting mantras. He infused his explanation of kundalini energy, based on ancient yogic understandings of divine power, with modern scientific language. Divine kundalini energy, emergent from the power of sacred speech, thus becomes within the temple framework indistinguishable from a chain of biological reactions.

In the end, science may explain, but it cannot explain away seemingly miraculous experiences attributed to ritual or mystical forces. For Aiya, scientific discovery, far from undermining the possibility and potency of ritual and yogic power, helps to confirm it. As he suggests, today's tabloids and pot-smoking teenagers are not reporting or experiencing anything new but rather are rediscovering and renaming what the ancient seers, or rishis, knew long ago.

Plainly, scientific discovery has not had the same effect on many other religious thinkers who grapple with the problem of supernatural power. The Protestant theologian Rudolf Bultmann put forth a classic Christian response, developed in light of Hume's famous definition of a miracle as "a violation of the laws of nature" that renders miracles and, therefore, God an impossibility (Hume [1777] 1975, 656). Bultmann shared Hume's definition and disregard for miracles, yet rather than give up on God altogether he proposed that divinity participates within rather than outside of natural history (1958, 16). Bultmann's position is fairly standard today among mainline Christian theologians who reconfigure traditional theology to fit modern parameters of science and nature. Aiya, while embracing a scientific worldview, does so on different terms by seemingly extending science to divine proportions. Bultmann's formula allows him to keep a grip on faith while maintaining Hume's view of the miraculous, whereas Aiya's religio-scientific framework does something slightly different.

A Christian approach similar to Aiya's is a postmodern theology proposed by the process theologian David Griffin. Like Bultmann and Hume, Griffin rejects the category of the supernatural but differs in his view of so-called supernatural events themselves. Griffin argues that a range of paranormal activities occur naturally and furthermore provide a welcome challenge to our modern scientific worldview. Griffin identifies our current classification of the supernatural as arising, in part, from an ecclesial agenda put forth in the late seventeenth century. At this time, the church promoted the notion that activities such as spiritual healing and clairvoyance were not natural but supernatural—that is, "miraculous"—thus attempting to claim and control the power of such practices. Advocates of Hermetic and other "magical philosophies" posed a threat to church authority through their insistence that such events were natural and therefore available outside Christian structures. Early modernism's resulting dualism between the natural and the supernatural order ("supernaturalistic theism") led to late modernism's rejection of the supernatural altogether ("naturalistic atheism"). Griffin notes that conservative Christians typically maintain early modern views of the supernatural, while those in academia largely adhere to the atheism of late modernity (1997, 21–23).

Somewhat supportive of the possibility that science can accommodate mystical experiences is Neo-Vedantic philosophy, prevalent today in urban South Asia, particularly in ashram settings. However, following the teachings of Patanjali, author of the Yoga Sutras, and his commentators, many Neo-Vedantans are nontheists who consider divine intervention unnecessary (Davis 1998, 10). Distinguishing itself from these past and present Hindu traditions is the Sri Vidya belief that divinity can also be distinguished from—and shower grace upon—the earthly, embodied domain. The fact that divinity within Sri Vidya is synonymous with both the transcendent and the seemingly mundane realms makes for a complex theology similar in many ways to Griffin's postmodern theology, which is both theistic and naturalistic.[5] As this chapter will argue, this nondualistic view also makes for a correspondingly complex conception of the miraculous.

On a number of occasions while listening to Aiya wax eloquent about the science of ritual and meditational practices, I wondered about the grace-filled aspect of transcendent divinity seemingly missing from the picture. Sometimes I would wonder aloud: if everything can be explained and understood scientifically, where does God go? More pedantically put, it seems that the beneficent Mother Goddess whom Aiya describes in intensely personal and devotional terms recedes into obscurity when science envelopes all. During these discussions Aiya often described this aspect of the goddess as residing in the inexplicable leaps between science lessons or between clusters of empirical evidence: between ritual power and meditational experiences or between a yantra's geometrical design and its capacity for generating energy.

As I view it, a preliminary understanding of the miraculous in a religious context where so much is explained relies upon the aspect of divinity that resides in the interstices, one that rests more comfortably in questions and mystery than in answers. Once when I suggested to Aiya that faith appeared to rely a great deal upon mystery, he agreed, yet he qualified his assent by adding, "She supplies it; we don't." Aiya seems compelled to supply explanation in abundance, yet he revels in divine mysteries and miracles that lie beyond his reach. Over the years, various encounters and experiences have indeed increased his faith, but so have they extended his reach. Although not always explicable in scientific terms, these formerly miraculous and mysterious experiences have become anticipated events that, for him, have narrowed the potential for the unexpected—if not the inexplicable—and thus, conventionally speaking, for the miraculous.

Making Room for Miracles

Not surprisingly, Aiya has come to inhabit a world so saturated with divine activity that little surprises him. Although he enthusiastically relates experiences conventionally construed as supernatural or mystical, only twice have I heard him explicitly use the term "miracle" to describe such an event. In one instance, on a midweek, mid-March evening in 1999, he and his wife Amma were driving to the temple for the evening *puja*. About forty yards ahead of them they saw a green van with three Euro American adults in it slowly approaching and then entering the temple driveway. The van stopped at an angle in the parking lot and then drove back out again, passing Aiya and Amma on the way. Figuring they simply had made a wrong turn, Aiya and Amma thought no more of it, performed the evening *puja*, and headed home.

The next morning, Aiya was back on the road to the temple, stopped just opposite the driveway, his left blinker on, waiting for a clump of morning traffic to clear. He noticed the same green van heading his direction, this time with one middle-aged gentleman inside. The man turned into the temple driveway, and Aiya followed. Once in the parking lot, the man asked Aiya if he had a little girl. Not one to give simple answers, Aiya said yes: his little girl was now grown but would always be a little girl to him. The man then notified Aiya that the previous night—it was around seven and almost dark—he and two family members had seen a little girl who looked to be from India riding her bike on the side of the road. When they saw her turn into the driveway, they wanted to warn her parents that, as Aiya put it, "this is a beautiful village and everything, but it isn't perfectly safe." The man explained that by the time they drove down the driveway they had lost sight of her and figured she had entered the house.

As the man wrapped up his account, Aiya's heart was pounding and his mind was racing. He knew no Indian families lived anywhere nearby, and he also knew who this man had seen. As he put it, "As soon as the guy drove off, I marched straight into the temple and yelled at Her! 'How dare you show yourself to this American and not to me!!!'" Based on accounts from temples in India as well as stories from Rush devotees, a typical divine manifestation at Indian goddess temples is one in which she appears as a little girl to bless those with eyes of faith. Aiya's wonderment over this particular sighting of a little girl on the bike, who he was certain was the goddess, is twofold. One, she appeared to people totally unaware of her existence; and two, it seems she blocked two of her most ardent devotees from view. Although they were driving only a short distance behind the green van, neither he nor his wife saw anyone riding a bike that night.

In the goddess-apparition stories recounted in this chapter so far, two types of context determine their meaning. First, cultural context forms expectations that allow group members to anticipate and appreciate an event as a miracle (see Davis 1998, 5). Whether appearing as a Dalit woman or as a little girl, the deity was recognized as such by her devotees, since South Asian goddess traditions offer precedent for such appearances. The non–South Asian passengers in the green van, lacking the appropriate cultural cues, understood the little girl on the bike to be just that—a slightly confused and underprotected little girl, perhaps—but nothing more.

A second level of context has to do with an individual's prior experiences and perceptions. In contrast to a cultural context that anticipates certain agreed-upon themes, personal context requires an element of surprise: the event must in some ways run contrary to expectation in order for it to be considered, in Rush temple parlance, miraculous. In the case of the little girl on the bike, most devotees found her appearance on wintry North American terrain to be surprising and wondrous in itself, and therefore miraculous. Aiya, on the other hand, was not so much surprised by her appearance—apparitions are not particularly surprising or miraculous for Aiya these days. He was confounded more specifically by her revelation to complete or, at least, apparent strangers, and for this reason he explicitly described the event as a miracle. During a weekday morning discussion on the subject the following September, Aiya describes the wonder of the event for him, associating it with the mysterious breach between ritual power—generated at the temple by the yantra lying beneath the goddess's form—and mystical manifestation:

> Now somewhere in between the scientific generation of Her power and the perception of that energy—somewhere in between is a leap where the manifestation has occurred. Now, that manifestation is the mystery that is associated with any temple, any church, any holy place.
>
> And if that leap has happened to you, then you always hold the possibility at the back of your mind that this was a figment of your imagination because you are continuously revolving around that statue and the temple and the lamps and the smell of incense and all that. Now, when that manifestation happens to somebody who has no idea what this place is about, has absolutely no knowledge of what is going on here, doesn't even know that there is a deity here that is female or anything like that, who had no idea that

there was even a temple here—because at that time there wasn't even a board up there—that tells you that there is something . . . a leap from the material plane into the divine, if you will, into the spiritual realm. And my job, as far as I'm concerned, is to keep that engine [the yantra] working in there.

Amid all the excitement generated by the little-girl-on-the-bike incident, Aparna, a Euro American devotee in her mid-thirties, involved for decades with Hindu traditions and gurus and with her own history of mystical experiences, reacted very differently to the event. In an e-mail she sent me soon afterward, Aparna seemed confused by the level of excitement displayed by temple devotees. A widespread interpretation that the goddess appeared in order to strengthen the faith of those who did not see Her seemed particularly problematic. Aparna felt that the three Americans in the van were not pawns in a larger game meant to increase devotees' faith, but were led to the temple for their own reasons. As she put it, "I believe this incident is true. I just don't get why it is so significant." For someone who not only has had prior experience with goddess apparitions but with non-Indian Hindus, the event lacked the element of surprise necessary for her to classify it as a full-fledged miracle. Based on this and other exchanges with Aparna, I decided that very little surprises her; she is hard-pressed to label anything a miracle—at least the kind that, as I define it, would radically reframe her world. I was therefore taken aback two summers later when, after mentioning to her my plans for writing about temple miracles, Aparna piped up, her brown eyes gleaming, "I have a miracle story!"

The event took place in late spring during the 2001 *pratishta* festival marking the third anniversary of the temple's consecration. Aparna sat by the *homam* fire, pouring milk, *abhishekam* style, over one of eight Ganesh *murti*s stationed nearby. When the *homam* was over, devotees circumambulated the fire and, as Aparna was making her rounds, Vijitha, a college-aged Sri Lankan–born devotee, motioned to her and whispered, "Aparna, come here! Ganesh is drinking milk!" Aparna nodded at her, not wanting to be distracted, but Vijitha persisted, saying, "Come on Aparna, he's drinking milk!" Aparna stopped and sat next to Vijitha, where she saw devotees placing spoons full of milk under Ganesh's tusk. She watched as the milk slowly disappeared and, as she put it, she could not believe her eyes. After witnessing about ten to fifteen offerings, she tried it herself.

When I reminded Aparna of her reaction to the little girl on the bike two years earlier, she remembered and laughed. She admitted that the experience with Ganesh, unlike secondhand visions of the Devi—which she nonetheless believed wholeheartedly—took her completely by surprise. While she claimed to take in stride the goddess's constant and yet sometimes unexpected presence around the temple, her experience of Ganesh physically consuming something before her eyes was altogether different. As she described it, the event forced her to readjust her thinking about the way the world worked.

My final miracle story involves participants who, somewhat like the three passengers in the green van, were largely disconnected from a cultural context and cues that anticipate miraculous temple events. Furthermore, the experience they perceived as miraculous would be less than wondrous for many temple devotees and easily explained by Aiya through the use of temple-science terminology. The event involves a friend of mine whom I will call Linda, a Catholic nun and professor of Christian ethics currently living in Massachusetts. Linda had met Aiya at an ecumenical gathering in Rochester and, finding mutual appreciation for each other and each other's work, he invited her to visit the temple.

We attended morning *puja* soon after, led by Aiya, and performed in the ordinary fashion—except for one small detail. When Aiya approached Linda with the camphor flame he had just offered to Rajarajeshwari at the start of the *puja*, she was supposed to receive blessings from the goddess by wafting her hands over the flame and toward her body. Instead, Linda looked at the flame in front of her and then back up at Aiya, not sure what to do. He chuckled and wafted the flame's blessings over her, afterward laying his right hand on top of her head in a fatherly fashion. It occurred to me that this gesture went against protocol. As I had learned at the previous winter's *puja* workshop, the person performing *puja* is not supposed to touch anyone until the conclusion of the ritual so as not to lose his or her electromagnetic charge. I took note but did not consider it again until later.

That night Linda called me from Massachusetts. Thinking she was just checking in, I asked her what she had thought of the temple visit. Rather than engaging in light conversation, she began with a nervous laugh and replied, "Actually I was calling for a reality check." After asking if I noticed Aiya place his hand on her head at the beginning of the *puja*, she described, slowly and methodically, as if recalling them, the sensations triggered by his touch, "It was the strangest thing. I felt this intense burning, electric sensation throughout me." After stopping to think for a few seconds, she continued, "It burned the strongest at the base of my spine, in the pit of my stomach, in the middle of my chest, the base of my neck, in the middle of my forehead, and on the top of my head where he put his hand." After another brief pause, she added, "The palms of my hands and bottoms of my feet also felt like they were on fire."

Stunned at the other end of the line, knowing that Linda had very little exposure to Asian religious traditions, I told her that she had practically given me the textbook description of the chakras located at different points along the spine. Burning hands and feet I was not familiar with. Taking this in and continuing, Linda described how, as Aiya performed *puja* at the different deities' stations, she felt different chakra points in her body burn with the same electric heat. When he performed his customary blessing of a life-sized picture of Kamakshi, holding up the camphor flame in front of different parts of her body, Linda felt the corresponding regions of her own body lighting up with heat.

Although Linda is one of the most levelheaded people I know, I was amazed she could sit next to me during *puja* and hide the fact that fireworks were erupting inside her. On the phone, she seemed rattled by her experience, hoping to understand it in order to have some semblance of control. I could tell her what chakras were on paper, that *shaktipat* was the descent of a guru's sacred energy into an initiate, and that each main temple *murti* is meant to emit a certain type of energy. I could even recite back to her Aiya's physiological explanation for internal yogic energy as well as his description of electromagnetic temple forces. Yet this kind of explanation seemed altogether unhelpful, given the event was so unexpected to both of us. For me, this kind of experience was something that happened to other people, primarily people I read about in books. Although I should probably have known better, I had no idea Aiya could do this.[6] Furthermore, Linda lacked the cultural context that anticipated chakras opening up, let alone allowing for their existence to begin with. It felt as though something unknown had grabbed us from behind and set us down in a whole different place—one with a dramatically different view.

Concluding Reflections:
Making More Room for Miracles

The *Skeptic's Dictionary*, found at www.skepdic.com, posits that miracles are induced by the power of suggestion. To some extent, based on the above accounts, this is true. A Dalit goddess who blesses a Marxist renegade, a bike-riding apparition who graces three outsiders, a stone Ganesh who draws in milk, or chakras that open and ignite were experienced as miraculous by those whose cultural frames of reference allowed—at least eventually—for such an interpretation. Yet distinguishing these accounts as miraculous is a certain defiance of suggestion, as well. As I have defined them, miracles are events initially thought by an individual to be implausible, if not impossible.

As proposed above, while initial experiences transform the impossible into the plausible, subsequent similar experiences function more as affirmations of divine presence than as framework-shattering miracles. Miracles thus narrow the range of events considered, in the same sense, miraculous. Viewing this paradox from another angle is the fact that Sri Vidya simultaneously encourages and discourages perceptions of the miraculous, delineated here as transformative experiences of wonderment and impossibility. In other words, the system that ideally dissolves miracles, defined as wondrously impossible, into nonexistence is formed and properly stretched through experiences of the same. This paradox, moreover, leaves the door open for yet another layer of miracles to consider.

The week before I presented an abbreviated version of this chapter to the 2005 Conference on the Study of Religions of India (CSRI) held in Albion, Michigan, I made a visit to Rush. During one of my chats with Aiya I took the opportunity to explain my theory on the miraculous to see what he thought. In the affirming style to which I have grown so accustomed, he enthusiastically concurred with my definition of miracles as events that radically alter one's perceptual framework such that they make room for divine activity previously considered impossible. Aiya also agreed that when these so-called miracles reoccur they become anticipated and thus lose their miraculous quality; as the impossible increasingly becomes possible, they eventually cease to exist.

With that settled, I decided to narrate a different scenario to Aiya to secure my sense that we were in agreement. I asked him what he thought of seemingly mundane coincidences in which, for instance (I paraphrase), "I drive into an overflowing parking lot. Next to me in the passenger seat is an elderly person for whom walking is difficult and thus, wishing for a spot near the building, I say a little prayer as I drive. As we near the building, it so happens that the perfect parking space opens up." Before I could even stop my narrative to ask his opinion, Aiya interjected, "That would be a miracle!"

Needless to say, Aiya's assessment was like a wrench thrown into my smoothly spun theory in which miracles ultimately and ideally shed their miraculous quality. Our conversation soon veered into a different direction, so I was left thinking: "Must I now discard my miracle theory entirely? Or can I fix it somehow so it still works?" I have chosen the latter option in part because I hate to throw away useful theories—after all, Aiya readily welcomed my definition before seemingly contradicting it. I also have chosen to tinker with the original, because it seems that Aiya's wrench is actually a crucial caveat to my original definition of miracle as a perception-altering mystery. I thus conclude by making room for mundane blessings—fortunate events, perhaps, but not necessarily mysterious or even surprising—as integral to the category of miracle within the Rush temple context.

With this in mind, I return to some of my earlier stated questions to Aiya: "What if repeated experiences of the miraculous alter one's framework such that wonderment and the wondrous, associated above with divinity, get edged out completely? What if science is stretched to fit divine parameters such that the sacred and the mundane become inextricable?" Aiya's answers accommodated me at the time by allowing mystery to exist in the spaces between empirically understood phenomena.

Yet these questions can also point to the Sri Vidya goal of sacred saturation in which these spaces ideally get edged out. This process that eventually eliminates divine mystery can also be a process within which divinity, rather than fading away, begins to imbue everything. The perspective that everyday blessings are unmistakable signs of divine presence—experienced as unequivocally miraculous—is, in this case, a privileged view, gradually acquired and contingent in part upon repeated encounters with the unanticipated miraculous. Two weeks after the little-girl-on-the-bike episode, Aiya introduced the subject to Anusha, a student at UCLA, and me as we sipped sweet milky tea outside the temple kitchen: "Now, after this thing with the little girl, I'm beginning to realize every hour is a miracle. Because now it's slowly beginning to hit: how the hell is this place keeping up? I shouldn't be able to make ends meet."

As Aiya paused, I chimed in, "Yup. It puts things in a different relief."

Aiya concurred and continued: "Different, very different. Every blossom that comes, every bit of fruit that somebody brings into the temple, something is being moved in a particular way. You won't believe me, Corinne, if I tell you. For the past thirty years—three-zero, not thirteen, three-zero years—I have never bought a bottle of oil for the temple, I have never bought incense sticks for the temple, I have never bought camphor. That's a *long* time ago. Right from the start, it's been taken care of. And just when you are running out of flowers or fruits or something like that, somebody will walk in with a box of something to keep you going. She keeps it going. She is the Master Planner."

Although Aiya has undoubtedly perceived the hand of the Divine Mother in his life for decades, long before the Rush temple existed and when he and his wife conducted rituals from their home, miracles such as the appearance of the little girl on the bike have helped to radicalize this view. It is through such framework-altering events that room is made for daily blessings to be taken just as seriously—as miracles in their own right.

Miracles emerging from these two different registers—one traditionally tied to transcendent mystery and the other easily confused with happy coincidence—are, with proper perspective, folded into one another. This collapsing of registers parallels the perspective that Sri Vidya practitioners aspire to uphold, one in which the distinction between miraculous and mundane, transcendent and immanent, realities are obliterated. Key to this perception is the knowledge that all things, in the end, are divinity manifest. As described by Brooks, "Where one *stands* in relation to others and the divine counts for everything in Sri Vidya. Sri Vidya's only incontrovertible truth is that the universe is a divine self-manifestation of power in which events are different in degree and kind only from an ordinary (i.e., ignorant) point of view. From the privileged vantage point of the Sri Vidya practitioner, the world is nothing but divine power or shakti" (1992, 148–49).

Central to Aiya's teaching is the idea that divine feminine power, or shakti, imbues all. Framework-altering miracles, rather than being ends in themselves that deepen life's mysteries, are meant to bring the practitioner to greater knowledge of the divine feminine's earthly presence. Although Aiya enthusiastically recounts this type of miracle as a means for building faith, he dedicates himself more fully to teaching his students temple science and ritual mechanics. He encourages knowledge and direct experience rather than disengaged awe because, ideally speaking, he knows that mystery only exists to a certain point. One evening at the temple before a final few of us headed home, he described the precarious existence of mystery as follows: "What is mystery? The entire world is Her—what you see, what you can't see, what you feel, what you don't feel. It's all Her. So what is mysterious about it? The intellectual understanding that everything is the Mother is already there. The only thing lacking is the experience of it. And I'm trying to bring people to that experience."

As this chapter has argued, temple participants, Aiya included, understand dramatic, unanticipated experiences of divinity as vital trail markers along the Sri Vidya path. Just as Sri Vidya teaches that external rituals are essential to the enhancement of—and are eventually and ideally replaced by—internal practices and experiences, framework-altering miracles ideally enhance and eventually are replaced by the perception that all is divinity. Unanticipated miracles are ultimately meant to transform, as Aiya put it, "the intellectual understanding that everything is the Mother" into something more real and radical—into a miracle-imbued reality that is certain of and anticipates the Divine Mother's hand in all things. This in many ways resonates with David Griffin's proposal for a postmodern theology, mentioned above. According to Griffin, the understanding of God as a natural force within the universe is one that relies upon serious consideration of paranormal events not as supernatural but as natural. Rather than proposing a nontheistic panentheism, Griffin's naturalistic theology, like Aiya's, does not therefore erase divinity. Griffin asserts that when so-called miracles are viewed as natural, God permeates reality as "the dominant member of the universal society, providing the overall order, and the supreme recipient of value, feeling both the delights and pains of the creatures" (1997, 276).

It is fitting that this final layer of the mundane miraculous is something I have worked into this chapter as an afterthought; the perspective required to see it as such is a privileged one, not naturally assumed by most people. If one is tempted to think that this latter type of miracle lacks the requisite zing for its inclusion within the category of the miraculous, this is, from the Sri Vidya perspective, a product of ignorance. From the vantage point of the spiritually privileged for whom unanticipated mystery has nearly been phased out, the mundane miraculous reflects a world entirely charged with divine energy—

one that, in the end, is no less powerful or dramatic. Parking-lot fortune and bike-riding apparitions are, at this point, equally valued signs of divine presence. Divine grace and electromagnetic energy are, in the end, the same thing. They are miracles inasmuch as all of reality is a miracle.

Notes

1. Although I have heard Aiya relate this story in a variety of contexts, this particular quoted reflection comes from a written account of the event, part of a short spiritual biography he wrote about a decade ago. In oral accounts, Aiya often mentions his transformation while cycling home, but not in so much detail.

2. This miracle story and several other stories included in this article also appear—but in a different order and framed for different purposes—in my book, *The Goddess Lives in Upstate New York*, which describes Aiya's temple and its emphasis on ritual power, its unconventional democratic practices, and its emergence within the realities of diasporic Hinduism.

3. Srividya is a tantric tradition developed in Kashmir and today practiced secretly and largely by Brahmins in south India and Sri Lanka. It is a tradition that honors the Great Triple Goddess Tripurasundari and places great emphasis on ritual power. For a detailed description of the development and practices of Srividya, see Brooks 1992.

4. A parallel practice at the Rush temple is that of menstrual restrictions. Women are discouraged from entering the Rush temple while menstruating due to the potential harm that temple energy can cause her reproductive organs during this time. The issue of purity and pollution, typically associated with menstrual taboos, does not come into play here. See Dempsey 2006, 138–39.

5. For Griffin's discussion of the place of God within his postmodern spirituality, see chapter 9 of his book. A fuller comparison of Sri Vidya with Griffin's theology would require a separate article. See Long 2007 on the interplay of process theology and Vedanta.

6. It turns out that the reason Aiya performed *shaktipat* on Linda had to do with his decision to give her a "jump start," to help her in her spiritual progress. Unlike some gurus, Aiya rarely performs *shaktipat*, reserving it only for very special cases. See Dempsey 2006, 29, 66.

References

Brooks, Douglas Renfrew. 1992. *Auspicious Wisdom: The Texts and Traditions of Srividya Sakta Tantrism in South India.* Albany: State University of New York Press.

Bultmann, Rudolph. 1958. *Jesus Christ and Mythology.* New York: Charles Scribner's Sons.

Davis, Richard. 1998. "Introduction: Miracles as Social Acts." In *Images, Miracles, and Authority in Asian Religious Traditions*, edited by Richard Davis, 1–22. Boulder, CO: Westview.

Dempsey, Corinne. 2006. *The Goddess Lives in Upstate New York: Making Home and Breaking Convention at a North Indian Hindu Temple*. New York: Oxford University Press.

Griffin, David Ray. 1997. *Parapsychology, Philosophy, and Spirituality: A Postmodern Exploration*. Albany: State University of New York Press.

Hume, David. [1777] 1975. "On Miracles." In *Enquiries Concerning the Human Understanding*. Oxford: Clarendon Press.

Long, Jeffery. 2007. *A Vision for Hinduism: Beyond Hindu Nationalism*. I. B. Taurus.

PART III

Managing the Establishment: Miracles and Popular Expression

CHAPTER EIGHT

An Ethnographic Encounter with the Wondrous in a South Indian Catholic Shrine

SELVA J. RAJ

Introduction

On May 31, 2000, my nephew Charles—a chemistry professor with an abiding interest in popular religious practices and my local research assistant that summer—and I were scheduled to take the overnight Nellai Express train from Tiruchirapalli to Tirunelveli en route to the shrine of St. Anthony at Uvari, where I had planned to conduct month-long field research studying the miraculous events and powers attributed to its patron saint. Our plan was to catch an early morning bus at Tirunelveli for Uvari—sixty miles southeast of Tirunelveli—and attend the flag-hoisting ceremony inaugurating the thirteen-day religious festival. However, due to some strange mix-up in our train reservation, we were not allowed to board that train. Worried and anxious that we might miss the flag-hoisting ceremony and doubtful of the prospects of finding alternate transportation at that late hour of the night (it was 12:30 a.m.), we sought any and all available transportation, including taxis, private cars, and even trucks. Finally, around three o'clock that morning we managed to get seats in a bus bound for Madurai, a major commercial city midway between Tiruchirapalli and Tirunelveli.

As I sat in the bus contemplating the comedy (more accurately, the tragedy) of errors that night, I could not help but wonder—despite my decade-long training in the Western academy—if there was a hidden message for me. "Is someone trying to thwart my trip? Is some unknown power sending me a mysterious sign? Is there a divine conspiracy to jinx or block my academic project? Is the academic study of miracles and the miraculous a futile or fruitful exercise?" These questions lingered in my mind as we made our way to Madurai.

When we reached Madurai around six that morning, my nephew led me to the home of a business associate who owned a taxi rental business. Though sympathetic to our plight and willing to deploy a taxi and a driver immediately, the owner nonetheless demanded an exorbitant rental fee. With limited options at our disposal, we had no choice but to rent the taxi and proceed on that hot summer day toward Uvari—a tiny coastal village on the Coromandel coast—150 miles south of the city of Madurai. After a six-hour drive on national highways and narrow rural roads, we finally reached Uvari late in the afternoon when there was hardly any life in the village. The entire village seemed to be enjoying the afternoon siesta. As we made our way through deserted village streets to the sandy premises of the shrine of St. Anthony— just a hundred feet from the beach—the shrine premises too seemed empty except for some lingering pilgrims. Soon we learned that the flag-hoisting ceremony presided by Rev. Irudayaraj—the senior priest of the shrine—had concluded earlier in the day. But we saw the gigantic flagpole overlooking the waters of the Bay of Bengal. Over sixty flags of various colors and stripes that adorned the pole fluttered in the blue sky, proclaiming the official beginning of the festival to all and sundry. Modeled after Tamil Hindu temple festival tradition, the flag-hoisting ceremony—typically celebrated with great pomp and fanfare by Parava Catholics in southeast Tamil Nadu—sets the festival season in motion (Younger 2002). Though we were disappointed by the strange turn of events that precluded our attendance at the flag-hoisting ceremony, we were happy to have finally arrived at Uvari, which became my research site and temporary home for the next four weeks.

Later that evening I met with Rev. Irudayaraj in the rectory and explained my research interests and plans. Not only did he seem genuinely thrilled about my research interest in his shrine, but he also enthusiastically endorsed it and extended warm and generous hospitality to me, offering room and board at the rectory. He went out of his way to provide assistance and assigned a staff member to take us around the village and introduce me to local leaders, residents, and visiting pilgrims, who would prove immensely helpful. The initial days entailed routine field-research tasks: familiarizing myself with the local religious and cultural landscape, customs, and practices; talking to villagers, clergy, and pilgrims; and interviewing them in both structured and informal contexts. Thus, despite some initial setbacks, Uvari and its famed shrine ultimately proved to be a rich resource for numerous miracle stories, which the villagers and pilgrims enthusiastically and, on occasion fervently, narrated to me.

In this chapter, I relate two miracle stories told and enacted by St. Anthony's devotees who maintain and participate in shared conceptions about miracles and the miraculous, derived, in turn, from a shared indigenous religious worldview and epistemology. In light of these narratives, I propose to explore the social processes and themes embedded in this miracle discourse, themes that, in my view, create grassroots ecumenism, and I will reflect on the theological and perspectival disjunctions between the religious elite and the enthusiastic masses in understanding the relevance and mechanics of miracles.

The Shrine, Saint, and Devotees

The shrine of St. Anthony at Uvari on the Pearl Fishery coast—thirty miles north of Kanya Kumari at the tip of the Indian peninsula—is a popular Catholic pilgrimage center in Tamil Nadu, south India. Known as the "Padua of the East" and "Padua of South India," Uvari is a coastal village of coconut trees and fishing boats situated on the shores of the Bay of Bengal. According to the 1995 village Panchayat census, the total population of the village numbers approximately sixteen hundred Catholic families of the Parava (fishing) caste group— also known as *bharathar* and *meenparavar* (literally, "Paravars who catch fish" to distinguish them from pearl-fishing Paravars)—a "low-ranking fishing and boat-handling population" (Bayly 1989, 321).[1] So, as in other coastal villages of southeast Tamil Nadu, fishing is the main occupation for its residents. While men venture into the sea, women help sell fish in village and neighborhood markets. In recent years, a small group of men has migrated to urban areas like Bombay in western India in search of better jobs and lifestyle. The Catholic community at Uvari proudly traces its Christian heritage to the missionary work of such notable Portuguese Jesuits as St. Francis Xavier, who is said to have spent several days in the village during one of his missionary trips. A kilometer away from Uvari is "Nadar Uvari," a Hindu village that boasts of a large shrine known as Swayambulingasamy temple, dedicated to the god Shiva.

Four towering churches, each dedicated to a different Catholic saint, dominate Uvari's physical and religious landscape.[2] Among these four churches, the recently renovated shrine of St. Anthony is undoubtedly the most prominent when measured by the number of pilgrims it attracts and the wondrous miracles attributed to its patron saint. While many south Indian Catholic shrines—like the popular shrine of Velankanni in northern Tamil Nadu—are known for fertility and healing, the shrine of St. Antony, a one-stop complex for various spiritual and human needs, is famous for healing demonic possession, various forms of black magic and sorcery, and psychological disorder and distress. Once a simple wayside shrine (*kurusadi*) cared for by a Hindu family, this shrine is now under the jurisdiction of the

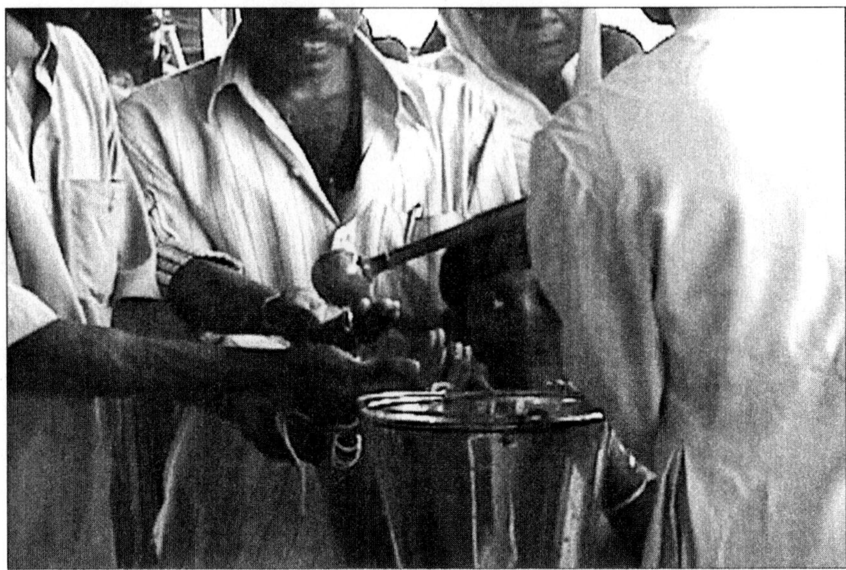

FIGURE 8.1. Devotees receive (and drink) blessed water, hoping for St. Anthony's miraculous aid. Photo by Selva Raj.

Catholic Diocese of Tuticorin and administered by its diocesan clergy. Local residents never tire of telling pilgrims and visitors the Uvari legend that recounts the shrine's humble yet wondrous beginnings.

Marion—an eighty-year-old retired catechist—enthusiastically recounted the following legend to me. Long, long ago, nearly three or four hundred years ago—so goes the legend—Uvari had a small harbor town known as "Obeer" where local villagers traded with incoming ships. The crew of a Portuguese ship approaching Uvari contracted cholera, and the crew lost some of its members to this deadly disease. Upon seeing this misfortune, a sculptor on board the ship began chipping a block of wood and carved the image of St. Anthony. As soon as he completed the sculpture the entire crew was miraculously healed from cholera. The ship then was docked at Uvari for some days. In gratitude for the miracle, the sculptor and sailors installed the miraculous wooden statue on the shores of Uvari against the backdrop of a huge rock and instructed the natives to pray to him in times of trouble. That is how St. Anthony made Uvari his home, said Marion. Around the eighteenth century a modest hut made of coconut leaves was built to house the saint's wooden statue under the care of a Hindu family. A full-fledged shrine dedicated to St. Anthony was built in 1940 and remodeled in 2003. From its modest beginnings in a humble village, the shrine has grown into a famed regional pilgrim center.[3]

Uvari residents assert that the wooden statue of St. Anthony enshrined on the present altar is the same wooden statue originally installed by marooned Portuguese sailors. This tiny wooden statue is one of the major spiritual attractions for pilgrims. Rev. Irudayaraj told me that a glass stand on the altar contains the relics of St. Anthony sent from Rome to the local bishop Gabrielle Francis Roche in the 1960s. Every Tuesday—considered sacred, since St. Anthony died on a Tuesday—pilgrims flock to the shrine to see the wooden statue and the relics. The two annual festivals—observed in February and mid-June—attract tens of thousands of pilgrims of all castes and creeds. According to a conservative estimate, the February festival draws over one hundred thousand pilgrims from far and near. During the festival season, streams of devotees stand in long lines to touch the glass case containing St. Anthony's relics or have an item blessed by the saint by placing it on the wooden statue.

St. Anthony, the shrine's patron saint, was a native of Lisbon, Portugal, but was commonly referred to as the saint of Padua since he spent his mature years as a Franciscan friar in the thirteenth century in the Italian city of Padua. He is well known throughout the Catholic world as the "patron saint of lost things" and bestower of fertility (see Foley n.d.). However, at Uvari, as noted above, he is especially reputed for his ability to ward off the ill effects of black magic and sorcery as well as for his powers over demonic spirits and malevolent Hindu village deities like Issakkiyamman and Cutalaimatan, who command the religious attention of a vast number of local Hindu and Catholic devotees (Raj 2004b, 33–44). Although his iconography is consistent with St. Anthony of Padua's typical representation in the Catholic world, where he is portrayed in a Franciscan habit and holding a book and the infant Jesus in his arms, Uvari Anthony's sacred persona and powers are radically recast to reflect indigenous assumptions concerning sacred figures and the existential human and spiritual needs of his local devotees. This recasting enables Uvari Anthony's religiously pluralistic clientele to embrace the European saint as their chosen clan or family deity (*kula teiyvam*) equal in power and attributes to such popular Hindu tutelary deities as Mariyamman, the Tamil goddess of disease and healing. Known as the Parava saint to distinguish him from St. Anthony of Puliampatti—about seventy miles northwest of Uvari—where Nadar caste groups constitute his principal clientele, this indigenized saint of European descent also reflects and supports such local social realities as caste. "Million Miracle Worker" (*koti arputar*), "Wonder-worker" (*putumaipunithar*), "Padua Saint" (*pathuvaipunithar*), and "Wondrous Healer" or "Superdoctor" (*athisaiyavaidiyar*) are some of St. Anthony's affectionate, indigenous titles. So powerful and revered is St. Anthony that numerous wayside shrines are dedicated to him throughout the coastal region of southeast Tamil Nadu. The spectacular annual chariot (*chapparam*) procession of St. Anthony's statue through the streets of Uvari powerfully reveals his protective role and function in the village.

Though located in the caste-conscious Parava Catholic village, the shrine's appeal extends beyond its geographical, religious, and caste boundaries. According to some unofficial estimates, nearly 40 percent of St. Anthony's loyal devotees are Hindus. Throughout the year, visiting pilgrims flock to the shrine on Tuesdays to perform vow rituals locally known as *asanam* that involve a wide array of ritual actions including—but not limited to—fasting, ritual sacrifice of goats or chickens, hair-shaving, and feeding the poor. Their number escalates during the two major annual festivals. Of those who visit the shrine on Tuesdays, many arrive early in the morning by bus, rented vans, or private cars, spend the day at the shrine to complete the rituals, and return by dusk, while others stay in the church guesthouse for an extended period that can be anywhere from two days to three weeks. As a rule, those suffering from demonic possession and psychological distress tend to stay for two to three weeks. When at the shrine, devotees willingly subject themselves to physical hardships, forgoing the usual comforts and conveniences of home by eating simple meals and sleeping on the ground in front of the shrine.

FIGURE 8.2. A young woman offers a coconut sapling to St. Anthony as down payment for the gift of a child. Photo by Selva Raj.

The modes and medium of social and religious interaction between local residents and visiting pilgrims merit our attention. Miracle stories and legends about the shrine and its patron saint provide an entree for initial social interaction between the two groups of devotees, which are ordinarily divided by caste, religious, and social distinctions. Thus, the saint and the shrine act as the primary reason and medium of interaction/exchange between the two groups of devotees. In this sense, the locals who regard him as a member of their "village family," claiming a filial relationship to him, play host to visiting pilgrims with a feeling of "ownership," as they regard him as "their" saint. The ritual hospitality offered by the villagers to visiting pilgrims is most prominent during the two annual festivals when Uvari residents offer free accommodation in their own homes to pilgrims traveling a long distance. In the process, the host families subject themselves to some physical hardship and inconvenience in hopes of garnering additional spiritual and/or earthly blessings from the saint. The caste-conscious Parava Catholics suspend caste-restrictions for the duration of the festival, sharing their home and food with Hindus and Catholics of the Nadar caste, who are generally avoided in daily life. Several villagers proudly told me that they consider it a great honor to extend hospitality to pilgrims. Extending hospitality to pilgrims, they say, is tantamount to extending hospitality to the saint himself. Others view it as a way of expressing gratitude to the saint for favors already received. Given that this remote village has limited lodging facilities, the hospitality tradition devised by the laity is also a creative and pragmatic adjustment to local economic realities. Mutuality and reciprocity characterize the hospitality tradition at Uvari. It yields spiritual and positive social benefits to hosts and guests alike as it helps expand their social network. In many cases, new friendships are forged between host and pilgrim families, while in other cases old bonds are renewed and strengthened, since host families tend to welcome repeat pilgrims. Pilgrims reciprocate by inviting the hosts to their homes. Thus, the origins of the shrine and the charismatic profile of its patron saint, his cult, and his cultic constituency are all firmly grounded in miracle narratives.

Encounters with the
Wondrous/Miraculous: Two Accounts

It was June 13, 2000—the titular feast of St. Anthony that marks the second annual festival at the shrine. Bright illuminations, religious songs on loudspeakers, and makeshift shops gave a festive look to the otherwise quiet, sleepy village of Uvari, transforming it into a site of intense social commerce, ritual activity, and religious devotion. Several thousand devotees had traveled long distances to attend the vespers presided over by the local Catholic bishop, Rev.

Peter Fernando, and the colorful procession that followed. Shrine officials estimated that nearly one hundred thousand pilgrims had gathered for the occasion. After attending both events, I wandered around the shrine for a few minutes as pilgrim families prepared to sleep in front of the shrine. Assuming that nothing unusual might transpire at that late hour—it was eleven o'clock—I returned to my room to retire for the night.

A half hour later, my field assistant knocked at my door to say that a possessed woman was performing some unusual feats. With camera and tape recorder in hand, I rushed to the shrine, where a small crowd of onlookers had gathered around a young woman in her mid-twenties. Dressed in a fine silk sari and expensive jewelry, the woman was kneeling on the sandy ground in front of St. Anthony's statue in the church vestibule. Hands folded behind her back, she proceeded to sketch—with her tongue—a large, eight-by-six-foot rectangular frame, and what appeared like an entryway to the frame. Painstakingly, she made sure that the lines were perfectly symmetrical, removing with her tongue any debris or paper on the ground. When the lines turned crooked, carefully she erased them with her tongue, and resketched the frame. After she completed the outer lines, she gently entered the interior surface and drew—again with her tongue—twelve crosses on the sand, eight vertically positioned and four horizontally positioned, creating a giant cross. After drawing twelve crosses, she paused for a moment and remained still.

At this time, a man in the crowd shouted aloud that she should draw one more cross. Visibly upset by the male instruction, she shot back sharply: "You don't need to tell me that, you worthless idiot; I know St. Anthony needs thirteen crosses. I was reserving the last one, the special one, for the door. Go, get me a rosary." The man rummaged through his bag, retrieved a rosary, and handed it to her. Then, she drew the thirteenth cross on the imaginary door and draped the rosary around it. Upon completing the final sketch, she entered the box, knelt on the sand with hands behind her back, and addressed St. Anthony in formal, literary Tamil, mimicking the tone and manner of a stammering child. The content of her speech alternated between abusing the saint and begging him to free her from her affliction. This lasted about five minutes. Then she emerged from inside the box, carefully tied the end of her sari around her waist, and stood silently for several minutes in front of the sketch she had drawn, periodically gazing intently and imploringly at the statue of St. Anthony enthroned in the church vestibule in the backdrop. As she stood there, I got a close look at her. I saw drops of blood trickle down from her tongue. I turned around to observe the audience that appeared visibly enthralled and awestruck.

Suddenly, the young lady did something that caught everyone by surprise; she did a forward somersault and landed perfectly inside the frame she had previously constructed with great care. She lay inside this frame like a human cross with outstretched arms and face turned to the sky. Eyes closed—as if in a trance—she remained in this position for about five minutes as the audience stood spellbound. A short while later, she opened her eyes, as if coming out of a trance; she seemed exhausted yet serene. Seeing the crowd of onlookers, she became self-conscious, rose, dusted off the sand from her sari, and ran to rejoin her family. I followed her, hoping to get a firsthand account. Since it was late in the night and since the woman appeared exhausted, the family thought that I should instead talk to her husband, Joseph, who just a few minutes back was the target of the woman's abusive tirade. He was more than willing to talk, and his wife sat silently by his side.

I learned from Joseph that the woman—whom I will call Mary—was born in a relatively wealthy Nadar (merchant caste) Catholic family near Tirunelveli, finished high school in a Catholic parochial school, and married into an equally affluent family. Though married for four years, the couple had no issue. Her husband said:

> Mary had been suffering from an unknown disease for the past three years; she complained of intense pain in her body, and she would scream and beat her head against the wall, roll on the ground, and say abusive things. In the middle of the night, she would get up and cry uncontrollably. We took her to several doctors for treatment, but to no avail. At our Hindu neighbors' suggestion, we consulted a *mantravati* (sorcerer/medicine man) who said that she has been possessed by two Hindu village deities (Cutalaimatan and Issakkiyamman) and instructed us to sacrifice two goats. As per the sorcerer's prescriptions, we sacrificed two goats, but there was no change in her behavior. A year ago, we heard about St. Anthony's miracles [*putumai*], came here on a pilgrimage, and promised to offer *asanam* when she is healed. After we took the vow, she has shown some signs of improvement. This is our third visit to St. Anthony's shrine.

Having never seen or heard of such a spectacular public display of possession behavior during my many field researches in Tamil Nadu, I asked Mary—who by this time had voluntarily joined the conversation—why she drew the frame and the crosses and why she acted the way she did. She said: "St. Anthony made me; he told me to sketch the frame. It is St. Anthony's sacred kiln charged with his special powers; the crosses represent his powers. After I finished my prayer, an inner voice instructed me to throw myself into the kiln if I wanted to rid myself of Issakkiyamman and her tortures." The fact that she fell perfectly inside the frame in the shape of a cross was a sign, her husband added, that Issakkiyamman now had no way to escape from Anthony's sacred fires. He commented that Mary's trancelike state inside the kiln signified the fiery destruction of the malevolent Issakkiyamman. At this point, I turned to Mary for her comment. In typical south Indian fashion, she vigorously nodded her head in assent and said: "Yes, now Issakki is gone, thanks to St. Anthony. I feel so light now as if a huge load has been lifted off; but Cutalaimatan is still there inside me; I have to keep praying so that Anthony will destroy him, too. I know he will when it is the right time. But I have to be faithful to St. Anthony."[4] The following day the couple returned home. Since I did not see them again, I cannot determine if the reported healing was spontaneous and temporary or long-term.

The second case concerns a twenty-one year-old unmarried Hindu woman whom I will call Subha. A native of Thisayanvilai—three miles west of Uvari—Subha, who belongs to the Nadar (merchant) caste group, had no more than an elementary school education. Her parents were unskilled laborers doing odd jobs. I met Subha and her mother a few days after I began fieldwork at Uvari. I learned from the shrine lay staff that she and her mother had been at the shrine for three months. I had seen her several times in front of the shrine; I had seen her roll on the ground, do *pey attam* (possession dance, literally "devil/ghost dance"), and vigorously swing her head in clockwise fashion nonstop for nearly an hour. I had also seen her say the rosary and attend Mass. One evening I saw her run to the flagpole and hit her head on its concrete base for several minutes. After observing her for several days, I met her mother and got her permission to talk to Subha. Though initially reticent and shy, she slowly warmed up to tell her story:

> When I was nine years old, I was possessed by a woman who had committed suicide in our village. Later, when I turned sixteen, Issakkiyamman took hold of me. My mother said it was because I violated the menstrual taboos and visited Issakkiyamman's temple when I had my period. Now I am tormented by these two spirits. My mother took me to several Hindu *pujari*s, magicians and sorcerers who performed numerous *puja*s to our *devata*s, but there was no change or improvement. We spent over Rs.20000 in the process.
>
> Then we heard about Uvari St. Anthony and came here three months ago. Since then I have been diligently performing all the rituals my mother and relatives have instructed me to do—attend Mass, say the rosary, circumambulate the shrine, rub my head daily with St. Anthony's oil, and eat *Anthoniar puthumai* [Anthony's miraculous medicine, balls of neem paste]. After I started doing these things, I began to feel better. Earlier, I used to run naked and do all sorts of crazy things. I do not act that way anymore, but the demon has not left me as yet. Issakki still tortures me and sometimes my head is ready to explode when she torments me. Once every day I go into possession frenzy and dance. Otherwise, I feel much better now.

> I want to be fully free, and only Anthony can drive this demon away. I know he will. We have renounced our former *kula teiyvam*s. Now St. Anthony is our *kula teiyvam*. My mother and I have promised Anthony to offer a goat and observe *asanam* when I am fully cured.[5]

When I visited the shrine a year later, by sheer coincidence I ran into Subha and her mother. Beaming, Subha cheerfully told me that she no longer suffers from chronic headaches or other afflictions. She and her mother had come to the shrine to offer St. Anthony the goat they had promised.

Since both women were said to be possessed by Issakkiyamman and Cutalaimatan, a brief description of the myths, personality, and powers of these low-ranking village deities of the Tamil Hindu pantheon is in order. Legends and folklore about Issakkiyamman in circulation in Tirunelveli District trace her origins to a *devadasi* (divine/temple prostitute) family. When she was a young woman, the local Brahmin temple priest (*pujari*) used to visit her, often bringing gifts of jewelry stolen from the temple. Initially, Issakki refused to accept them but, at her mother's persuasion, she eventually began accepting his gifts. As a result, a romantic relationship developed between the temple priest and Issakki, and Issakki became pregnant. When he learned that she was pregnant, the *pujari* killed her by hitting her with a rock and pushing her into a well. Not long after, the *pujari* also died and was reborn in a Chettiar (merchant caste) family. Issakki, who was also reborn, took revenge on the Chettiar family and the entire Chettiar village. She is called *neeli* and *thusta devatai* (evil goddess).

Menstruating and pregnant women are forbidden to pass by her shrine. Black bangles, saris, thread, and oil are the common votive items offered to Issakkiyamman. Women seeking offspring usually tie black bangles on her temple doors in hopes of getting a child. Pigs and goats are the common sacrificial items offered to this goddess. Some stories of her origins describe her as an avatar of the pan-Indian Hindu goddess Parvati, the domestic spouse of the god Shiva. Unlike Parvati, Issakkaiyamman is said to be a destructive, vengeful goddess, yet protective of her devotees and those who please her through animal sacrifices. In her ambivalence, she resembles another local goddess in Tamil Nadu, Mariyamman, the goddess of disease and healing.[6] Issakkiyamman and Cutalaimatan (to whom I will turn shortly) are two of the most feared village deities in Tirunelveli District. Although Issakkiyamman and Cutalaimatan are frequently placed next to each other in many village and roadside temples, and although some variants of their legends treat them as cousins and others as consorts, there is no relationship between them.[7]

Cutalaimatan ("Fierce God of the Cremation Ground") is regarded as a son of the Brahmanical pan-Indian god Shiva, born from his third-eye. Some legends and myths also consider him to be a manifestation of Shiva (Mines

2005, 134–35). Treating a village deity as a manifestation of Shiva is a well-known Hindu religious strategy to relate and induct a non-Brahmanical god into the Brahmanical tradition. Cutalaimatan is notorious for his wrathful temperament (Mines 2005, 134–35). Members of washer-men (*dhobi*) caste revere him as their patron deity. As Mines observes in her study of fierce gods in southern Tamil Nadu, "[I]f the fierce Cutalaimatan becomes angry at the humans who worship him, he can wreak vengeance in many ways, including death," earning him the title of Fierce God (144). Mines argues that while Brahmanical gods like Shiva and Krishna are "soft," fierce gods such as Cutalaimatan and Issakkiyamman are "cruel or fearsome." While the former are calm, stable, and beneficent, the latter are wild, unstable, and unpredictable (125). According to Mines, fierce gods like Cutalaimatan and Issakkiyamman "live on the margins of village territory, outside residential areas, out in the fields or beyond in the wasteland (*katu*) (131). In myth and ritual, "these gods are often subordinated to the village goddesses as guardians who live near but outside her temple, much like the humans who live outside the central village residential area are thought to be subordinate . . . as well" (131).[8]

To return to the present case studies of possession and healing, Subha and Mary—the two principal figures in the case studies—are neither isolated nor exceptional cases but typify the bulk of St. Anthony's devotees seeking healing from possession. According to church authorities, nearly 80 percent of these are Hindus—more precisely, Hindu women. What is noteworthy about this particular cultic constituency is that almost all of them claim to be possessed by one or more of the malevolent Hindu village deities like Issakkiyamman and Cutalaimatan. Many say that first they seek relief through familiar Hindu and secular sources such as medicine men, magicians, sorcerers, doctors, and Hindu *pujari*s. When these fail, as a last recourse they turn to St. Anthony.

Two features, however, distinguish these narratives from one another. First, whereas Subha, the Hindu woman, had made the Catholic shrine her temporary home for over three months, as if to familiarize herself with the powers, temperaments, likes, and dislikes of an alien, Catholic, sacred figure and to manifest the extent of her physical afflictions to the saintly physician, the Catholic devotee had only made several one-day trips to the shrine. But they apparently reaped similar results. Second, the "kiln metaphor" that gains ritual prominence in Mary's miracle narrative is conspicuously absent in Subha's or similar narratives involving Hindus and Catholics. Having never before witnessed such a spectacular display nor heard about the kiln metaphor at Uvari or any other Catholic shrine in Tamil Nadu, I am inclined to think that the kiln metaphor is peculiar to this particular Catholic family and their village. Regardless of the manner and method of Anthony's victory over these spirits, all devotees—Hindu and Catholic alike—stress his power to effect miraculous healing.

Despite minor variations in ritual procedure, these narratives reveal that neither the dynamic of possession nor the dispensation of healing and miracles seems to respect religious boundaries. Both women—one Catholic and one Hindu—possessed by two non-Sanskritic Hindu village deities receive miraculous healing from St. Anthony of Uvari, an indigenized Catholic saint of European descent. Their personal and religious odyssey serves as a textbook case for the confluence of two different miracle discourses, each influenced— if not shaped—by the religious worldview and epistemology of the other. It vividly illustrates the complex negotiations and *multiple, complex* sharing occurring at Uvari.

The Social Subtext of Uvari Miracle Discourse

Echoing Victor Turner's suggestion that ritual is a social drama, in *Images, Miracles, and Authority in Asian Religious Traditions* Richard Davis delineates several social aspects of miracles. For Davis, these include the attribution of agency, miracles' role as signs and communications of the supernatural prompting recommunication and recirculation among humans through stories and anecdotes, and their role in constituting claims to religious authority and power. It seems to me that the authority-establishing role of miracles is particularly relevant in understanding the miracle discourse at Uvari. "Miracles seem to occur" writes Davis, "most frequently at moments of challenge and conflict" produced by differing systems of beliefs and practices (1998, 11). Davis detects this feature, for example, in the religious career of the Buddha, who engaged in "many contests of supernatural feats" with rival ascetics that helped establish the Buddha's religious authority over his rivals (11).

In the case of St. Anthony, however, the challenge and conflict come not from human virtuosi but from indigenous Hindu supernatural beings that traditionally had exerted and continue to exert power over local inhabitants, whether Hindu, Christian, or Muslim. This perceived challenge evokes different responses from St. Anthony's two principal constituencies—namely, the institutional guardians of the cult of St. Anthony and the saint's religiously pluralistic lay clientele, each emphasizing a specific trait in the saint's sacred persona. While lay devotees stress the miraculous and supernatural power exerted by this European Catholic saint over Hindu village deities, official religion and its institutional leaders emphasize the saint's authority, specifically his spiritual authority, and by extension the truths and teachings of the Catholic Church. Thus, it appears that the attribution of miraculous agency to St. Anthony by official, institutional religion, which markedly differs from the focus and concerns of the laity, is a way to establish the European, Catholic saint's authority and power over indigenous Hindu village deities like Issakkiyamman and Cutalaimadan. By extension, it shows the superiority of Christian teachings in an alien religious geography, the preeminence of its sacred sites, and the social power of its institutional leaders to garner for the saint his local cultic constituency.

In the process, indigenous deities and their powers are subjugated and dominated by a Christian sacred power. For, as Mullin suggests, in the Catholic world, miracles are "not merely a sign of God's activity, but as a sign of the true church and rebuke against all imposters" (Mullin 1996, 112). In his ethnographic study, R. L. Stirrat highlights how this top-down strategy is popularized and perpetuated in Sri Lankan Roman Catholicism (Stirrat 1977, 133–57; 1981, 183–200). Although this conflict and conquest discourse was originally a top-down strategy instigated by foreign Christian missionaries, today it is popularized and perpetuated by clerical leadership—through sermons and official shrine brochures and pamphlets, whereas Hindu and Catholic lay devotees stress—through stories, testimonials, and anecdotes like the ones discussed in this chapter—almost exclusively the saint's miraculous powers. In other words, what is being recognized and spread by St. Anthony's Hindu and Catholic devotees is not the good news of Christianity but the healing power of the Christian saint.

While past and current ecclesial leadership emphasizes—consciously or unconsciously—the conquest discourse, St. Anthony's grassroots devotees espouse a dialogical discourse. This is most evident in the fact that these lay devotees—Hindus and Catholics alike—also reconfigure and reconstruct a distinctively local identity and persona for the European saint, one that resonates with their indigenous religious worldview and epistemology. They achieve this by investing in St. Anthony miraculous powers and attributes traditionally associated with Hindu tutelary deities and by expressing their faith through native—frequently vernacular—ritual idiom (Flueckiger 2006, 3). At the metalevel, therefore, the Uvari miracle discourse simultaneously represents the coexistence of both conquest and dialogue discourses as well as the confluence—some might say collision—of two distinct, Hindu and Catholic, worldviews and epistemologies transformed into a shared worldview and epistemology that provides the theological framework for Anthony's multireligious, pluralistic clientele. Together these multiple discourses illustrate the localization, or what anthropologists like Singer (1980) call "parochialization," of an alien tradition and its sacred figure.

A reverse example would help illustrate the authority-establishing function of miracles. For it I turn to Ammachi, a prominent Hindu female guru known for her miraculous powers of healing. Although Ammachi herself refrains from speaking about the miracles attributed to her, her devotional biographies never fail to emphasize her supranormal powers. She is said to make "the blind see, the deaf hear, and the barren produce children" (Woodward 2000, 381; Raj 2004a). Anecdotes and stories of Ammachi's miracles abound in devotees' accounts of her first visit to the United States in 1987 and her subsequent annual tours. In the United States, Ammachi's packed evening *darshan*s (spiritual sessions involving spiritual hugs of devotees by Ammachi) are invariably interspersed with moving testimonials by Western devotees regarding Ammachi's miraculous powers. Ammachi's miraculous powers and performances are key instruments in establishing her religious authority and the legitimacy of an ever-growing global religious organization; they also help build a growing national, transnational, international, multiethnic, and multireligious clientele (Raj 2005, 123–46).

Woodward suggests that "Ammachi identifies her miracles of God-consciousness with love[,] giving these manifestations of her divinity a quasi-Christian cast" (Woodward 2000, 381; Raj 2005, 140–41). The ethnographer in me discerns in this miracle narrative an ingenious attempt by Ammachi, her growing global religious movement, and her Euro-American followers—most whom have strong ties to the Christian tradition—at the localization (more precisely, the transnationalization) of a Hindu religious teacher's authority, charisma, and message through religious idioms familiar to her audience. As with St. Anthony, Ammachi's miracle narrative has served as an effective instrument for establishing her charisma, lending authority to her teachings, and garnering followers. Unlike the conflict/conquest discourse that marks St. Anthony's initial interaction with his indigenous supernatural rivals (Issakkiyamman and Cutalaimatan), this is a harmonious, conflict-free process of localization of a foreign spiritual power in an alien cultural and religious landscape.

While scholars continue to be divided on what constitutes a miracle, most acknowledge its public character since, as Davis and Mullin remind us, "miracles are more than private experiences" that have importance to a larger community, and since the fruits of the miraculous occurrences trickle down to the larger society (Davis 1998; Mullin 1996, 6; Woodward 2000, 366). To return to St. Anthony, apart from legitimizing the European saint's spiritual authority in the alien cultural and religious soil of India, devotees' public ritual display of faith in his miraculous powers and the saint's own public demonstration of supernormal power for a predisposed audience serve to enhance his spiritual repute among the wider public. These also help to reinforce the spiritual authority of institutional leadership that acts as his earthly representative.

The Uvari ritual tradition and miracle discourse also provide valuable clues to the dynamic of shared religious culture and ritual exchange across boundaries that defines much of grassroots religious life in India in general and in south India in particular. In her recent study of vernacular Islam in the neighboring Indian state of Andhra Pradesh, Flueckiger provides fresh corroborating data from the field. She writes: "Resorting to multiple religious healing systems/healers for a persistent illness or family trouble . . . is typical of many, even most, Hyderabadis. Spiritual healing characterizes vernacular religious traditions in India, creating a shared plane of experience and assumptions of spiritual powers that impact physical bodies across lines of educational, class, caste, and religious differences. But each healing site is uniquely created by who 'sits' in it and the means through which they claim authority to be there" (Flueckiger 2006, 4). This dynamic of shared religious culture in turn effects—I submit—a grassroots ecumenism not only among diverse devotees but also among disparate deities

The View from the Pew

While the ritual exchange and religious behavior of Hindus and Catholics at the shrine of St. Anthony provide compelling evidence for the shared miracle discourse at work in grassroots religion in India, the problem of miracles—the thematic center of gravity in this volume—that still looms large warrants a closer look. In many, if not all, religions, the religious masses' assertions of the miraculous not only might differ—even deviate—from official definitions and understandings, but they can challenge, expand, or unsettle established theologies, epistemologies, and traditions. This is true of the miracle discourse at Uvari as well, where institutional definitions and requirements of the miraculous—set by the Vatican and monitored by local religious leadership—are invariably at odds with the religious folks' experience and understanding of the possibility of miracles, what constitutes a miracle, how it works, and how devotees experience the miraculous. At Uvari, Catholic and Hindu devotees alike implicitly assume that miracles can and do occur and understand how they work, based, in some cases, on prior personal experience and, in other instances, the experience of family members and relatives. In this regard, St. Anthony's Tamil devotees are not unlike their counterparts elsewhere in India. Flueckiger's recent study of healing practices among south Indian Muslims articulates the common Indian devotee's understanding of and approach to miracles and healing. She writes: "Why and how religious healing works across religious boundaries is implicitly assumed and understood by patients; these issues are of more concern to scholars and students outside this local context than to Muslim and Hindu participants who interact with Amma [a Muslim spiritual healer in Hyderabad, Andhra Pradesh]" (Flueckiger 2006, 9). She continues: "[I]n the healing room, religious distinctions and identities are not those that matter most. Patients know, understand, and accept the contours of the religious landscape and identities encoded in practice and performance at this site of vernacular practice" (10).[9]

At Uvari, however, devotees' miracle claims are frequently met with strong skepticism and disapproval—if not disdain—by church leaders. For example, while most priests strongly affirm faith in Anthony's sacred powers, they are particularly skeptical of alleged incidents of possession and healing. Many explain such claims away in psychological terms. Trained in clinical counseling in a North American university, Bishop Peter Fernando of the Diocese of Tuticorin, which has jurisdiction over the Uvari shrine, said to me that nearly all incidents of possession at Uvari are psychosomatic cases requiring clinical treatment. Having said that, he paused to add: "But if the people feel they are healed by St. Anthony, who am I to challenge their simple faith?"[10] The senior pastor of the shrine echoed the bishop's sentiments. This demonstrates that at St. Anthony's shrine the miraculous is contentious not because there is disagreement between Hindus and Catholics, since they share a common, pragmatic worldview and epistemology, but because there is tension and disagreement between the priests and pilgrims on what is salvific and redemptive. In other words, the theological disjunction and contest between the clergy and the laity is grounded in their respective, divergent, religious frameworks, foci, and needs.

While priests stress soteriological ideals and goals attainable through an internal, enlightened, "adult" faith nourished and nurtured by the Gospel and sacraments, the laity focuses on such mundane, earthly goals as healing and fertility attainable through external display of devotion and miraculous agency. As Ruth Behar's work on popular religiosity in post–Franco Spain clearly demonstrates, the religious masses' focus on mundane needs and tangible results is neither peculiar nor unique to Tamil Catholics but fairly widespread in European peasant Christianity and throughout the Catholic world (Behar 1999, 76–112). Schooled in Western rationalist tradition and post-Vatican liberal theology, Tamil priests, however, tend to view—and often disavow—the religious folks' approach to religion in general and to the miraculous in particular as unreflective, unenlightened, and premodern. As institutional guardians and teachers of faith, they are charged with cultivating an interior, enlightened faith and practice among the religious masses. Therefore, these priests are under institutional pressures to resist the miraculous or the supernatural manifestations and irruptions into the mundane. It is not surprising, therefore, that the priests seek to maintain an intellectual, theological distance, "a separation between the "simple faith" of the people . . . and the "adult" faith of the priest" (Behar 1999, 106).

Fulfilling this task, however, is not without its ambivalent moments and attendant pastoral challenges. As native priests born and bred in India with strong ties to the indigenous religious culture that tends to acknowledge—even celebrate—the miraculous and inexplicable irruptions of the sacred in the mundane world, they resonate, on a personal level, with the religious instincts and yearnings of the masses. Many of these priests have encountered miracle claims—similar to those reported at Uvari—among family members and relatives. Thus, while culturally they feel a certain predisposition to accept miracles, their official position, training, and obligation require them to adopt a carefully cultivated skepticism toward devotees' miracle claims.

Consequently, these priests find themselves in theological and pastoral liminality. They are caught between their professional obligation to defend and implement institutional norms, canons, and prescriptions of which they themselves may not be convinced, the pastoral realities on the ground that demand greater sensitivity to the religious sensibilities of their flock that go against (if not defy) official prescriptions, and their own cultural conditioning and professional training. This explains why priests feel compelled to provide the ritual context and space and pastoral affirmation for the public demonstration of miracle narratives, as well as to document the laity's claim of miraculous occurrences in the shrine's official records, even though they are reticent about fully endorsing such claims.

Perhaps a comparative look at the two miracle discourses discussed in this chapter (the Uvari miracle discourse and the miracle discourse in the Ammachi movement) might shed some additional light. A common feature in the cult of Ammachi and St. Anthony is that in both cases devotees—Euro-Americans and Indians, Hindus and Catholics—exhibit an openness, even a predisposition, to the possibility and even reality of miraculous powers and manifestations. What distinguishes these two groups is that while the secondary leadership in the Ammachi movement, who form Ammachi's immediate and trusted circle of disciples of Euro-American and Indian descent, not only do not show any resistance to stories and testimonials extolling Ammachi's miraculous powers but actively and enthusiastically endorse, publicize, and perpetuate such stories by providing an official venue and platform to disseminate them during crowded evening *darshan*s and by publishing them in their official literature. In other words, Ammachi miracle stories are allowed to flow with abandon with institutional approval and validation. As noted above, devotional biographies are filled with anecdotes and testimonials testifying to and reinforcing devotees' faith in her supranormal and miraculous powers. But one cannot say the same about the religious leadership at Uvari. Thus the Catholic priests' attitude to miracles is not only at odds with their own laity but with that of religious leadership in other traditions as well.

What might account for the attitudinal difference between Catholic priests and the religious leadership in non-Christian traditions like the Ammachi movement? As I have suggested earlier, an important variable in miracle claims and discourse is their potential role in augmenting or challenging established religious power relations and structures. While devotees' miracle stories help cement and reinforce Ammachi's personal charisma, her centralized authority, and the power structures within her movement, Catholic laity's miracle stories have the potential to wean devotees away from institutional centers of power and authority. More importantly, as noted above, there is a radical difference between priests and laity on what constitutes a miracle, its mechanics, and its occurrence. While Ammachi's devotees and Catholic laity place a huge premium on individual, personal, tangible experience, priests rely almost exclusively on institutional prescriptions, approval, validation, and legitimacy. Another contributing factor that accounts at least in part for the attitudinal difference between the two groups of religious leaders is their inherent structural variance. Unlike the Catholic Church, which has an institutionally established centralized office and system for processing, verifying, and authenticating miracle claims, miracle claims in the nascent Ammachi movement are dependent—solely and exclusively—on the authenticity and legitimacy of an individual devotee's experience. It seems reasonable to assume that when the process of routinization that Max Weber mentions sets in, similar tensions between devotees and religious leadership within the Ammachi movement are bound to follow. Shifting our focus from and beyond these illustrative case studies, at the metalevel this conflict between the miracle discourse of the priests and the laity, between the elite and the masses, that is pronounced in institutionalized religions is ultimately an index and metaphor for the tensions and power relations between the center and the periphery.

Seen from the standpoint of power relations between earthly and supernatural figures, the reluctance to endorse devotees' miracle claims—some scholars theorize—might also be based on institutional leaders' fear of losing their power and control over the laity to a saintly competitor. For example, in his study of the cult of St. Sebastian at Mirisgama in Sri Lanka, Stirrat discerns this competition between earthly and saintly powers. He writes: "Now that the saint is here on earth he can begin to challenge the role of the priest as the prime mediator between man and God, the channel through which 'grace' flows to man. And thus the division of labour between priest and saint develops into a competitive relationship, as each offer alternative paths to salvation" (Stirrat 1981, 185). At one level Stirrat's argument does have some intrinsic merit and appeal, since clerical rejection of devotees' miracle claims is designed to protect proper sacred protocol and to solidify, in turn, the institutional church's—and, by extension, their own—mediating role.

Nevertheless, the possibility that the priests work in concert with the saint rather than in competition is evident in their systematic and conscious effort to extol the saint's spiritual virtues and sacred powers. It is the priests who promote and institutionalize the saint's cult through public sermons, private spiritual counseling, published literature, and shrine brochures. But the kind of sacred powers they invest in St. Anthony are radically different from those invested by the masses. In so doing, however, they are guided not only by spiritual motives but by material considerations as well, since the saint and his shrine yield much desired economic and social dividends. In other words, on the more mundane plane, the clergy's reluctant endorsement—despite personal and theological reservations—is inspired, it seems to me, by two related factors. First, miracle stories help confirm popular faith in Anthony's spiritual powers, prestige, and status, and, by extension, the shrine's spiritual fame and reputation. Second, such approval generates welcome revenue to the shrine and social recognition for the institutional church.

Conclusion

As mentioned in the Introduction to this volume, the writings of the eighteenth-century Scottish philosopher and historian David Hume—who regarded most miracles as human fabrications and deceptions—helped to discredit any evidentiary claims to the miraculous. Since then academic literature on miracles almost always allude to his influential essay "Of Miracles" in shaping the post-Enlightenment skepticism toward miracles and the miraculous. Scholarly skepticism notwithstanding, the human propensity for the miraculous finds outlets particularly among the religious masses. To quote Mullin: "The tenacity of the idea of the miraculous lies in the fact that it is linked in the religious imagination to a number of cherished beliefs such as the reality of a spiritual realm, the meaningfulness of prayer, and the ability of a personal God to respond to the word. Whereas outside of the religious world view the idea of a miracle might appear meaningless, from within it is not" (1996, 4–5). This propensity and desire to perceive the extraordinary and wondrous in the midst of the mundane is strong among the vast majority of Indians, argues Davis, regardless of religious and caste distinctions in such wise that they form, as it were, the brick and mortar, the bread and butter of popular religion in India (Davis 1998, 16).

Both Mullin's and Davis's positions warrant further modifications. Mullin's claim that the tenacity of the idea of the miraculous is linked to a specific worldview is not entirely reflective of the religious realities on the ground. I would argue that the tenacity of the miraculous is not simply due to a worldview or religious imagination that considers the miraculous important and meaningful, but to something more concrete: experience. According to people on the ground, the existence of the miraculous lies in their own experiences, which, for them, are unrefutable. Of course experience is only understood as such within a certain context/worldview/religious imagination; what sustains folks' discourse on the miraculous is not grounded primarily in their worldview as much as their concrete, lived experiences.[11]

This fact is well illustrated in the corroborating account Dempsey offers in her work on the cult of St. George in the neighboring state of Kerala. To quote: "A male board member at the St. George Catholic Church in Aruvithura laughed during a conversation about the saint's Vatican demotion, saying, 'The people sided with the saint, not the pope.' Overhearing our conversation from a few feet away, a nun added to it by stating that St. George is, for his Keralite devotees, 'their own.' Elaborating upon her interjection, she insisted, 'The people's negative reaction to the decree was based upon their own personal experience of his miraculous power. Such things the pope can never understand'" (Dempsey 2001, 48).

While Davis's contention that Indians exhibit a special propensity to see the miraculous amid the mundane, though not entirely preposterous, seems to be a broad generalization and essentializing of the tradition, given the internal diversity and intrinsic complexity that define Indian religious groups. For example, Ammachi commands a large number of credulous followers of her miraculous powers, many of whom are Euro-Americans schooled in modernity and scientific rationalism. On the other hand, there are many Indians, Hindus and Catholics alike, who are deeply cynical and skeptical of miracle claims. For example, there are Catholic priests in India, including the shrine priests at Uvari, who have little time or patience for possession and even for miraculous claims. For anthropologists and scholars of religions engaged in the ethnographic study of popular religion in India, the task and challenge is to make sense of the value, relevance, meaningfulness, and significance that religious practitioners—especially the masses—attach to their encounter with the miraculous in their specific social, cultural, and religious context.

In this regard, let me return once more to Stirrat's valuable studies on popular religiosity of Sinhalese Catholics in Sri Lanka. As Stirrat rightly observes in the case of Sri Lanka, in India too, "religion is inextricably linked up with culture, and to distinguish between 'religious concepts' and 'cultural concepts' is a hazardous operation. . . . Simply by being Sinhalese, Sinhalese Catholics share many concepts and constructs with Sinhalese Buddhists" (Stirrat 1981, 197). Similarly, simply by being Tamil, Tamil Catholics share many concepts and constructs with Tamil Hindus, and among these are the possibility and experience of miracles and miraculous happenings. Furthermore, miracles and miraculous events are "experienced realities" for St. Anthony's multireligious clientele. Their indigenous cultural and religious assumptions about miracles and sacred powers facilitate and authenticate their "experience" of miracles and the miraculous, which might seem to outsiders as premodern, unreflective, and unenlightened. Stirrat's earlier study (1977) on incidents of demonic possession and healing in Roman Catholic Sri Lanka sheds further light on the lived understanding and experience of miracles by St. Anthony's Tamil devotees. He argues that "at a logical level, the collective representations precede the actual incidence or events of possession. Very simply, one can only become possessed if one has a category of possession. If not, it is rather difficult to persuade others of the reality of possession" (Stirrat 1977, 155). What Stirrat says about possessions can be said of miracles and miracle claims at the shrine of St. Anthony at Uvari as well. St. Anthony's devotees experience miracles and miraculous events because they have the category of miracles and collectively assert their possibility and reality. Only those—academics, priests, and skeptics—who lack "their" category of miracles suspect the possibility and reality of miracles.

In the south Indian religious context, the miracle discourse at the shrine of the Uvari St. Anthony serves as a vivid metaphor for the complicated identities and complex negotiations of Catholics and Hindus, who draw from a shared religious worldview, a shared indigenous religious epistemology, a shared ritual data bank, and a shared grammar. What accounts for this phenomenon? In *Fluid Signs: Being a Person the Tamil Way*, Valentine Daniel suggests that materiality shapes a person's and a group's identity, knowledge, and spirituality. He writes: "To know who I am, I had to know the soil of the village which is, after all, a part of me" (Daniel 1984, 62). If we extend his insight to the miracle narratives popularized and perpetuated by St. Anthony's devotees, it seems to me that materiality—that is, tangible experience—is what miracles are made of.

To return to the comedy/tragedy of errors alluded to in the opening paragraph of this chapter, the questions I wrestled with during the bus journey illustrate the tension between the pressures of the scientific worldview advocated in the academy and the dictates, demands, and lessons of lived experience. This tension manifested itself during a transportation crisis when part of me—almost innately and intuitively—resorted to and leaned on my cultural legacy and upbringing, which sometimes attaches supernatural value and significance to lived, tangible experience. Like most academics schooled in Western academia, I had cultivated an intellectual distance between myself and the religious folk. Therefore, I ventured into this field research with a healthy dose of skepticism toward devotees' miracle stories. I was eager to study their miracle claims and accounts based solely on hard empirical evidence, on what the masses did and said, and what I myself observed, without much regard either to the experiential aspect of their claims or to my own cultural and religious experience. But ethnographic encounter does affect—if not transform—the worldview and epistemology of the ethnographer and consequently the scholar's conclusions and assessment of miracle claims and stories. In my case, while the ethnographic encounter with the religious masses at Uvari and their miracle claims has not made me a "born-again" devotee, reflection on the way that I intuitively suspected supernatural significance during an ethnographic crisis has allowed me a deeper and greater intellectual sensitivity to the experiential dimension of miracle claims. It has taught me that when one engages—albeit unwittingly—in the world of religious masses and "their" epistemological categories, miracles and miracle claims are not naive tales or fanciful fabrications, but are authentic, "lived" realities.

As such, the case studies documented in this chapter and my own ethnographic encounter suggest that supernatural agency is not just something people imagine (even though outside observers might accuse them of imagining); it is what devotees experience in their material lives. In other words, it is the "materiality of miracles"—namely, the tangible experience of St. Anthony's sacred, miraculous powers available and accessible to his religiously pluralistic clientele and their shared material religious culture on which Tamil Catholics and Hindus depend—that account, at least in part, for their shared religious worldview and epistemology enlivened and expressed in shared miracle discourse. The religious odyssey of hybrid devotees like Mary and Subha serves as a textbook case for the vitality of this shared discourse.

Notes

1. The Paravas are distinguished from the Mukkuvas, another maritime trading caste group who also are fishermen by occupation. In terms of caste ranking, the Paravas consider themselves superior to the Mukkuvas, though both groups are exclusively Catholic. For a fuller discussion of Parava and Mukkuva caste-ranking, see Bayly 1989, 268, 317–21.

2. While it is not uncommon to find multiple churches in a single Parava or Mukkuva Catholic village that reflect the religious piety and social politics of different neighborhoods, what is distinctive about Uvari is the Selvamatha (literally, "Our Lady of Wealth") Church, built in the shape of a ship bearing an airplane dedicated to Mary. This church is a tourist attraction as well.

3. Interview with Marion Courier at Uvari, June 4, 2000.

4. Interview with Joseph at Uvari, June 13, 2000.4. Interview with Mary at Uvari, June 13, 2000.

5. Interview with Subha at Uvari, June 6, 2000.

6. Based on interview with a temple priest at an Issakkiyamman temple near Nagercoil on June 23, 2000.

7. In his discussion of south Indian village deities, James Harnell sums up the central attributes and characteristics of Issakkiyamman. For a fuller treatment, see Harnell n.d.

8. Mines maintains that an important ritual variable differentiating the fierce gods and other Brahmanical gods and village deities is that "fierce gods are not paraded through the streets in processions, nor are they generally brought inside the house for worship" (Mines 2005, 131).

9. For a succinct analysis of Amma's healing powers, see Flueckiger's chapter (chapter 9 in this volume).

10. Interview with Bishop Peter Fernando in Tuticorin, June 20, 2000.

11. I am thankful to Corinne Dempsey, whose comments and insights on an earlier draft helped sharpen my analysis of the attitude of religious folk to the miraculous.

References

Bayly, Susan. 1989. *Saints, Goddesses and Kings: Muslims and Christians in South Indian Society, 1700–1900*. Cambridge: Cambridge University Press.

Behar, Ruth. 1999. "The Struggle for the Church: Popular Anticlericalism and Religiosity in Post–Franco Spain." In *Religious Orthodoxy and Popular Faith in European Society*, edited by Ellen Badone, 76–112. Princeton, NJ: Princeton University Press.

Daniel, Valentine. 1984. *Fluid Signs: Being a Person the Tamil Way*. Berkeley and Los Angeles: University of California Press.

Davis, Richard, ed. 1998. *Images, Miracles, and Authority in Asian Religious Traditions*. Boulder, CO: Westview Press.

Dempsey, Corinne. 2001. *Kerala Christian Sainthood: Collisions of Culture and Worldview in South India*. New York: Oxford University Press.

Flueckiger, Joyce, B. 2006. *In Amma's Healing Room: Gender and Vernacular Islam in South India*. Bloomington: Indiana University Press.

Foley, Leonard. n.d. "Life of St. Anthony of Padua." http://www.stanthony.org/aboutanthony/WhoIs.asp.

Harnell, James. n.d. *The Ancient Village Gods of South India*. n.d. http://www.antiquity.ac.uk/Ant/018/0078/Ant0180078.pdf.

Hume, David. 1902. "Of Miracles." In *Enquiries Concerning the Human Understanding and Concerning the Principles of Morals*. Oxford: Clarendon.

Mines, Diane. 2005. *Fierce Gods: Inequality, Ritual, and the Politics of Dignity in a South Indian Village*. Bloomington: Indiana University Press.

Mullin, Robert. 1996. *Miracles and the Modern Imagination*. New Haven, CT: Yale University Press.

Nadar, Ganesh. n.d. "The Village St. Anthony Calls Home: A Place of Miracles." http://www.rediff.com/travel/1998/dec/19chris.htm.

Raj, Selva. 2004a. "Ammachi: The Mother of Compassion." In *The Graceful Guru: Hindu Female Gurus in India and the United States*, edited by Karen Pechilis, 203–18. New York: Oxford University Press.

———. 2004b. "Dialogue 'On the Ground': The Complicated Identities and the Complex Negotiations of Catholics and Hindus in South India." *Journal of Hindu-Christian Studies* 19:33–44.

———. 2005. "Passage to America: Ammachi on American Soil." In *Gurus in America*, edited by Thomas Forsthoefel and Cynthia Humes, 123–46. Albany: State University of New York Press.

Singer, Milton. 1980. *When A Great Tradition Modernizes: An Anthropological Approach to Indian Civilization*. Midway Reprint. Chicago: University of Chicago Press.

Stirrat, R. L. 1981. "The Shrine of St. Sebastian at Mirisgama: An Aspect of the Cult of the Saints in Catholic Sri Lanka." *Man* 16:183–200.

———. 1977. "Demonic Possession in Roman Catholic Sri Lanka." *Journal of Anthropological Research* 33:133–57.

Younger, Paul. 2002. *Playing Host to Deity: Festival Religion in the South Indian Tradition*. New York: Oxford University Press.

Woodward, Kenneth. 2000. *The Book of Miracles*. New York: Simon & Schuster.

CHAPTER NINE

The "Deep Secret" and Dangers of *Karamat*

Miraculous Acts, Revelation, and Secrecy in a South Indian Sufi Tradition

JOYCE BURKHALTER FLUECKIGER

There is grave danger in the performance of miracles (*karamat*), a danger that lies, in part, in their position at the boundary between the physical and spiritual worlds and and, in part, in the tension between the secret and revelatory nature of the miracles performed by Sufi saints. *Karamat* are revelatory in that they are often the primary means through which Muslim saints (*pir*s), both living and dead, are first identified; this seems to be the case particularly for locally renowned saints rather than those associated with literary traditions and established saints' grave shrines (*dargah*s).[1] Disciples are often drawn to *pir*s through their reputation for performing miracles or through dreams in which the *pir* calls them. Not only do *karamat* identify the saint, but they are also indicative of the nature and strength of the saint's relationship with Allah—in a sense, *karamat* are the residue of that relationship, the *barakat* (blessings) of God made tangible in the acts of the saints. Amma, the spiritual healer with whom I have worked since 1989, attributes *barakat/karamat* specifically to the relationship of love between God and the *pir*, between her and God.

<hr>

This chapter was originally published as "The 'Deep Secret' and Danger of Karāmat: Miraculous Acts and Secrecy in a South Indian Sufi Tradition," *Comparative Islamic Studies* 1.2:159–76. Ed. Brannon M. Wheeler. Copyright ©2006 Equinox Publishers. Reprinted with permission.

However, these same revelatory miracles may also need to remain secret. According to some textual and oral traditions, *karamat* may need to remain hidden because their performance may lead to misunderstanding, controversy, and even heresy when unknowing witnesses attribute the power of the miracle to the saint rather than to Allah. To truly understand *how* miracles work is dependent upon deep spiritual knowledge and experience that most witnesses to miracles do not have. Some textual traditions make the distinction between *mujizat* and *karamat*—that is, between miracles performed by the prophets (and in Shia traditions also Hazrat Ali and the twelve imams) and intended to be public, and those performed by saints, intended to be secret or private. While the distinction between *mujizat* and *karamat* is often not maintained in contemporary, vernacular (popular) practice and may be linguistically conflated as simply *karamat*, these terms analytically help us to understand the dynamics and potential controversy of miracles in practice. This essay examines the tension between secrecy and revelation in the practice of miracles/*karamat* as expressed in the spiritual healing practice and rhetoric of a contemporary Sufi female healer in Hyderabad, south India.[2]

An Ethnographic Context of *Karamat*

The healer, called Amma by her patients, is married to a Sufi religious guide and teacher (*pir*), whose calling is to "show and teach the right path" to his disciples. Amma and Abba are primarily identified with the Qadari Sufi lineage, although they often remind their audiences that they "immerse themselves in the colors of all the seven lineages." Many *pir*s are both spiritual teachers and healers. However, Abba is not literate in Arabic, upon the writing which the healing system, called *abjad ka phal kholna* (lit., opening the mystery of numbers), depends. And thus, in a very unusual manner, he shares the ritual role of *pir* as healer/teacher with Amma; he is the teacher and she is the healer. It is unusual for a woman to serve as a spiritual healer who meets the public (including men and non-Muslims), but with Abba's permission and out of her own intellectual and spiritual curiosity, Amma learned the healing practice from her own *pir* and took up the public practice after her last child was born.

Amma performs *karamat* big and small through her healing practice: guaranteeing fertility, exorcising a house or human body from disruptive spiritual forces that cause all kinds of troubles, finding lost objects, banishing a fever. Amma makes very clear that she heals only illnesses or troubles caused by spiritual forces and that there are illnesses that are purely physical, such as poor eyesight, typhoid, heart disease, and cancer; for these, Amma prescribes a visit to an allopathic doctor. When a patient comes to her healing room,

FIGURE 9.1. Amma blessing a patient at the end of a healing session in 1991. Photo by Joyce Flueckiger.

Amma first asks him or her for his or her name and that of his or her mother. She writes out the name of each in the Arabic script. Each letter of the Arabic alphabet has been assigned by the tradition a numerical value; Amma adds up the values for each name along with the assigned numerical value for the day of the lunar month. She then divides the total by three or four (depending on what gives a whole quotient), and the final quotient identifies the cause of the patient's illness (specifically, the kind of evil eye—that is, whether cast by human or nonhuman forces) and determines its prescription. If the quotient is zero, the cause is determined not to be spiritual. Often patients still ask Amma for one of her amulets or series of prescribed rituals, "just in case."

Amma's primary prescriptions are Quranic verses, numbers, and symbolic geometric shapes on slips of paper to be folded into amulets or rolled into wicks to be burned or immersed in drinking water, on saucers, on unleavened breads to be fed to dogs, on gourds to be laid next to the weakened bodies of newborns who are failing to thrive, or on pieces of uncured leather to be burned. Her table is lined with stacks of different kinds of amulets, held down by glass paperweights; a pen is always in hand or resting in the inkwell. As Amma once exclaimed, "There would be no world without paper and pen!"

The public nature of Amma's *karamat* and the strength of oral transmission of stories of Amma's healing successes draw up to forty or fifty patients a day—Hindu, Muslim, and Christian—to her healing room on the campus of Osmania University. Abba is not associated with an established *dargah* and an associated institutionalized spiritual lineage through which disciples may be drawn to him. It is significant that he has become known primarily through Amma's miraculous (healing) acts, *karamat*, and his disciples are drawn primarily from among her patients. Only after his death in 1998, at the site of his grave, have his disciples and others begun to experience *karamat* that are specifically associated with him (including a glowing light from his grave at night and his presence in dreams).

Abba's grave site has become a *dargah*, and Amma was buried there, too, in 2001. The *dargah* has been built far from the healing room in which Amma practiced, in a newly developing neighborhood where none of Amma and Abba's disciples lives. Large numbers of nondisciples who visit the *dargah* have not met Amma and Abba, and one can imagine that the biographical details of their lives, like those of many saints whose small green-painted grave-site shrines (*dargah*s) are scattered across the urban landscape of Hyderabad, may be lost over the coming years. What will remain may simply be the *karamat* experienced at their *dargah*s.[3]

Many highly educated Muslims I met during the course of my fieldwork often questioned why I was spending time learning about traditions that they did not consider to be "true Islam." Some suggested that I spend time studying the Quran with a "learned person"; others wanted me to read what they considered reputable books about Islam instead of talking to people about their experiences. They specifically identified the *karamat* of healing and vow fulfillment experienced in Amma's healing room either as manifestations of the influence of Hindu culture, as cultural superstition (therefore not truly "religious"), or as *shaytani* (acts of the devil).

While *karamat* are relatively easy to identify, they are less easily understood; and the *ways* in which these miracles "work" are rarely publicly discussed or explained, either by the saints, the beneficiaries of *karamat*, or their critics. Amma often said about such matters, "Jo-ice, it's a deep *raz* [secret]; I'll tell you one day when we have time." Or, "it's a very heavy thing," implying that miracles are outside the understanding of ordinary people and that true understanding comes only with deep spiritual knowledge gained through relationship with a *pir*. Without such guidance and insight, a beneficiary of or witness to *karamat* simply sees the surface; he or she may happily experience healing or he or she may misuse or misunderstand the external rituals and manifestations of *karamat*. And hence my title: "The deep secret and dangers of *karamat*."

Public and Private Miracles in
Islamic Traditions: *Mujizat* and *Karamat*

In Islamic analytic and literary traditions, miraculous deeds—acts that break with the natural order of things, or, in Arabic, acts that "tear the custom [of God]" (Schimmel 1975, 206) [khariq ul-'ada] have come to be identified by two words: *mujizat* and *karamat,* words distinguishing the miraculous deeds of prophets and imams from those of the saints. The *Encyclopedia of Islam* defines *mujizat* as public acts that should be proceeded by a "proclamation [*da'wa*] and a challenge [*tahaddi*], by means of which the prophet demonstrates incontrovertibly the impotence of his hearers to reproduce likewise the miracle . . ." (Van Lent and Bearman 1997, 615). These miracles are a public confirmation by Allah of the identity and proof-of-mission of his messengers, performed with the intention of rendering adversaries "weak and feeble" (Houtsma 1987, 624). The miracle as challenge, in contexts in which rival traditions seek to claim superior authority, is, of course, also common in numerous other religious traditions (including biblical and Buddhist traditions; see Davis 1998 and Dempsey 2005).

The ultimate miracle in Islam is that of the Quran itself, the beauty of which is considered to be unsurpassed and unable to be imitated.[4] It is distinguished from other miracles of the prophets (*mujizat*) in that it is everlasting and does not require eyewitnesses, as do other prophetic miracles (Cragg and Speight 1980, 17–18, quoting Al-Suyuti, b. 1445). Other miracles attributed to the Prophet Muhammad in the Quran (called *ayat*, lit., "signs," rather than *mujizat,* but analytically categorized as the latter) are the clefting of the moon, Muhammad's night journey from Mecca to Jerusalem, and the assistance given to Muslims at the battle of Badr. Various hadith also record numerous other miracles performed by the Prophet Muhammad in the presence of eyewitnesses.

Karamat, literally "acts of [God's] generosity," are bestowed on *awliya* (pl. of *wali*), friends of God/saints, and are distinguished in classical Hanifi school texts from *mujizat* in that they are not intended to be public (Ernst 1997, 61). The nature of *karamat* was a topic of frequent debate among early Muslim theologians. Some spiritual masters warned against public miracle-working as a hindrance on the path to union/relationship with God, in that the saint may be tempted by the sway of public opinion and the snares of the world (Schimmel 1975, 211–12). Carl Ernst writes that early texts about sainthood "insist that the saints are known only to God; they are not recognizable to each other and may not know even that they are saints." He quotes a tenth-century text, *Adab al-muluk,* (The Manner of Kings): "The sciences of Sufism are esoteric knowledge, which is the knowledge of inspiration, and an unmediated secret

between God (the might and majestic) and his friends [i.e., the saints] . . .
every outer has an inner; every inner has a secret; and every secret has a reality. This is what God the great and majestic gives to his friends [i.e., the
saints], as a secret by a secret. It is one of the signs of sainthood. The saints
subsist by that, and they live a wonderful life by it" (Ernst 1997, 62).

However, in contemporary Indian Sufi practice and many oral and written biographies/hagiographies of the saints, *karamat* begin to approximate,
or are conflated with, *mujizat* in that they *are* intended to be public acts that
identify the religious power and authority of the saint. It is through these
miraculous acts, including dreams, visions, and healing, that many (even
most) disciples identify and find their *pir*. When Amma used to ask me
about one or another *pir* or *piranima* (wife of a *pir*) whom I had met, her
first question was nearly always something like, "What does he or she *give?*"
not "What is his or her lineage," "Who is his or her *pir*," or "What does he
or she teach"? Amma identifies the legitimacy of *pirs* first and foremost by
their "works."[5] These miraculous works may be the only thing known about
a saint, particularly after death. The saint's teachings may be transmitted
through his successor and among his close circle of disciples; but in my
experience of eliciting narratives at the tombs of saints in Hyderabad, these
teachings may soon be disassociated from the person (more specifically,
from the *place* or physical presence) of the saint, particularly if that saint is
not literate and/or his teachings have not been written down. *Karamat* often
remain the primary external manifestation of an internal reality that is hidden or secret.

The hidden nature of true knowledge is central to Sufi experience, writing, and thought on numerous levels—including the distinction between eso-
teric/unmanifest and the exoteric/manifest, whose exact relationship must be
kept secret. The twelfth-century theologian al-Ghazzali warns that once the
Sufi disciple begins to ascend in the path of knowledge, it becomes dangerous
to attempt to articulate what is beyond language, as it will only be misunderstood and thus, of necessity, be erroneous: "But the word of Lovers Passionate
in their intoxication and ecstasy . . . must be hidden away and not spoken
of. . . . In relation to the man immersed in this state, the state is called, in the
language of metaphor, "Identity"; in the language of reality, "Unification." And
beneath these verities also lie mysteries which we are not at liberty to discuss"
(al-Ghazzali 1924, 106–18, qtd. in Ewing 1997, 240).[6]

Amma and Abba, too, often remind their disciples and patients (and the
ethnographer) that to "know" is not to understand; they warn against the futility of accumulating external knowledge in one's search for inner spiritual
knowledge. In a discussion about my writing a book about her practice, Amma
reminded me, "Allah has decreed that even if you use up all the ink of the
water of the oceans and all the pens from the trees of the world, even then,

you won't have finished the history of the *kalma* [the Muslim creed of faith, but here used to refer to "true" knowledge]. . . . No matter how many books you write, Jo-ice, that knowledge will be incomplete. No matter how much you write, it won't be enough. Even if you used all the trees in the universe as pens, even then."

Understanding the Deep Secret through
Relationship and Ritual Performance

How then are we to know the deep secret of God, the true nature of reality? Abba repeatedly teaches, "We know God's love only through observing the love between humans," most particularly through the relationship with the *pir*. One of Abba's disciples elaborated, "The most important thing is love; it's simply loving your fellow human being as an equal. When you see someone on the side of the road and stop, *that's* what makes you a human being rather than just a person." This love is most publicly "performed" during the monthly *sama* held in Abba's courtyard; Abba presides over it and in it his closest circle of disciples participates. The *sama* is a ritual of devotional song (*qavvali*) and remembrance and recitation of the names of God (*zikr*); the purpose of the ritual is to arouse mystical love among those assembled and move them closer to the *pir*, the saints, and God.[7] The highlight of the *sama* is when the mystical experience of love manifests itself in the ecstatic trance state of *wajd*. While *wajd* is not indigenously associated with *karamat*, it falls on a continuum of acts that manifest the generosity of God. God is "generous" to the devotee who has entered a deep relationship with him; *wajd* is an externalization of that generosity, of *barakat*.[8] And like *karamat* of healing, *wajd*, too can be misunderstood by the uninitiated.

When one of Abba's disciples enters trance at the *sama*, he stands up and begins to twirl, whereupon Abba, too, stands and embraces him, the pair then twirling together. According to the tradition, trance is an indication of the presence of the saints, and so, to honor them, when trance is manifest, all the rest of the disciples present at the *sama* stand as well. The circle of disciples join hands around the twirling couple in the middle, to keep them from losing their balance and falling over if the twirling becomes vigorous. Amma says that the disciples "lose themselves" when the poetic lines of the *qavvali* are "good"; but performatively the disciple in trance is kept, quite literally, grounded in Abba's embrace, which absorbs the potentially dangerous heat (*jalal*) of *wajd*. The love of God is physically revealed/manifest through the love (embrace) of the *pir* and disciple.

One verse sequence repeated by the *sama* musicians reiterates the message that we only know God's love by witnessing it between/in humans:

Look for God in man; see if his reflection is there.
    The one you're looking for is there, in your own house.
Look for God in man; see if his reflection is there.
    The one you're looking for is there, in your own house.
You won't find God through external knowledge;
    This is a deep, deep secret [raz].
You won't find God through external knowledge;
    This is a deep, deep secret.

Beauty and all that; they're just words, just words.
    Look for God in man; see if his reflection is there.
Beauty and all that; they're just words, just words.
    Look for God in man; see if his reflection is there.

While women do not sit in the *sama* courtyard—rather, they sit behind a curtain—they, too, may experience *wajd*. In this state of consciousness, Amma says, Allah becomes close; her soul leaves her body and she receives visions of the saints. But, she says, she can describe it no further, because "it is a deep secret." We can see and describe the manifestations of the secret, but true understanding of what one has seen or experienced is possible only through development of the relationship with the *pir* and the performative bodily experience itself. Hence, like the deep secret of *karamat*, the secret of *wajd* also carries with it the potential for misunderstanding its source and motivation (conflating *wajd* with possession, for example).

Narratives of the Secrets of *Karamat*

A common strategy for Amma and Abba to talk about these spiritual mysteries is through narrative performance. Narratives can leave room for and image the tension and ambiguities of secrecy and revelation, of knowledge and understanding in relationship to *karamat*, in ways that non-narrative discourse often does not. One of Abba's favorite narratives (indicated by frequency of performance) addresses these issues of secrecy and the human desire to want to put words (external knowledge) to the secrets of *karamat*. Of importance to understanding the narrative is the distinction between the nature of Sufi saints as *jalali* (fierce, quick to anger, asocial) or *jamali* (cool, easygoing, cheerful). Both saints of this narrative, Shams and Ghaus-e-Azam, are known for their particularly *jalali* nature. And Abba, too, characterizes himself as *jalali*, often barking orders to his disciples or young children in his store, although his rough voice is usually accompanied by a twinkle in his eye. Amma is said to be his opposite, *jamali*, and many patients come to her specifically because of her reputation for patience and having a loving nature. The names of Allah are also characterized as *jalali* or *jamali*, and the invocation of God's *jalali* names in *zikr* (ritual recitation of the names of God) can be dangerous for the novice (Ernst 1997, 97).

Now back to the miracle story of the founding *pir* of the Qadari lineage, Ghaus-e-Azam Dastargir (Sheikh Abdul Qadir Jilani, d. 1166 CE), to whom Abba traces his own authority (via the famous saint of Ajmer, Gharib Nawaz, also known as Khwaja Muinaddin Chishti, d. 1236 CE). The story's two main characters are Ghaus-e-Azam and one of his contemporaries, Shams Tabriz, most likely a conflation of the same Shams who was the mystical teacher and beloved friend of the thirteenth-century poet Jalaladdin Rumi and the saint from Multan, Shah Shams Multani. Abba begins, with interjections by Amma and a male patient, as we were all sitting around the healing table:

ABBA: [The Ajmeri *pir*] Gharib Nawaz's hand is only on India, whereas Ghaus-e-Azam's hand is over the whole world. Wherever you go, you'll see the green flag [the latter's symbol]. But, it's like this. When people used to take Ghaus's name, their heads would fall off.

MALE PATIENT: He means that if a person was not pure or took his name without thinking—

ABBA: —the head would separate from the body.

MALE PATIENT: The head separated. But who was he?

AMMA: Shams-i Tabriz.

ABBA: There was an important person called Shams-i Tabriz. He used to play with tigers in the jungle. With tigers—in the same way we might play with ten to twelve dogs—he used to play with tigers in the jungle. Do you understand? One day a king had a baby.

AMMA: He couldn't have children; the king's wife couldn't have children. The astrologer had told them that even if they did have children, the children would all die during childbirth itself.

ABBA: The king asked, "Then who will inherit my throne? How can my children be kept alive?" The astrologer told the king, "In the jungle, there lives a *faqir* [Muslim ascetic] who is blind. His name is Shams-i Tabriz. He has the power to bring people back to life."

The queen delivered; she delivered a baby son who died soon after. They hung a curtain and put the child behind it. The king called the army and said, "Go to the jungle and bring back whoever's there [i.e., the *faqir*]." He was playing in the jungle with nine tigers. They surrounded him and caught him. And what did they say? "Come with us; it's the order of the king that you should come." "Why me? I can't come." "No, no, we've been ordered to catch and bring you!" "O.K., let's go then."

They took him and went back. They pulled the curtain back. "Bring this child to life." What did the king say? "Bring this child to life." He [Shams] responded, "O.K. Get up by the order of Allah." But the child didn't get up. Then he said, "Get up by my order." The child shook himself [as if from sleep] and got up.

The king asked, "What is your secret [*raz*]? Why didn't the child get up by the order of Allah, but got up by your order? What is the secret, tell me." [The *faqir* answered,] "What can I say?" "No, no, you have to tell me" [the king insisted]. He called for the executioners and said, "Come and pull off his skin."

The roly-poly executioners came to pull off his skin, but it didn't come off; they couldn't get a hold of it. So what did he tell them? "Once, when I was sitting to pee, a drop fell here. Grab my skin from here and pull it off." Then they pulled off his skin, all of it. They pulled it off, and the king ordered him to leave the city.

Covered with flies, filth, and stench, he began to beg from people, but no one gave him anything. So he went to a butcher. "I'm hungry; give me something," he said. And the butcher gave him a piece of raw meat and told him to have someone else cook it for him. But no one would cook it; no one let him come close because of his bad smell.

People were afraid of him. After all, he was only raw flesh, right? There were flies buzzing around him.

AMMA: He was only raw flesh, right? Wouldn't people be afraid of him?

ABBA: The poor soul gave him a chunk of meat and said, "Take this chunk of meat and cook it." But whoever saw him told him to move on [no one agreed to cook it]. So he got very angry; being angry, he didn't say anything.

MALE PATIENT: He went to a mountain.

AMMA: Then Tabriz said, "I'm going to call *shams* [Arabic, sun; called down to cook his hunk of meat]." Saying this, he called the sun. He said, "*Shams*, come down." But just before the sun came, Ghaus-e-Azam came and stood before him. "Don't call it down; don't call it down! If the sun comes down, the whole 'public' will be burned into ashes."

How did he [Shams] respond? "O.K., I won't call *shams*. But whenever anyone takes your name, his head separates from his body [i.e., your *jalali* nature is as dangerous as mine]. You, too, shouldn't use the power of your tongue like that." So Ghaus-e-Azam said "O.K." and went away. Now, raising his [Shams's] hand [toward the sun], the meat was cooked. He ate it and went away, and Ghaus-e-Azam went the other way.

ABBA: Earlier it was like that: whenever someone took Ghaus-e-Azam's name, his head would separate from his body. Shams asked him to control his *jalali* [fierce nature]; only then he, too, would stop [asking the sun to come down]. So he agreed. When someone is in pain, he says a lot of things; he may say anything [i.e., he may call out the name of the saint Ghaus-e-Azam]. Earlier, in this situation, if you took his name, your head separated from the body.

AMMA: Now look, even in troubled conditions, we didn't use to take his name, didn't say, "*Ya Ghaus,*" because as soon as you said it, your head separated from the body.

Abba first told me this story as a means through which to position himself in the same spiritual lineage as its two powerful protagonists; its performance indirectly confers the authority of the lineage—even the *jalali* nature of its founder—upon Abba. The narrative's repeated performance also helps to create, elicit, and solidify assumptions of patients about the intercessory power of the *pir* by dramatically exteriorizing this power: the *pir* can cause heads to fall off with the mere mention of his name, can play with tigers, raise the dead, and call down the sun. Because Abba and Amma follow in the lineage of Ghaus-e-Azam, at some level they share in the possibilities of saintly miraculous power, albeit in a diffused (even diluted) intensity. If audiences (disciples and patients) of this narrative can accept the possibility of these dramatic *karamat*, then it is seemingly a small step to ask them to accept the possibility of spiritual healing that will bring home a lost child, lower a child's fever, effect fertility, or heal an abusive or otherwise fractured relationship.

The story also indirectly addresses the debate and ambivalence among some Muslims about the miracles of saints. Let's first look at the various levels of miraculous action in this narrative and interweave them with similar levels of *karamat* displayed by Amma in her healing practice. The first miraculous act is that whenever anyone says out loud the name of Ghaus-e-Azam, his or her head falls off. This is not an actively motivated miracle on the part of the saint, but is inherent to his very nature as a *jalali* saint. Although miraculous, it is so natural to who he is that actors in the social world of the narrative seem to accept it without question; they do not ask what its secret is. It is part of the natural order in the same way as are storms and drought, which may have similar inherently destructive elements that are not actively directed toward humans but nevertheless affect them. The second miracle, Shams's ability to play with tigers, is of a similar kind. It is a natural outcome of saintly nature; similar communications with wild animals (and control over them) are reported in the hagiographies of many saints (Schimmel 1975, 207–8). Again, this miraculous power is not actively directed, but inherent to the nature of the saint.

Amma periodically refers to her own inherent spiritual power in similar ways. She attributes her close connection to and love of animals—albeit not wild ones, but domesticated ones: goats, chickens, rabbits, cows—to her spiritual awareness and sensitivities. (One of the miracle stories told in her healing room tells of Amma's ability to "shut a [threatening] dog's mouth" simply by looking at him. She never explained *how* she did this, as she rarely explained about any *karamat*, but simply said that she had the power to do so.) Amma told me her very presence in her neighborhood protected it, most particularly from crime and political activity such as communal unrest. Furthermore, because of who she is, Amma asserted that she and her family do not need to wear the protective amulets (*taviz*) she writes for her patients. As she said, "I *am* the *taviz*." When some of her patients were surprised I was not afraid to accompany Amma to a house exorcism she was performing (thinking I might be afraid that the offending spirits or devils would "come on me"), she interjected, "Why would she be afraid? She's with me." These kinds of miracles are not controversial either in the narrative or, more broadly, in the Muslim world of South India. While this class of miracles of Shams is publicly known, they remain on one level "secret," because they are passively enacted and seemingly "natural."

The potential controversy seems to develop when miraculous power is actively manipulated and directed by the saint. In the narrative, the *pir* Shams is reluctant to come forward to perform the miracle of raising the dead; he complies only under duress. He first orders the dead child to rise up from the dead in the name of Allah, but nothing happens. Then he says, "Get up by my order," and "The child shook himself and got up." The king notices this discrepancy—that the saint's name is seemingly more powerful than that of God—and demands that Shams explain why the child did not get up in Allah's name. Interestingly, the king is interested in more than the *result* of the miracle (his living child); he wants to know *how* and *why* it occurred the way that it did. In this way, the king is very different than Amma's patients. Never have I seen a patient actually read the amulets Amma writes or ask her exactly how they work. They are concerned with the mechanics of their ritual manipulation (when they should be burned or where they should be placed) and results, but seemingly they have little interest in the reasons why or how they work. They have heard about and on some level trust Amma's spiritual powers as something necessary to effect change in the spiritual world that has impinged negatively on their physical and/or social bodies—however that may happen. When I asked Amma for explanations of her healing system, she often tried to explain the externals of the name-number mathematical calculations of her diagnoses, but usually ended her explanations with a comment like, "Even a parrot can perform these. It's understanding that's the [difficult] thing." The exact ways in which this spiritual understanding "works," the ways in which spiritual knowledge is cultivated, manipulated, performed, and effected, is what Amma calls the deep secret or *raz*.

Shams refuses to reveal to the king the secret of his miracle of raising the dead boy. Although we are not told this explicitly, the king himself is presumably not initiated and therefore would be unable to understand the secret even if he were told. Shams's refusal leads to the unfolding of the rest of the story, in which he himself is quite literally exposed in the most dramatic way—by being skinned alive; but his secret remains intact. Instead of attracting disciples by dint of his miraculous acts, as is the case for many saints, he becomes repellant to others. No one will come close enough even to offer him a fire over which to cook his raw meat. The narrative, then, would seem to serve as a warning about publicly performed, actively directed *karamat*: one should only reluctantly perform them, their interior explanations should be kept secret, and even so, their external manifestations may be misunderstood.

At the end of the narrative, Ghaus-e-Azam agrees to put an end to heads falling off when his name is taken (*this* is the agentive act, rather than causing them to fall off in the first place); and Shams agrees not to perform the miracle of calling down the sun to cook his raw meat (and thus destroying the earth). A truce of sorts is called on miracle-making. Presumably, Shams returns to the jungle and withdraws from the social world. This is one model for the Sufi saint.

However, for the contemporary *pir* who chooses to live in the world, whose role it is to show the correct spiritual path to disciples, this withdrawal to the jungle is not an option. Disciples need a means through which to identify their *pir*, and most of them come to know him through his *karamat*. Although most of Abba's disciples have initially been drawn to him through the *karamat* of Amma's healing practice, Amma talks about the necessity of restraint in performing miracles, as they may be misunderstood. She often told me she *could* do more, but has chosen not to, knowing the problems these could cause: for example, predicting the future, naming exact persons who have cast evil eye on her patients, and even raising the dead.

The Dangers of Making Public the Acts of *Karamat*

While Amma's spiritual healing acts—her *karamat*—are not controversial among her Hindu and Muslim patients (at least not when they are there sitting at her healing table), they are controversial for some Muslims outside the context of the healing room. Among contemporary critiques of *karamat* (specifically, regarding the kinds of healing practices performed by contemporary, living *pir*s) is their potential to breach a central concept in Islam: that of *tawhid*, the singularity of God. Some critics fear that when a saint displays such power, his or her disciples may be tempted to not simply honor him or her or learn a spiritual path from the saint, but to worship him or her—to attribute the saint's power to the performer of *karamat* rather than to Allah, who has given him or her this power. This may be true of the miracles both of the living saint as well as of the one who is approached at the site of his or her *dargah*. In a context like India where both Muslim and Hindu patients come to *pir*s for healing, the misunderstanding by Hindus may be particularly likely. In Hindu cosmologies, lines of distinction between human and deity are permeable—these firm identities lie on two ends of a continuum, at whose middle can be found living gurus and saints and the deified dead (including gurus and saints, but also martial heroes and others who have died violent or premature deaths and who linger as troubling ghosts until they are propitiated). Performatively, Hindus may identify the *pir* or *piranima* who has left the physical body with deified dead, as the *source* of *karamat* experienced at the *dargah*, since one worships at the tomb of the *pir* in ways similar to the ways one worships the image of a Hindu deity: by offering flowers and incense or tying a string on a gate as a tangible record of having made a vow to the deity, and receiving in return blessings of the deity through sweets, ash applied to the forehead or eyelids, or the "pat" of a peacock feather, administered by the caretaker of the shrine.

The fear over possible confusion as to the source of the miraculous power is also present, however, for Muslim patients, disciples, and beneficiaries of a wide range of *karamat*—as well as for those who witness these miracles and practices indirectly and do not understand their mysteries. For example, a statement such as one I heard from one of Abba and Amma's disciples, "For me, my *pir* is God," using the English word "God," could suggest misplaced identity and authority. For Western scholars and students of Islam, perhaps the best-known example from Sufi traditions of the potential for misunderstanding and accusation of heresy for making such statements is the execution of the Sufi al-Hallaj (b. 857), for his exclamation, "ana al-Haqq," for which a standard translation is "I am Truth." Haqq is also one of the ninety-nine names of God, and he was accused of claiming to be God. Narratives of this incident do not recount that al-Hallaj gave any justification or explanation for his statement; its meaning was seemingly a secret beyond ordinary human understanding. Some later Sufis understood the cause of his death to be that he had revealed what should have been kept secret (Williams 1994, 120).

A second danger of *karamat* is that they may be imitated, in contrast to the *mujizat* of the prophets. Witnesses to imitative acts may attribute them to positive spiritual power (literally, light knowledge) or God when, in fact, they may be based on manipulations by sorcerers/magicians of spiritual knowledge to an evil end (literally, light knowledge)—and thus witnesses or recipients of the miraculous acts may be deluded, and worse, drawn down the wrong spiritual path.[9] Amma described similar potential confusion when I asked her about the distinctions between two Urdu words used for altered states of consciousness/trance, *wajd* and *hal*. Although the two states look very similar in performance, she attributes *wajd* to God and *hal* to the devil. While a more traditional Sufi usage of *hal* is to identify it as a state that originates from God, and even Amma on other occasions uses the term in this way, the importance here is the distinction between the *sources* of two different kinds of states that manifest in the human body in similar ways. Amma explains: "*Hal* is the dance of the devil [*shaytan*]. What we are talking about [here at the *sama*] is *wajd*, *wajd-zikr*. . . . The dancing at the *dargah*, that's *hal* [when persons are possessed by devils/satans and come to the shrine for healing]. What happens at the *sama* is *wajd*. There's a distinction between things of the devil and things of God. When you get possessed, you dance and dance. But when you get lost in Allah, that's *wajd*."

In his treatise concerning appropriate action for women, *Bihishti Zewar*, the early twentieth-century Indian scholar Maulana Thanawi similarly cautions about the dangers of this kind of confusion and thus against miracle-making altogether: "Whoever is against the *shari'at* cannot be a friend of God. If anything amazing appears by the action of such a person, it is either magic of the work of that person's lower soul (*nafs*) and of Satan. It should be rejected" (qtd. in Metcalf 1990, 70). Thanawi goes on to distinguish the miracles of magic from the miracles of God by their distinct origins and methods. Magicians force spiritual powers or agents to come to their service through particular ritual actions, whereas the miracles of saints (what he calls "openings/*kashf*" or "illuminations/*ilham*")[10] come unelicited from God ("while awake or asleep") to the saint (Ewing 1997, 140). However, Sufi teachers would argue that both the danger of *shirk* (associating another being/deity with God) and inability to distinguish light and dark knowledge can be countered by entering discipleship with the *pir*, which protects the disciple from possible heresy. Gradually, the disciple's relationship with the *pir* deepens, his or her spiritual knowledge increases, and he or she fully enters the "deep secret." Ironically, once the disciple has entered such a relationship, the explanations for and mechanics of miracles matter little, unless the disciple himself or herself wants to practice such healing knowledge. When a young male disciple was pressuring Amma to show him how to effect some negative changes in the lives of some of his coworkers through manipulation of amulets, Amma said to me in an aside that with knowledge comes responsibility for using it wisely. She implied that this young man did not have such wisdom, and she did not give him the technical knowledge that he wanted.

↾

Historically, Sufi traditions have openly acknowledged the dangers of many of their own practices—the dangers of acting upon internal realities that can only be witnessed or experienced by others (noninitiates) on an external level. This is the danger of *karamat*. Shams and contemporary *pir*s (teacher/healers) such as Amma and Abba recognize the limits of human understanding. To *explain* is not necessarily to reveal; to hear explanations is not truly to know. Nevertheless, not all who experience the generosity of God can or do retire to the jungle, where their *karamat* would remain unseen or secret (and even then, the jungle seemingly cannot hide all secrets; Shams's miraculous nature comes to be known by the king). Furthermore, *karamat* are necessary for the disciple to identify his or her *pir*, and narrativizing the *pir*'s miracles helps both to build the *pir*-disciple relationship and relationships *between* disciples. However, many aspects of how these miracles work must remain secret until the disciple himself or herself reaches an advanced spiritual understanding. Until such time, the *pir*-disciple relationship safeguards against potential dangers of *karamat* vocalized by their critics. The dynamics of *karamat* as practiced on the ground (in the healing room) are complex; *karamat* are needed to reveal and identify, but they are inherently beyond understanding and must remain at some level secret. And it is this same secrecy or lack of understanding of *karamat* that are often the source of controversy and worse—for Shams, being skinned alive.

Postscript: Fieldwork and Matters of Secrecy

I entered the fieldwork context of Amma's healing room knowing little about this level of vernacular Muslim practice, with its specialized vocabulary and ritual. Initially I asked what must have seemed like many naive questions. Amma patiently answered these questions both directly and indirectly. She often answered my questions about the mystical or symbolic significance of names, numbers, and letters she had written on her healing amulets with something like, "These are very heavy matters." Her answer implied that I had not yet reached sufficient spiritual maturity to understand these matters, that they were beyond my understanding for other reasons, and/or that this was not the time and place for such explanations. Sometimes she would answer, "I'll explain everything sometime when we have time"; but the explanation would not be forthcoming, either because she forgot about it, because extended time alone was rarely available, or she had decided it should remain secret. Once she explicitly told me that there were some things she could not tell me, as she had not been given permission to do so by her own *pir*. As I was writing the book that resulted from my relationship with Amma, I found myself thankful that there were some "secret" things that I did not know, because, were I to know them, I would not ethically be able to write publicly about matters that could be understood fully only by initiates who had years of experience in relationship to Amma and Abba.[11] Like *karamat*, their revelation could lead to controversy and misunderstanding. While I was interested in all aspects of the healing practice and person of Amma, the specific content of these "mystical secrets" was not crucial to answering questions that became central to my work: the ways in which a "universal" religious tradition found local (vernacular) expression in a specific geographic/cultural locale.

But Amma and Abba's teachings about the difference between knowledge and understanding led me to make decisions to leave out some of the data/information that I *did* know, decisions I might not have made earlier. For example, I made decisions to not write about certain family matters that may have been interesting to readers, even titillating, but that did not impact my theoretical concerns. Further, family dynamics were always shifting, and thus to write about some family tensions would be to freeze them in time, when on the ground they were more fleeting. There were other descriptions of people or places that may have added to local color in my writing, but that, left uncontextualized or explicated at length, might have created "false knowledge" and misunderstanding for a reader unfamiliar with South Asian social and physical landscapes, and so I did not include them. Finally, Amma's teachings about the deep secrets of spiritual life and relationships encouraged a degree of humility among those with whom she interacted. She invited me into her healing room and home, encouraged my research, and was excited about the possibilities of a book with her picture on the cover (Abba teased, "She'll be on exams in America."); but her eyes twinkled when she cautioned, "No matter how many books you write, Jo-ice, that knowledge will be incomplete."

Notes

A version of this essay appears in the *Journal of Comparative Islamic Studies* (2006, Equinox Publishing Co.). A preliminary version of the paper was delivered at the American Academy of Religion Annual Meeting in San Antonio, 2004, on a panel entitled ""Revealing and Creating through Miracles: Ethnographic Encounters with the Wonderous in South Asian Traditions." The research upon which this essay is based was supported by grants from the American Institute of Indian Studies, Fulbright, and the American Academy of Religion. I thank two anonymous readers for the *Journal of Comparative Islamic Studies* for their perceptive reading of this essay and suggestions, many of which I have incorporated in this version.

1. See Ernst and Lawrence 2002, 71–71 for a list of "traits" often associated with medieval Sufi saints/masters in biographical literature. The performance of miracles is only one of numerous other traits (including birth into a well-established family, reli-

gious/Quranic education, performance of hajj, etc.). Amma and Abba—and they are not anomalous in Hyderabad—represent a level of Muslim practice not associated with literary traditions and lineages connected to (or founders of) well-established shrines (*dargahs*) and institutions. At this level of practice and sainthood, traditions are preserved primarily orally, and the external criteria of sainthood, at least as they circulate in the oral traditions, seem to be based primarily on charisma and *karamat*.

2. I use the ethnographic present as my narrative tense, although the healer, Amma, died in August 2001. I do so in part to help re-create the vitality of the interactions in Amma's healing room. Furthermore, my use of the present tense is intended to honor the indigenous Sufi belief that Amma and Abba (and other saints) have not actually died, but have passed beyond the veil/curtain (*pardah*) and are living in a different reality that continues to intersect with the human world. See Dakake 2006 for a relevant analysis of the tension between secrecy and revelation in Shiite Islamic traditions. Here the tension is that between glorified martyrdom (exemplified in the massacre of Ali's son, Imam Hussein) and the protection through secrecy of the imams and their disciples, and hence the protection of the truth that they embodied.

3. My book *In Amma's Healing Room* (2006) is currently the only written document narrating the lives of Amma and Abba. It is not yet accessible to non-English-reading audiences. Amma and Abba's son Khalid inherited Abba's *khilafat* (right of succession) and is the caretaker of his *dargah*. He also learned the healing practice from Amma. It will be interesting to observe in the coming years whether he becomes "known" as a healer/performer of *karamat* or through his ritual position as holder of the *khilafat* and miracles experienced at Amma and Abba's grave site.

4. See Martin 1980 for a discussion of the development of debate around the "miracle of the Quran" as a sign of Muhammad's prophethood.

5. In contrast, Carl Ernst characterizes early saints' hagiographies as emphasizing the teachings/sayings (words) of the saints and edifying narratives (1997, 63–64); see also Ernst and Lawrence 2002, 71–72 for other characteristics of medieval saints' written biographies. Katherine Ewing writes of the efforts of the Auquf Department in Pakistan to purposely manipulate the narration of the lives of saints to *eliminate* miracles from their life stories, published as pamphlets on the occasion of the saints' *urs* (death anniversary celebrations) at major shrines. These "describe in detail the historical circumstances in which each saint lived, his individuality in appearance, and his social and political activities. In sharp contrast to most hagiographies, they do not give accounts of the miracles performed by the saint. Rather, they stress the saint's pious actions, actions that are within the capacity of the ordinary man, actions that do not violate a modern, scientific worldview" (1997, 71).

6. See also the poet Attar (thirteenth century, author of *Parliament of the Birds*) on the necessity of secrecy regarding union with God: "But who can speak of this? I know if I betrayed my knowledge I would surely die; if it were lawful for me to relate such truths to those who have not reached this state, those gone before us would have made some sign; but no sign comes, and silence must be mine" (Attar 1990, 229).

7. See Flueckiger 2006, chapter 7, for a fuller description of the *sama* held monthly in Abba's courtyard.

8. During one *sama* in Abba's courtyard, a newly initiated Hindu disciple went into *wajd*. The women with whom I was sitting complained that he "didn't know anything. This isn't right. He's just become a *murid* [disciple]. What does he think?! Not *everyone* achieves *wajd*. It's a matter of time [experience]." They assumed that *wajd* was an indication of a high level of spiritual knowledge and relationship with God that a new initiate simply would not have had.

9. This distinction between spiritual miracles and magic is made in other traditions, as well. Augustine makes this distinction when he comments on the contest between Pharaoh's wise men and Moses (in the book of Exodus) as being the contest between "magical acts and incantations to which the evil spirits or demons are addicted" and those made possible by the help of angels (Davis 1998, 6).

10. An alternative standard translation for *kashf* is "uncover" and for *ilham* is "inspiration."

11. For discussion of the ethics of writing about esoteric/secret traditions, see Hugh Urban 1998.

References

Attar, Farid al-Din. 1990. *Muslim Saints and Mystics: Episodes from the "Tadhkirat al-Auliya'"* (*"Memorial of the Saints"*). Translated by A. J. Arberry. London: Arkana.

Cragg, Kenneth, and Marston Speight. 1980. *Islam from Within: Anthology of a Religion*. Belmont, CA: Wadsworth Publishing Company.

Dakake, Maria. 2006. "Hiding in Plain Sight: The Practical and Doctrinal Significance of Secrecy in Shi'ite Islam." *Journal of the American Academy of Religion* 74, no. 2:324–55.

Davis, Richard. 1998. "Introduction: Miracles as Social Acts." In *Images, Miracles, and Authority in Asian Religious Traditions*, edited by Richard H. Davis, 1–22. Boulder, CO: Westview Press.

Dempsey, Corinne. 2005. "Nailing Heads and Splitting Hairs: Conflict, Conversion, and the Bloodthirsty Yakshi in Kerala, South India." *Journal of American Academy of Religion* 73, no. 3:111–32.

Ernst, Carl. 1997. *The Shambhala Guide to Sufism*. Boston: Shambhala.

Ernst, Carl, and Bruce Lawrence. 2002. *Sufi Martyrs of Love: The Chishti Order in South Asia and Beyond*. New York: Palgrave Macmillan.

Ewing, Katherine. 1997. *Arguing Sainthood: Modernity, Psychoanalysis, and Islam*. Durham, NC: Duke University Press.

Flueckiger, Joyce Burkhalter. 2006. *In Amma's Healing Room: Gender and Vernacular Islam in South India*. Bloomington: Indiana University Press.

Ghazzali, Abu Hamid al-. 1924. *Al-Ghazzali's "Mishkat Al-Anwar"* (*"The Niche for Lights"*). Translated by W. H. T. Gairdner. Lahore: Sh. Mohammad Ashraf (Royal Asiatic Society).

Houtsma, M. 1987. Th. *E. J. Brill's First Encyclopedia of Islam*. Leiden: E. J. Brill.

Martin, Richard. 1980. "The Role of the Basrah Mu'tazilah in Formulating the Doctrine of the Apologetic Miracle." *Journal of Near Eastern Studies* 39, no. 3:175–89.

Ratke, Bernd, ed. 1991. *Adab al-muluk fi bayan haqa'iq al-tasawwuf* (*The Manners of Kings: Explaining the Realities of Sufism*). Beiruter Text und Studien 37. Stuttgart: Franz Steiner Verlag.

Schimmel, Annemarie. 1975. *Mystical Dimensions of Islam*. Chapel Hill: University of North Carolina Press.

Urban, Hugh. 1998. "The Torment of Secrecy: Ethical and Epistemological Problems in the Study of Esoteric Traditions." *History of Religion* 37, no. 3:209–48.

Van Lent, J., and P. J. Bearman. 1997. *The Encyclopedia of Islam*. New Edition. Leiden: E. J. Brill.

Williams, John Alden. 1994. *The Word of Islam*. Austin: University of Texas Press.

CHAPTER TEN

Media of Miracles, Miracle of Media

Clairvoyants and Commercials on South Asian Television in the Diaspora

NEELIMA SHUKLA-BHATT

During the years 2004–2007, it would hardly have been an exaggeration to call three miracle workers—Ajmeri Baba, Pundit Maharaj, and Peer Syed Sahib—the "patron saints" of Zee TV USA, a popular television channel from South Asia that has been available in the United States since 1998. A first-time viewer of this channel would have been amazed at the frequency with which commercials for these miracle workers/spiritual healers/clairvoyants appeared on its shows, giving an absolute guarantee of solutions to life problems though the "help" of the masters within a short period of time.[1] The commercials also provided a phone number in the United Kingdom (and not in the United States) to call. In a half-hour show, the viewer would have heard messages from all three masters or may have received repeated *darshan* (sacred viewing) of one. A master could be the sole sponsor of the show or he could be its cosponsor, sharing the honor with powerful financial institutions like ICICI Bank, New York Life, and Metlife.[2] Commercials for these masters appeared on Zee TV USA's Canadian counterpart, ATNZee, as well. For a long time, they also appeared on "Asia 1" of the United Kingdom.[3] Similar commercials for other wonder-workers have been seen with comparable frequency on other South Asian TV channels in North America such as SONY.[4] Surprisingly, these commercials avoid the word "miracle." The nature of their messages and the titles of the masters, however, clearly indicate that they are commercials for miracle working. While some in the South Asian diaspora

187

community are sharply critical of the commercials, their frequency on popular television—particularly during the years 2004–2007—points out that the product they advertise, miraculous help, does have an appeal for many.

In view of the general perception of South Asians as a highly successful immigrant group in North America, excelling in the science-based professions of medicine and technology, these commercials raise interesting questions: Why does the belief in miracles persist in this community? How do these commercials modify understandings of miracles among their prospective viewers by using the power of television as a medium? How do they help us to understand "miracle" as a religious category? What do they indicate about the intersection of religion and business in the context of globalization? This essay explores these questions through an examination of the commercials for Pundit Maharaj, Peer Syed Sahib, and Ajmeri Baba that frequently appeared, in recent years, on Zee TV USA. I draw on insights provided by Mark Corner (2005) and Robert Mullin (1996) about miracles as a persistent theme in human religious experience, ethnographic studies of saint cults in South Asia, analyses of television advertising, debates about globalization, and Max Weber's concept of routinization of charisma. The following examines how these commercials demonstrate the hold miracles have over human imagination. It furthermore analyzes the implications of globalization—marked by movements of people, advances in technology, and the spread of consumerism—for an immigrant community's understandings of miracles at the beginning of the twenty-first century. To this end, it is helpful to look first at the context that makes these commercials possible.

The Context: Globalization

My attention was first drawn to the commercials of spiritual healers as products of globalization in late 2004 during a lighthearted conversation at a friend's home in New Jersey as we watched a popular Zee TV show. After seeing a few cycles of the commercials of the three masters, someone remarked, "How come these masters, who claim to solve everybody's problems, cannot solve their own problem of seeking clients across the globe and depend so much on the TV screen?" That was an interesting remark, pointing out the dependence of miracle workers on the power of media in the context of a global market—an inversion of the traditional image of a saintly person in South Asia who depends solely on God and helps the needy miraculously by mediating divine grace. As scholarly works show, oral and written hagiographic narratives in various South Asian traditions are full of allusions to saints as transmitters of grace (Werbner 2003, 143; Hawley 1987, 59). This traditional understanding is radically challenged by miracle-worker commercials in the context of a global market and the rapidly spreading commercial culture of our times.

The religion scholar David Chidester views global market culture as dangerous because, in its realm of influence, multinational businesses are able to effectively promote consumerism as a universal religion for their own profit. He contends that multinational businesses from developed countries—businesses such as Coca-Cola, McDonald's, and Disney—attempt to spread their empires by creating a mythical aura around their products by incorporating local cultural symbols into their marketing plans, especially their advertisements.[5] Using symbol systems that have a powerful appeal for local people, such businesses present the consumption of their products as an uplifting experience, creating "One Market under God."[6] By associating their own products with powerful symbols of local cultures, they subtly influence people's sense of identity and orientation in the world, two features traditionally associated with religion (Chidester 2003, 150–55, 163).

While Chidester focuses on the tendency for multinational businesses to adopt religion-like rhetoric, Jereme Carrette and Richard King critique the converse: globalization's use of business strategies in the realm of religion. They note how contemporary "spirituality" traditions offer exotic bits and pieces from far-off religions to individual seekers for a fee and, as such, privatize and commodify religion. Such traditions, they maintain, provide avenues for the new wave of capitalism that is "infiltrating all other dimensions of human life, translating and transforming everything in its wake into the language and philosophy of consumerism." This, in turn, leads to a "commodification of life itself." Commodification of religious practices for individual consumers encourages narcissism and displaces traditional, community-based, religious value systems that teach concern for others (Carrette and King 2005, 174–75).

Commercials for miracle workers on South Asian TV channels stand at an interesting juncture in this global market environment. Like the multinational businesses discussed by Chidester, they attempt to build global customer networks by appealing to the cultural and religious sensibilities of their viewers. Like the spirituality traditions critiqued by Carrette and King, they also commodify what traditionally belongs to the realm of faith. In some important ways, however, they counter global market trends discussed by these scholars. First, they market a cultural/religious product from a less-developed part of the world and primarily target immigrants from that world region who have moved to more developed countries. Second, rather than appropriating local cultural symbols for business expansion, they effectively appeal to nostalgia and reassurance. Furthermore, unlike the spirituality traditions that import exotic religious practices from far-off lands for the local elite, they market a component of popular religion—miracle working—from back home for the culturally dislocated. This reinforces a belief in miracles among viewers, while it modifies their understanding of miracles. A close look at the texts of selected commercials reveals several aspects that make them successful in the global context.

The Texts: The Commercials

The four commercials sketched below are only a sampling of the many interesting commercials for the three masters aired during the fall of 2005. In terms of frequency on Zee TV USA, the commercials for Pundit Maharaj, Peer Syed Sahib, and Ajmeri Baba are comparable. With regard to variety, content, and format, however, they are considerably different. Pundit Maharaj repeats a single, dense and carefully constructed commercial. Peer Syed Sahib and Ajmeri Baba air multiple commercials of varying lengths. Peer commercials are remarkable for their variety of human figures, and Ajmeri Baba commercials display variety and complexity in their format.

Pundit Maharaj

As the commercial begins, a young South Asian man appears in a frame in a corner of the screen, looking distraught. His mood is matched by leafless trees in the background. The voice-over (male) asks, "Are you worried, depressed? Have you failed in a love relationship?" Next, a young South Asian woman is seen sitting sadly by a window. The voice-over asks, "Are you separated from the person you love?"

In the following two frames a man appears in an office. In one he is working; in the other he is looking at a photograph. As the voice-over asks, "Do you have problems with your business, finances, children, or health?" the words "Business," "Finance," "Children," and "Health" appear under the frames one by one. Next, another man shakes his head in desperation. His wife stands in a corner, looking helplessly at him. And the voice-over asks, "Do you see your problems increase day by day?"

Then, an Indian astrological chart covers the whole screen. The voice-over asks, "Have you been disheartened by various gurus, astrologers, and spiritual healers?" Instantly, the screen is covered with an image of sunrise. Hues of gold, orange, and pink spread across a blue sky with scattered clouds. In large italicized letters appear the words:

Pundit Maharaj
has
Good News

The voice-over repeats the message, making it more personal for the viewer: "Pundit Maharaj has Good News *for you*."

In the scenes that follow the mood is celebratory. The man and woman who appeared sad at the beginning reappear, walking hand in hand in a park. As the man places a ring on the woman's finger, she is ecstatically happy. The desperate man from an earlier scene enters his home smiling and is welcomed warmly by his wife. A series of captions appear on the screen, reinforced by the voice-over: "All problems solved in 7 days Guaranteed," "Black magic removed in 72 hours," and "Officially established in UK since 1952." The voice-over gives an additional detail: "Pundit Maharaj has been televised by BBC."

The penultimate screen shows four smiling faces, including one of a Caucasian person. The commercial ends with the reappearance of the sunrise image. Superimposed on the image is the caption, "Ring Pundit Maharaj immediately 011-44-796-796-7968." An off-the-screen female voice says in a reassuring tone, "Call Pundit Maharaj immediately at 011-44-796-796-7968 and all your problems will be solved forever."

Peer Syed Sahib

The scene opens with two men and a woman. The woman stands in the middle. All are dressed in stylish Western clothes and look very tense. The eyes of both men are on the woman. The woman looks at the man on the right. A male voice-over asks: "Do you want a marriage of your choice?"

On the second screen, two hands, one of a man and one of a woman, are shown moving apart, faintly reminiscent of the hands of God and Adam in the famous Michelangelo painting. The voice asks: "Is the person you married drifting away from you?" Now, the banner "Peer Syed Sahib, 011-44-1723-507749" starts rolling at the bottom of the screen. A few screens follow, each showing a desperate man. He is either in an office surrounded by files or at home. In some, the man holds his head in his hands and shows extreme stress. The voice-over asks a series of intense questions: "Are you facing problems due to your children? Are you sick or is your life suffering from black magic or evil spirits?"

Presently, a vignetted photograph of a bespectacled, old, and holy-looking Peer Syed Sahib appears on a green background. Underneath the photograph is his phone number—011-44-1723-507749. The voice-over says: "Stop worrying. Contact Peer Syed Sahib, the name that will put an end to your worries in a few days."

The next screen shows the man in the office happily high-fiving his partner. Once again, the screen with the Peer Syed Sahib picture appears, and the voice urges: "Call 011-44-1723-507749 now."

Ajmeri Baba (Two Commercials)

The first commercial is in minidrama format, presenting scenes from stressful life in the diaspora. Each scene is associated with a specific problem and appears with a label. The initial segment is set in a well-furnished living room and is labeled "Family problems." A woman says angrily to her husband in Hindi: "Lagta hai phirse pi rakhi hai!" (It looks like you are drunk again!) The man retorts: "Oye! Chup!" (Hey! Shut up!) The woman walks away, grumbling: "Pata nahin kyaa hoga is ghar ka." (I don't know what will happen to this family). An offscreen male voice asks in a sympathetic tone: "Do you need help?"

The second clip is labeled "Extramarital problems." At first, a man and a woman in a sari (apparently his wife) are seen walking together, engaged in a pleasant conversation. In the next screen, the wife looks sadly out the window of her apartment. Her husband next appears with a woman in Western clothes on a mall escalator, laughing. The last screen of this segment shows the wife sitting on a sofa with her phone in her hand and shaking her head.

The third set of problems is "Financial problems." First, the offscreen voice asks, "Are you in business difficulty?" Then, in an office with many stacks of files, an employee hands files to his boss, who is sitting in a chair. The employee asks, "Boss, we are running out of money. How are we going to take care of these payments?" The boss shakes his head and answers, "I don't know what we are going to do this month."

Now, a woman in *salwar-kamiz-chunni* (loose pants, long shirt, and scarf), the traditional attire of Punjabi women, appears in a frame. Speaking softly in Punjabi, she conveys a message that translates: "All these difficulties can be resolved only by Ajmeri Baba: A gift of nature that, in itself, acts like a Raambaan [the unfailing arrow of Ram, the epic hero of the Ramayana]."

The next screen has a blue background in which a picture of Ajmeri Baba appears. He is a middle-aged man with a beard, dressed in white attire of unspecific nature, and wears three bead necklaces that can be associated with any number of religious groups. In the background the words "success," "prosperity," and "happiness" appear. Under the portrait appears the logo "Ajmeri Baba, Spiritual Healer. 40 Broadway, Cheshire, England SK73BU (U.K.). Telephone: + 44797-746-4013." The offscreen voice repeats the information. The commercial ends with the woman in *salwar-kameez* urging in Punjabi, "Go to Babaji and all your troubles will go away."

The second commercial opens with a man who looks like a professional or a businessman sitting uneasily at one end of a sofa in a nice living room. He opens and shuffles the contents of his briefcase on a coffee table. Meanwhile, an offscreen male voice asks: "Have you lost your peace of mind? Are you worried, stressed, or depressed?" The man exclaims, "I can't believe this is happening. All this is happening to me. What am I going to do?" His hand gestures and facial expressions, along with his tone, convey extreme agitation. Suddenly, he notices the TV remote control on the coffee table and turns on the TV, where a commercial for Ajmeri Baba is airing. In this commercial within the commercial, the screen is covered with the beautiful eyes of a woman. As they open slowly, the words "AJMERI BABA" appear in large letters across the screen, as if this logo is a revelation to the eyes. An offscreen voice says, "Open your eyes to the world of Ajmeri Baba."

Next a street with glittering lights appears, and the voice says, "Ajmeri Baba has helped thousands of people just like you from all over the world." On each of the next four screens one word in large letters appears on different wallpaper reinforced by the voice-over: DOMESTIC, FINANCE, MARITAL, BUSINESS PROBLEMS.

At this point, the screen changes, and a window opens, releasing the words: "100% Guaranteed." The voice continues, "Ajmeri Baba can guide you to good fortune and ensure your future." Now, a yellow phone with the word "Call" written on it flips on the screen. The voice says: "So, what are you waiting for?" Next, we see the man on the phone. The expressions on his face change gradually from extreme anxiety to happiness. In the last screen the man sits in a garden surrounded by his friends and family and is laughing heartily. The voice commands, "Call Ajmeri Baba today at 011-441723-507749 to help solve your problems."

Each of these commercials is followed by an express disclaimer from Zee TV USA, giving an ironic twist to their rhetoric of guarantee.

The Subtext: The Power of Television and Commodification of Miracles

Even though there is no explicit mention of fees or even of miracles in the commercials sketched above, their rhetoric of guarantee and the expressed disclaimer by Zee TV immediately following them convey a subtext that is not hard to fathom: problems can be solved through unexplainable help—that is, holy persons can perform miracles. Miracles no longer belong exclusively to the realm of faith, however; they are also a commodity for purchase in the global market, just like other consumer products. To effectively convey this subtext to prospective viewers, commercials must skillfully make use of two building blocks: (1) a persistence of faith in miracles as products of divine or saintly intervention; and (2) the power of television advertising.

The commercials for Pundit Maharaj, Peer Syed Sahib, and Ajmeri Baba stand in a special category of commercials—faith-based commercials that offer solutions to complex and devastating life problems that claim a supernatural (often divine) source for the solutions. Commercials in this category attempt to provide an aura of profundity to their message that differentiates them from other commercials.[7] However, since commercials for many consumer products also tend to present their products as having profound effects on the lives of their consumers, as suggested by Chidester, these pose a challenge to faith-based commercials. In order to be effective, faith-based commercials must have the right blend of elements so that they will appeal to their viewers' religious/cultural sensibilities as well as to their sensibilities as consumers. Commercials for miracle workers examined here combine culturally specific understandings of miracles from South Asia with standard television advertising techniques of the global market. As these building blocks come together in the creation of commercials, they strengthen each other at some points of intersection while simultaneously transforming each other in significant ways.

An important feature shared by miracles and advertisements is a myth-like quality. Each has a powerful appeal to the imagination. Miracles, as Manabu Waida points out, are understood by communities as manifestations of sacred powers of divine or charismatic human beings that cannot be understood empirically or rationally (Waida 2005, 6049). Due to miracles' appeal to the imagination, belief in them has continued to prevail in human history since antiquity, despite challenges by the rationally oriented in various contexts. In the mid-1990s, Sandra Gurvis catalogued fifty places associated with the miraculous in the United States, several of which are typically visited by educated and affluent believers (Gurvis 1996). The persistence of "magical thinking" among such seemingly unlikely people as modern professionals leads Michael Brown to wonder if the miraculous should be recognized as an "enduring quality of the human imagination," related to "a search for authentic experience" (Brown 1997, 130–31).

Even though television commercials have appeared only recently in human history compared to myths and miracles, they are markedly similar to these latter in their mode of functioning. As Bernice Kanner's analysis in *The 100 Best Commercials* shows, they appeal to the imagination and dreams of their viewers, promising results that are beyond belief (Kanner 1999).[8] A severe critic of commercials, Leslie Savan also recognizes their appeal to the human psyche by suggesting that even those viewers who do not buy a product "buy the world that makes the product seem desirable" (Savan 1994, 8). Commercials share an additional quality with myth. Like myths that present primordial models for human action, commercials subtly influence worldviews and provide a model for activity. Through countless images of healthy, energetic, confident, and happy individuals, commercials forcefully advocate an ideal of success that can be achieved through the use of the products being advertised. The products are projected as magical objects offering neat resolutions to problems. The appeal of commercials is aided by the easy availability of credit cards or imaginary wealth that makes one feel that the realization of one's dreams is only a phone call away. Often, following a commercial, one purchases what one cannot afford.

In addition to their mythlike quality, miracles and television commercials share two other features that make them compatible. Both require the involvement of two parties and are associated with spreading the word. As Waida points out, miracles require both the miracle workers who claim spiritual inspiration and the people who have faith in them. The latter often engage in the spreading of the word about the former (Waida 2005, 6049). A commercial, whose raison d'être is the spreading of the word, conveys an appealing message regarding a product by using hyperbolic rhetoric. It would have no meaning, however, without at least some viewers responding to it with an action: buying. In a sense, as Savan suggests, viewers are coproducers of commercials whose memories and desires have to be factored in order to make commercials effective (Savan 1994, 9, 2).

Factoring in the Expected Viewers

If frequency of commercials during the period under consideration is any indication of success, the producers of commercials for South Asian miracle workers know their viewers extremely well. They are keenly aware of the tendency of South Asian immigrants to re-create their homeland in foreign environments in concrete and symbolic ways.[9] They attempt, therefore, to appeal to the imagination of prospective viewers in this group by linking miracle workers to authentic experiences in the homeland left behind. The power of cultural memories over the imagination of the dislocated provides an important avenue of appeal for these commercials. Along with memories of the native land, these commercials also focus on the dreams of immigrants for success in new homelands that entice them with their affluence. Every commercial for a spiritual healer interweaves memory and hope through selected elements.

The most important markers of continuity and authenticity are the names and titles of the miracle workers—Pundit Maharaj, Peer Syed Sahib, and Ajmeri Baba. For a South Asian, each of these is symbolic of a long spiritual tradition. Both *pundit* (learned man) and *maharaj* (lord) are titles associated with religious authority in Hindu traditions—the former with ritual and intellectual authority, and the latter with piety. *Peer*, the term for a Muslim Sufi spiritual master, is associated with the miraculous; *sahib* (master) is a term of respect. The title or surname Syed is closely associated with sainthood (Werth 1998, 80). Even though the religious identity of Ajmeri Baba is difficult to discern just from the title, the term *baba* (elder) is associated with piety in many traditions of South Asia as in the title of the famous Satya Sai Baba.

"Ajmeri" (from Ajmer) alludes to the city where the shrine of Sufi saint Moin-uddin Chishti, famous for its miraculous powers, is located. (On his Web site, Ajmeri Baba indicates his lineage to be the oldest family of spiritual healers in the world.) For migrants from South Asia, each word in the titles of the masters suggests personal piety associated with miracles. The titles implicitly convey the guarantee that is given explicitly at the end of the commercials.

Additionally, the titles of the masters enhance the effectiveness of television commercials. South Asians are accustomed to hearing stories about the miraculous powers of yogis, *pundits*, *peers*, and *baba*s for centuries. Since ancient times, followers of holy persons in a variety of traditions in India have told stories about their masters in both oral and written hagiographies.[10] To this day, the testimonials of people who claim to have found solutions to their problems through the blessings of a spiritual master are routinely circulated by the followers of the master through word of mouth and sometimes in print media. Commercials about spiritual healers, filled with characters testifying to the miraculous help they received from the masters, can be viewed as a continuation of those traditions. Unlike food commercials, for which there is no long and continuous tradition back home, these can be seen as having a deeper cultural grounding.

In addition to the title of the master, each commercial integrates some other cultural symbols to remind the viewer of the homeland. The Pundit Maharaj commercial, for example, has an Indian-style horoscope chart covering the screen for a few seconds, reminding viewers of family astrologers back home. The last commercial of Ajmeri Baba sketched above interweaves many cultural allusions. Even though set in the living room of a modern South Asian man in the diaspora, it bears an interesting resonance with the story-within-a-story format used extensively in ancient Indian epics and religious texts. In this format, when a character is faced with a perplexity, he or she puts the question to a *rishi*, a seer, who has insights into the reality of things. To answer the question, the seer begins a new story. The utterly distressed man in the television commercial does not ask a sage a question; he presses the button on his remote control. And surely, an Ajmeri Baba commercial is going on—a story within a story. Here the screen is covered with two large and beautiful eyes that open slowly, releasing the words "Ajmeri Baba," alluding not only to the ability of ancient "seers" and medieval holy men of all faith to penetrate reality, but also to prominent eyes of the goddess and to the eye-opening ceremony in Hindu temples.

Viewers' sensibilities are also factored into the commercials by creating a sense of affinity with the help seekers on the screen. Most figures in the commercials appear to be people of South Asian origin. An immigrant, required consistently to cope with difference, feels a sense of solidarity with the characters who are portrayed as struggling with some of the same problems he or she is facing, especially with regard to professional and financial success. Often, a person who has lost the social standing he or she once enjoyed feels tremendous pressure not to lose face in the new social milieu where many of his or her compatriots are immensely successful. Keeping up appearances comes with the price tag of alienation. The problems faced by characters in the commercials give a South Asian viewer consolation that he or she is not alone. Importantly, the commercials convey that there is light at the end of the tunnel with the help of a miracle worker, just as there would be back home. This can be a source of reassurance for the distressed. With the use of audio and visual cues, the medium of television is especially suitable for creating a virtual bond between the viewers and the characters on the screen. If allusions to traditional elements appeal to cultural memory, virtual bonding evokes hope—the two strongest emotional anchors for a migrant.

Standardizing the Sales Pitch

While commercials for ethnic products in the diaspora must factor in cultural memories of expected viewers, they also need to stress a change in content, form, or packaging of the product that makes the sales pitch more appropriate for the new context.[11] Commercials for the miracle workers in question tap into cultural memories of miracle working in South Asia in some important ways, but by presenting miracles as purchasable products that anyone can buy in the context of the global market, they radically modify the signification of miracles for the viewers. An important factor in this modification is what Lawrence A. Babb terms "standardization." Standardization here refers to the presentation of a standard version of a South Asian religious or cultural product in modern media, especially television, which minimizes its rich cultural diversity in order to appeal across class, caste and geographical boundaries and create large viewer communities (Babb and Wadley 1995, 2–5). While Babb's reference is to television programs produced in South Asia, standardization is at work on many levels in the commercials for miracle workers in the diaspora as well. It plays a pivotal role in the modification of miracles into purchasable products.

First, aside from mentioning the titles of the masters to add force to the standard commercial rhetoric of guarantee, the commercials give no information regarding the master's spiritual lineage, attainments, or personality. This is in sharp contrast to traditional narratives about miracles performed by holy persons in South Asia, where the help seeker is given extensive details about these matters, prompting the listener or reader to approach the saint if he or she is living and his or her shrine if the saint is deceased. While some tropes such as the transmission of grace by a holy person are found in miracle narratives from many different traditions of the subcontinent, every narrative reflects some concepts and vocabulary specific to the tradition of the master. A Hindu holy person's miraculous powers, for example, would be described using terms such as *tapas* (asceticism), *bhakti* (devotion), and *kripa* (grace). The narrative would reflect an understanding that miracles happen when a person of great spiritual achievements—through asceticism or devotion—bestows grace on a supplicant. Thus, *Bhakta Shri Jalaram*, a hagiographic book about a Hindu saint that is sold on many roadside stalls in Gujarat, includes numerous details about his relationship with his guru, Bhojalram, his bhakti to Ram, as well as many testimonies from his devotees about his *kripa* (Rajdev n.d.). Similarly, as Pnina Werbner's essay on Zindapir of Ghamkhol Sharif in Pakistan shows, narratives about Muslim saints contain the recurrent use of terms such as *awliya* (friends of God), *dua* (supplication), and *barakat* (grace). They convey an understanding that a miracle occurs when a saint, a friend of Allah, mediates his grace to a person in need (Werbner and Basu 1998, 104–11). In the television commercial format, such details have little place. Except for one commercial of Pundit Maharaj that uses the term *kripa*, the commercials for these miracle workers are marked only by an emphasis on guaranteed results, creating a standardized miracle worker for the consumer market.

Standardization of the image of a miracle worker in the commercials under consideration is comparable to what Max Weber has termed "routinization of charisma." It happens when charisma, which is based in personal qualities in its pure form, becomes a hereditary or official position that meets the continued ideal and material needs of both followers and masters, creating a stable community (Weber 1968, 54—57). Of the two types of routinization discussed by Weber, hereditary and official, the standardization of miracle workers is closer to the routinization of charisma into an official position, which is based on an effective execution of an important function in the community. A miracle worker's commercials highlight the master's ability to provide miraculous help rather than his personal qualities. There are, however, important differences. Standardization of a miracle worker does not happen in the context of a community of followers; it happens in the global market of individual consumers. Nor do commercials aim at creating a stable community; they are oriented toward onetime transactions between individual clients and masters.

The second standardized component in the commercials for miracle workers is provided by the human figures who appear as South Asian immigrants striving for success. These are marked by a complete lack of specificity regarding their regional or religious affiliations within South Asia.[12] It is difficult to make out whether the person fluttering across the screen is Hindu, Muslim, or Sikh or is from Kolkata, Kerala, or Kashmir (the only exception being the Punjabi woman in the Ajmeri Baba commercial). While veneration and supplication to saints across regional and religious boundaries is common in South Asia, diversity among supplicants is stressed and not suppressed in spreading the word about the powers and kindness of a saint. In Corinne Dempsey's study of Christian spiritual healers of Kerala, she discusses an example of this in the story of a Muslim boy healed of his clubfootedness through a posthumous miracle of the female saint Alphonsa. In spreading the word about her, Bishop Valopilly of Thallassery in northern Kerala stresses that the boy remains a Muslim. As Dempsey observes, "Bishop Valopilly does tell this story to demonstrate his part in spreading good news throughout the region—but it is not the good news of Christianity. It is that of Alphonsa's healing power" (Dempsey 2002, 133). In the oral traditions of the saint Jalaram in Gujarat, stories about his miraculous help to non-Hindus are especially stressed. Interestingly, a Peer Syed Sahib advertisement for print media does make an attempt to stress diversity among his clients and even mentions his lineage ("Syed family, the oldest & most prestigious name from Ajmer Sharif in India"). In this advertisement, appearing regularly in the English monthly *Little India* and in the Gujarati weekly *Gujarat Times*, three "thank-you" notes are included—one from a Muslim woman in London, another from a Sikh couple in Australia, and the third from a Hindu family in the United States.[13] By contrast, TV commercials for the miracle workers do not emphasize the diversity of their clientele (except through a few Caucasian faces appearing here and there), but portray the common element of stress in the lives of individual immigrants worried about attaining success in various areas of life.

In addition to standardizing South Asian human figures in Babb's sense of the term, commercials for miracle workers are also standardized in accordance with television advertising techniques. An important means for standardization is the format for conveying the message. Most of these commercials are in the before-and-after format. While this format is now seen as prosaic by experts of television advertising (Kanner 1999, 3), it still seems to work particularly well for spiritual healers. In each of their commercials, the 180° turn in the facial expressions of the human figures—from unbearable stress to ecstatic happiness—within a span of thirty seconds brings into sharp focus the proclaimed miraculous powers of the master. Happy faces of the consumers on whose needs the commercials are focused eliminate the need to refer to the impressive spiritual attainments of the master.

With regard to the format, the "before" part of the commercials is marked by yet another type of standardization. There is no trace of unpleasantness in the portrayal of suffering. The characters shown on the screen are stressed individuals moving around in nice clothes and comfortable surroundings. While problems such as separation from a loved one, a financial crisis, and marital problems are dramatically portrayed in many slice-of-life-format commercials, visual representation of sickness, the most frequently solved problem in the traditional context, is altogether missing. This is a major departure from the traditional oral testimonies about spiritual healers, which tend to give detailed descriptions of diseases to highlight the healers' powers. Even in print, a large number of testimonies in the book about Jalaram give details of diseases from which the writers found relief (Rajdev n.d., 403, 418, 419). In the television commercials, even while stressing the healing powers of a master, their producers do not wish to disturb the sanitized neatness of the viewers' well-decorated living rooms, thus complying with standard television commercial etiquette.

Another standard element of television commercials adopted by the commercials of Pundit Maharaj, Peer Syed Sahib, and Ajmeri Baba is the phone number to be called by a prospective client. Each commercial repeatedly gives a phone number in the United Kingdom both on the screen and through the voice-over. As in many commercials for consumer products and services like insurance and medical help, the prospective client is asked to call the number with a sense of urgency. The Pundit Maharaj commercial urges, "Call Pundit Maharaj immediately." The Ajmeri Baba commercial asks, "What are you waiting for?" The Peer Syed Sahib commercial asks the viewer to call "now." Interestingly, however, none of the commercials makes reference to fees, as commercials for consumer products accepting phone orders do. Nor do they mention any expectation of faith from the caller. The standardized broadcasting of a phone number as a point of contact has important implications for the traditional understanding of miraculous help in South Asia. It disembodies the miracle worker and eliminates the requirement for reverence on the part of the help seeker.

As a number of essays in *Embodying Charisma: Modernity, Locality and the Performance of Emotion in Sufi Cults* (Werbner and Basu 1998) make clear, sacred powers of saints in South Asian Islam are embodied and largely associated with their shrines or tombs (*dargah*s). Shrines of Hindu and Sikh saints are also regularly visited by supplicants. In traditional understandings, visitation to a saint's shrine (or residence, in the case of a living saint) or some type of personal contact with him or her is required for miracles to happen. The availability of a phone number eliminates the requirement for visitation or direct physical contact. The more radical impact of contacting a spiritual healer by phone is that it challenges the traditional understanding that faith is central to the relationship between a master and a recipient of his or her grace. As traditional testimonies make abundantly clear, the miraculous is not just "beyond belief," it is also sacred, demanding the emotional commitment of veneration.

In 2004, during a rikshaw (three-wheeler cab) ride with my cousin, she began expressing to me her distress over not being able to buy a condominium in Mumbai. The Muslim *rikshaw* driver, who kept a picture of the shrine of Khwaja Moinuddin Chishti of Ajmer in his *rikshaw*, overheard the conversation and promptly suggested that with complete faith, she should make a *mannat* (a vow to do something if a desire is fulfilled) to visit the *dargah* (tomb) of the Chishti saint when she had bought a condo. He stressed that if she made such a *mannat*, there was no question of it not being fulfilled; he then proceeded to tell a couple of stories from his own experience. Whether my cousin actually followed up or not, it was made clear to her that faith was critical to the fulfillment of the *mannat*.[14] Similarly, on a Sufi Web site, the section on the saint Moinuddin's tomb refers to the custom of tying a thread on the lattice of the building as a way of making a *mannat* and untying it with gratitude when it is granted. It draws attention to how each supplicant makes a personal connection with the saint through the tying and untying of a thread. "Each thread tied is a wish and when it is granted, and it inevitably is, the person who tied it returns to untie a thread. The hot desert winds play with those threads, the sun leaches them of colour but the faithful return to tie and untie, in a cycle that never seems to end."[15]

Scores of Web site testimonials about the living Hindu saint Satya Sai Baba refer not only to his miracles, but also to the devotion of the recipients of his grace.[16] Even the letters in the Peer Syed Sahib print advertisement discussed above express gratitude and veneration. The television commercials have none of this. If absence of detail about the master's spiritual lineage and attainments standardizes a miracle worker, absence of any mention of expectation of faith standardizes miracles as market commodities, even when specifications about amount and manner of payment are strikingly absent. This leads one to wonder how the process of performing miracles initiated by a commercial works.

Modus Operandi

My understanding of the procedure for seeking help from the spiritual healers in question comes from a variety of sources: blogs and forums on the Internet, conversations with radio talk-show hosts, interviews with people who have contacted one of the masters, and helping a friend who had phone conversations with a master from my home.[17] The general pattern that emerges from these sources is that the first phone call from a help seeker functions as a sort of satellite prayer for the grace of the guru. When the phone is picked up, the caller is not asked about possession of faith, but rather possession of a credit card. The caller is asked to give the numbers of his or her credit card and phone. He or she is called back after verification of the credit card. In the first conversation, the credit card pays for the diagnosis. Once the root of the trouble is determined, fees for the solution to be brought about through rituals or prayers have to be paid. These fees may run into large amounts. Throughout the process, the ritual props linking the client and the master remain the phone and the credit card, unlike offerings of garlands, scarves, or coconuts back home. The process of problem solving—beginning with the initial viewing of the commercial and hopefully ending in a positive resolution—takes place entirely in a virtual space for the client. Commercials for a spiritual healer function as gateways to this impersonal relationship between the master and the recipient of his grace. It is significant that print advertisements for the three masters in the United States refer to the help seekers as "clients" or "customers" and not as "devotees" or "disciples" or simply "seekers of help."[18] It is not that material or monetary gifts are absent in master-follower relationships in South Asia. They are very much a part of miracle-working phenomena. In contrast to clients' payments to the miracle workers featured on television, however, gifts to saints are viewed as expressions of gratitude or veneration. Werbner points out that in the Sufi traditions of South Asia, a gift (*nazrana*) is seen as a "tribute to the saint," given with a clear understanding that the saint, like God himself, does not need it (Werbner and Basu 1998, 107). Similarly, followers feel gratified when gifts (*bhet*) offered as signs of reverence are accepted by Hindu saints. The commercials, in contrast, turn devotees into clients.

Critique within the Community

If spiritual-healer commercials rule the television screen on South Asian TV channels, discussions about them abound on the computer screen. The masters and their commercials have attracted a great deal of attention from computer-savvy South Asians who engage in some fairly insightful and humorous conversations about them in blogs and forums.[19] Even some newspaper columnists have found them interesting enough to write columns about them.[20] Unlike Web pages about healers like Satya Sai Baba and Benny Hinn, which include both testimonials of followers and criticisms by the unimpressed, most writings about the South Asian spiritual healers who advertise their services are less than favorable. Even though a few contributors recognize that the commercials can have an appeal for the depressed or the desperate, a large majority think of them as "frauds," "hoaxes" or "scams."[21] Some consider the belief in miracles to be foolishness or are critical of South Asian culture for nurturing such irrationality.[22] Some are suspicious of spiritual healers who run repeated ads in multiple media and directly ask for money when called.[23] Some poke fun at the virtual nature of credit card transactions over international phone lines.[24] The sharpest critiques in almost every blog and column are directed at the rhetoric of "guarantee" and the appearances of the phone numbers—the two features that firmly establish the commercials as part of the business world. Overall, those who question the possibility that a holy person can actually perform miracles are in the minority. Most seem concerned about the manipulation of desperate immigrants by fraudulent persons and about the changing chemistry of faith in ways that are less than desirable.

Miracles in the Age of Global Market: Some Concluding Thoughts

The fact that miracle-worker commercials constantly appear on South Asian TV channels in the diaspora yet exist alongside a profusion of criticism on Web pages creates a paradox of sorts, reflecting a debate within this migrant community about two things: a belief in miracles and the nature and implications of the commercials. The challenge to a belief in miracles comes from a few members of the community who see it as irrational baggage left over from the traditional culture of South Asia. For them, rationality is a mark of modernity. As the frequency of the commercials indicates, however, a belief in miracles persists among a significant number of people in the community. As Brown suggests, the hold of the miraculous on the human imagination is not shaken easily, even among the scientifically oriented. In the context of globalization, when entire faith movements are sometimes built around miracles geared toward success and prosperity, added anxiety about success in new homelands adds force to attraction for miracles among migrants.[25]

The other point of debate—the use of commercials by spiritual masters— arouses sharp responses and raises important questions. As the above exploration shows, commercials use the medium of television effectively to blend faith and business as well as to evoke memory and hope, standardizing miracle working for the global market in the process. Their success, as suggested by their frequency, exemplifies experts' views that effective commercials both reflect and shape people's desires (Savan 1994, 9; Kanner 1999, xvi). But an important question to ask is, "Which people's desires?" The analysts of television ads seem to think of viewers as vulnerable individuals and advertisers as impersonal businesses without a trace of vulnerability. The commercials of the spiritual masters show that, to the contrary, advertisements reflect and shape desires of both viewers and advertisers. They indicate that in the context of a global market, dreams of success hold as strong a grip on the imagination as does a belief in miracles. The desire for success among advertisers and viewers alike leads to a commodification of miracles.

The standardization of miracles in the commercials leads, as we have seen, to an elimination of traditionally crucial aspects of reverence and gratitude toward the spiritual master. While matters of faith are inevitably subject to transformation in every historical context, such radical commercialization of faith in the global market worries thinkers like Carrette and King as well as South Asian bloggers (Carrette and King 2005, 143). Savan is disturbed by the tendency of television commercials to downsize vital human emotions (Savan 1994, 3).[26] Viewing the commercials from the other end, Bernice Kanner admires commercials and writes, "Selling is the language of our time and advertising its boldest manifestation" (Kanner 1999, xvii). Looking at commercials of miracle workers from this perspective, it is possible to see them as adapting a faith practice to our times.

Standing at the intersection of faith, desire, business, and technology in the context of globalization, commercials for South Asian spiritual healers on international television channels like Zee reflect dilemmas and achievements of our own times as well as the power miracles have over the human imagination. With regard to our own times, on one hand, they point out the startling ways in which the global market culture commodifies faith, subjugating tradition to business. On the other, they reflect the ability of globalization to provide assurance to the dislocated and link cultures over vast distances, a quality admired by Jagdish Bhagavati (Bhagavati 2004, 106–20). Importantly, they demonstrate how the global market, using sophisticated media, is helpful in keeping cultural memories of the dislocated alive and in providing them reassurance. Globalization and commodification form only one aspect of the commercials, however. The other and perhaps more fundamental aspect of the commercials for a student of religion is belief in miracles.

With regard to miracles, commercials for miracle workers confirm the insights offered by Corner and Mullin, while pointing out new directions for inquiry. Their frequency in the face of critique from within the South Asian community validates Corner's idea that a belief in and debates about miracles have continued in culturally specific ways in all parts of the world since antiquity (Corner 2005, 177–97). Presenting miracles in their modified form as a service for purchase, they also support Mullin's observation that cultural debates and challenges modify rather than displace a belief in miracles in various historical contexts (Mullin 1996, 264).

Miracle-worker commercials thus point out an avenue for examining further implications of Mullin's insights. The fact that the global market plays such a crucial role in the emergence of miracle-worker commercials suggests a need for examining intersections of religion and business—two forces that fascinate and motivate people—for understanding the nature of religion in our times. Such an endeavor would prove helpful for understanding religious phenomena in other times as well. In recent years, much significant work has been done exploring the intersections of religion and politics. The intersections of business and religion are still not extensively explored. Since some aspects of business are integrated in all areas of life—including religion—in any historical context, intersections of faith and business provide a rich arena of exploration for students of religion. Only at such an intersection can we understand the dependence of the media of miracles on the miracle of media.

Notes

I would like to thank Corinne Dempsey, Selva Raj, and Bharat L. Bhatt for their careful reading of drafts of this essay and their immensely helpful comments and critique.

1. The terms "spiritual healers" and "miracle workers" are used synonymously in this essay to mean persons who perform miracles to heal or help others, claiming a spiritual basis for their ability to do so. The three masters whose commercials are discussed here use the first two terms synonymously in their commercials.

2. In January 2006, Pundit Maharaj sponsored *Sindoor Tere Nam ka*, Peer Syed Sahib sponsored *Sat Phere*, and Ajmeri Baba sponsored *Sa re ga ma pa*—three extremely popular prime-time shows.

3. As this essay was being written, the commercials for spiritual masters were discontinued by Asia 1 in the United Kingdom. Since the first draft of the essay (early 2006), however, another major change has occurred that offsets the discontinuation of commercials on one channel. In May 2007, each of these masters has a Web site. Pundit Maharaj's Web site: http://www.punditjimaharaj.com/home.html; Peer Syed Sahib: http://peersahibji.com/; Ajmeri Baba: http://www.ajmeribabasahib.com/.

4. In early January 2006, I saw commercials for a Sai Baba on SONY, also giving a phone number in the United Kingdom.

5. A good example is provided by a beefless burger—the Maharaja Mac—served at McDonald's in India. It appeals to the religious sentiments of Hindus who avoid beef and, at the same time, it presents itself as a dish fit for a king, a maharaja. An amusing instance of how internationally known brand-name products infiltrate all layers of life in remote corners of the world was provided by a news item on Alpha Gujarati news on January 10, 2006. In Ahmedabad, Gujarat, a male goat to be sacrificed on Muslim festival of Eid, which fell on January 12 this year, had been given Pepsi for two years by his owner, Moyuddin. The goat had developed a liking for this drink, and Moyuddin wanted to raise the sacrificial animal with care and affection in accordance with his religious beliefs.

6. Taken from the book title of Frank 2000, as cited by Chidester (2003, 147).

7. The First Church commercials that could be viewed on www.ingrammedia. com, for example, present the saving grace of God through Jesus as the solution to situations like attempted suicide. In these commercials (termed so by the owner of the Web site) profundity is conveyed through the tone of the voice-over, symbols like the cross on a church under an open sky, and a praying couple with closed eyes.

8. A good example of an appeal to the imagination is provided by a 1996 commercial that presents a well-known soccer player exploding a demon goalie with a fiery

ball hit with his Nike shoe. The scene is set in a Roman amphitheater, where popular players of today play against a whole army of demons on the opposing team. Wearing a Nike shoe makes a veritable hero of our times victorious not only in a game, but also against the forces of evil across eras. The founder of Nike called this ad an appeal to "the idealized serious athlete who dwells in the imagination of millions of people" (Kanner 1999, 80–81).

9. For a discussion of a construction of homeland in the diaspora, see Paranjape 2001, 9–11.

10. As W. L. Smith shows, beginning with biographical sketches of the Buddha in the Pali canon and of the Jinas in the *Kalpa Sutra* in the centuries before the Common Era, the hagiographic literature in South Asia has continued to grow and is often termed "endless" (Smith 2000, 1–8).

11. The phrase "sales pitch" is adopted from Leslie Savan, who suggests that there is no human emotion or experience that cannot be reworked into a "sales pitch" by advertisers (Savan 1994, 3).

12. This is in sharp contrast to some impressive food commercials, such as those for "Ashoka Parathas" and "Vadilal Quick Treat," that try to link the products to the authenticity of regional recipes. The first bite of the food product transports the eater imaginatively to a specific region, home of both the eater and the recipe. In each of their many commercials, a person in the attire specific to the region from which the recipe comes vouches for the authenticity of the dish in the regional accent only to discover that it was made with Gits mix by someone totally unfamiliar with the recipe.

13. This ad can be seen with considerable regularity in *Little India* and *Gujarat Times*, such as in the September 2005 issue of *Little India* and the July 29 2005, issue of *Gujarat Times*.

14. This incident happened on October 16, 2004.

15. http://www.pilgrimageindia.net/muslim_pilgrimage/ajmer_sharif.html.

16. See www.satyasaibabalinks.org/saibabamiracles.htm. A particularly interesting testimony is from Dr. Kishan Gadhia of London. It mentions many incidents in which Dr. Gadhia received miraculous help from Satya Sai Baba, each of which increased his devotion for the saint. The most impressive of these is the incident in which he was held at gunpoint by an African soldier of Idi Amin in Uganda. Dr. Gadhia took out the saint's picture from his pocket to offer his last prayer. The soldier saw it and let him go. Years later, he learned that the soldier also had become a devotee of Satya Sai Baba.

17. For Web sites, see http://hindustan.net/discuss/messages/16326/16327.html?1133664436, especially the first section titled "How does it work?" as well as postings by "Anonymous" dated October 25, 2005; by "Distressed Lady," dated July 14, 2005; and by "Angel," dated Nov. 10 2005. See also http://www.gsharma.com/2005/04/18/85/peer-Syed-sahib/, especially the post by "Ajay" dated October 31, 2005, and http://mannat123.blogspot.com/2005_03_13_archive.html. A radio talk show aired on WCNJ 89.3 FM in July 2004 in which many callers talked anonymously

about their experiences of seeking help from spiritual healers. In December 2005, I interviewed some people in New Jersey who had called one or more of these masters. In August 2000, a close friend of mine called one of these masters from my home for her health problems.

18. See the Peer Syed Sahib print commercials discussed above, the Ajmeri Baba commercial on the online version of *India Daily* (July 26, 2004), and the Pundit Maharaj commercial in *Gujarat Times* (November 11, 2005).

19. Two examples are provided by 1) http://www.gsharma.com/peer-Syed-sahib/; 2) http://mannat123.blogspot.com/2005_03_13_archive.html.

20. See the article "Overkill by Psychic's Advertisements in Indian TV Channels" by Dr. Jaswant Singh Sachdev in *Valley India Times* (published from Phoenix, AZ) online at http://www.valleyindiatimes.com/noqnews/nnqview.php?ArtID=149, dated March 24, 2003, and Khalid Hasan's column in *Pakistani Daily Times*, "Postcard USA: Pundit Maharaj Rules OK," dated March 11, 2002 at http://www.dailytimes.com. pk//default.asp?page=story_3-11-2002_pg3_6 . Hasan satirizes Pundit Maharaj and Ajmeri Baba. He does not mention Peer Syed Sahib.

21. See Poonam and Deepak Jeswal's postings on Mannat's blog (March 17, 2005). A comment by Jeswal is especially interesting: "As the rush of life of people continues, they try to find a quick-fix solution."

22. Among many who comment on the foolishness of people calling the spiritual healers, some are fairly strong in their expressions. On the hindustan.net forum discussion cited above, "Curious_person" refers to help seekers as "the dumbest on earth" (October 12, 2005). "Anonymous" calls them "stupid morons" (June 6, 2005). Among those who attribute such irrationality to South Asian culture are Mohan, who refers to the culture in which people believe in "things that don't exist" and "superstitions," and Mannat, who refers to such belief as "badly incorporated in our culture" (Mohan and Mannat's postings dated March 17 and 18, 2005, are on Mannat's blog cited above).

23. To cite only a few examples: on the hindustan.net discussion forum, "Curious_Person" wonders how the miracle workers can "afford to advertise every 5 minutes on international channels" (October 12, 2005). "A Concerned Mom" complains about being asked for $300 upon calling Pundit Maharaj (October 3, 2005), and "Jafar" expresses his anger at the "ugly commercials" appearing day and night (July 1, 2005).

24. Dr. Jaswant Singh Sachdev refers satirically to the impression given by the commercials that "one phone call can transform you into the happiest man on the earth" (*Valley India Times*, March 24, 2003). In a similar vein Mannat writes, "'Problems resolved' over the phone (jet age!) and they take your credit card # for payment" in his posting on his blog (March 17, 2005).

25. The cult of miracles associated with prosperity can easily be seen among televangelists in the United States. An excellent example outside the United States is the El Shaddai movement in the Philippines (Wiegele 2005).

26. Carrette and King are worried about the new market ideology "where religion is nothing but a tool for business and capital" (Carrette and King 2005, 143).

References

Babb, Lawrence A., and Susan S. Wadley, eds. 1995. *Media and the Transformation of Religion in South Asia*. Philadelphia: University of Pennsylvania Press.

Bhagavati, Jagdish. 2004. *In Defense of Globalization*. New York: Oxford University Press.

Brown, Michael, F. 1997. "Thinking about Magic." In *Anthropology of Religion: A Handbook*, edited by Stephen Glazier, 121–36. Westport, CT: Greenwood Press.

Carrette, Jeremy, and Richard King. 2005. *Selling Spirituality: The Silent Takeover of Religion*. Abingdon, UK: Routledge.

Chidester, David. 2003. "Cross-cultural Business: Cocacolonization, McDonaldization, Disneyization, Tupperization, and Other Local Dilemmas of Global Signification." In *Religion and Global Culture, New Terrain in the Study of Religion and the Work of Charles Long*, edited by Jennifer Reid, 145–66. Lanham, MD: Lexington Books.

Corner, Mark. 2005. *Signs of God: Miracles and Their Interpretations*. Hampshire, UK: Ashgate Publishers.

Dempsey, Corinne. 2002. "Lessons in Miracles from Kerala, South India: Stories of Three Christian Saints." In *Popular Christianity in India: Riting between the Lines*, edited by Selva J. Raj and Corinne Dempsey, 115–39. Albany: State University of New York Press.

Frank, Thomas. 2000. *One Market under God: Extreme Capitalism, Market Populism, and the End of Economic Democracy*. New York: Doubleday. Cited in Chidester 2003, 147.

Gurvis, Sandra. 1996. *Way Stations to Heaven: 50 Major Visionary Shrines in the United States*. New York: Macmillan.

Hawley, John Stratton. 1987. "Morality beyond Morality in the Lives of Three Hindu Saints." In *Saints and Virtues*, edited by John Stratton Hawley, 52–86. Berkeley and Los Angeles: University of California Press.

Kanner, Bernice. 1999. *The Hundred Best TV Commercials*. New York: Random House.

Mullin, Robert. 1996. *Miracles and the Modern Religious Imagination*. New Haven, CT: Yale University Press.

Paranjape, Makarand, ed. 2001. *In Diaspora, Theories, Histories, Texts*. New Delhi: Indialog Publications.

Rajdev, Saubhagyachand. n.d. *Bhakta Shri Jalaram* [in Gujarati]. Rajkot, India: Jalaram Jyot.

Savan, Leslie. 1994. *The Sponsored Life: Ads, TV, and American Culture*. Philadephia: Temple University Press.

Smith, W. L. 2000. *Patterns in North Indian Hagiography*. Stockholm: University of Stockholm Press.

Waida, Manabu. 2005. "Miracles, an Overview." In *Encyclopedia of Religion*, edited by Lindsey Jones, 6049–55. Detroit: Macmillan Reference.

Weber, Max. 1968. *On Charisma and Institution Building*. Edited by S. N. Eisenstadt. Chicago: University of Chicago Press.

Werbner, Pnina. 2003. *Pilgrims of Love, The Anthropology of a Global Sufi Cult*. Bloomington: Indiana University Press.

Werbner, Pnina, and Helene Basu. 1998. *Embodying Charisma: Modernity, Locality and Emotion in Sufi Cults*. London: Routledge.

Werth, Lukas. 1998. "'The Saint Who Disappeared': Saints of the Wilderness in Pakistani Village Shrines." In *Embodying Charisma: Modernity, Locality, and the Performance of Emotion in Sufi Cults*, edited by Pnina Werbner and Helene Basu. New York: Routledge.

Wiegele, Katharine. 2005. *Investing in Miracles: El Shaddai and the Transformation of Popular Catholicism in the Philippines*. Honolulu: University of Hawaii Press.

Contributors

CHAD M. BAUMAN is assistant professor of religion at Butler University, where he teaches Asian religions. His research focuses on the interaction of Hindus and Christians in India and the United States. His article "Singing of Satnam: Blind Simon Patros, Dalit Religious Identity, and Satnami-Christian Music in Chhattisgarh, India" appeared in the spring 2006 issue of the *Journal of Hindu-Christian Studies*. His book *Christian Identity and* Dalit *Religion in Hindu India, 1868–1947* is forthcoming with Eerdmans Publishing Company.

CORINNE G. DEMPSEY received graduate degrees from the Graduate Theological Union and Syracuse University. She teaches in the Philosophy Department at the University of Wisconsin–Stevens Point and has researched and written in the area of popular Christianity in India and diaspora Hindu traditions in North America. She has published a variety of articles and two books, *Kerala Christian Sainthood: Collisions of Culture and Worldview in South India* (New York: Oxford University Press, 2001), and *The Goddess Lives in Upstate New York: Breaking Convention and Making Home at a North American Hindu Temple* (New York: Oxford University Press, 2006). She coedited with Selva Raj *Popular Indian Christianity: Riting between the Lines* (Albany: State University of New York Press, 2002) and *Sacred Play: Ritual Levity and Humor in South Asian Religions* (Albany: State University of New York Press, forthcoming).

JOYCE BURKHALTER FLUECKIGER received her PhD in South Asian Language and Literature from the University of Wisconsin–Madison and is professor in the department of religion at Emory University. She specializes in performance studies, with a particular interest in gender. She has carried out extensive fieldwork in India, working with both Hindu and Muslim popular traditions. Her new book, entitled *In Amma's Healing Room: Islam,*

Gender, and Religious Identities in South India, was published by Indiana University Press (Bloomington, 2006). The book addresses questions of religious and gender identities and boundaries in the healing practice of a female Muslim folk healer in the south Indian city of Hyderabad. She spent the academic year 1999–2000 in Tirupati, South India, where she conducted ethnographic fieldwork on the goddess tradition of Gangamma. A book in progress based on this research is entitled *When the World Becomes Female: The Gangamma Goddess Tradition of South India.* She is also the author of *Gender and Genre in the Folklore of Middle India* (Ithaca, NY: Cornell University Press, 1996), and has published numerous articles on South Asian folklore. She is coeditor of and contributor to *Oral Epics in India* (Berkeley: University of California Press, 1989) and *Boundaries of the Text: Epic Performances in South and Southeast Asia* (Ann Arbor: South and Southeast Asian Center Publications, University of Michigan, 1991).

ANN GRODZINS GOLD is professor in the departments of religion and anthropology at Syracuse University. Since 2005 she has also been director of Syracuse University's South Asia Center. Gold's research in north India has focused on religious practices, gender, oral traditions, and ecological change, and her publications include numerous articles and four books: *Fruitful Journeys: The Ways of Rajasthani Pilgrims* (Berkeley: University of California Press, 1988); *A Carnival of Parting: The Tales of King Bharthari and King Gopi Chand* (Berkeley: University of California Press, 1992); *Listen to the Heron's Words: Reimagining Gender and Kinship in North India* (Berkeley: University of California Press, 1994) (coauthored with Gloria Raheja); and *In the Time of Trees and Sorrows: Nature, Power and Memory in Rajasthan* (Durham, NC: Duke University Press, 2002) (coauthored with Bhoju Ram Gujar), which in 2004 was awarded the Ananda Kentish Coomaraswamy Book Prize from the Association for Asian Studies. Gold's current work concerns origin tales and miracle tales at rural shrines to regional deities whose healing powers are linked to protected landscapes and natural beauty.

SUNIL GOONASEKERA is visiting associate professor in the Departments of Religion, Sociology, and Anthropology at Bowdoin College in Maine. He previously taught sociology at the University of Peradeniya, Sri Lanka and at the University of California, San Diego. He received a law degree from University of California, Hastings College of the Law, San Francisco, and a doctorate in anthropology from University of California, San Diego. His publications include *Walking to Kataragama* (Colombo: International Center for Ethnic Studies, 2007) and *George Keyt: Interpretations* (Kandy: Institute of Fundamental Studies, 1991). He has published articles and book chapters in the areas of Buddhist practice and interreligious exchange in Sri Lanka, pre-

and postcolonial Silk Road trade in Sri Lanka, the art and interpretation of George Keyt, and Jainism. Goonasekara is currently compiling a Festschrift volume in honor of Gananath Obeyesekere.

WILLIAM P. HARMAN teaches in the Department of Philosophy and Religion at the University of Tennessee in Chattanooga, Tennessee. He writes about ritual, temples, and religious devotion, especially in India, though many of his scholarly works are concerned with issues of comparison. He is author of over twenty scholarly articles, of *The Sacred Marriage of a Hindu Goddess* (Bloomington: Indiana University Press, 1992), and is editor of *Religion in Tamilnadu* (Madura, India: DeNobili Press) and coeditor (with Selva J. Raj) of *Dealing with Deities: The Ritual Vow in South Asia* (Albany: State University of New York Press, 2006). He has held fellowships from the National Endowment of the Humanities, the American Institute of Indian Studies, and the Fulbright Foundation.

SELVA J. RAJ, who received his PhD in the History of Religions from the University of Chicago, is Stanley S. Kresge Professor and chair of Religious Studies at Albion College. His research interests are in the areas of ritual exchange between Hindus and Catholics in south India, the Indian Christian diaspora in the United States, Hindu women saints, and contemporary women's movements in India. Author of numerous articles, he has coedited three volumes. With Corinne Dempsey he coedited *Popular Christianity in India: Riting between the Lines* (Albany: State University of New York Press, 2002) and *Sacred Play: Ritual Levity and Humor in South Asian Religions* (Albany: State University of New York Press, forthcoming). With William Harman he coedited *Dealing with Deities: The Ritual Vow in South Asia* (Albany: State University of New York Press, 2006).

ROBIN RINEHART received her doctorate from the University of Pennsylvania and teaches in the Department of Religious Studies at Lafayette College. Her research and publishing interests include religious movements in medieval, colonial and contemporary Punjab, including Neo-Vedanta Hinduism, Sikhism, and Sufism, and their interrelationships. In addition to writing numerous scholarly articles in this area, she is author of *One Lifetime, Many Lives: The Experience of Modern Hindu Hagiography* (New York: Oxford University Press, 1999), and is editor of *Contemporary Hinduism: Ritual, Culture, and Practice* (Santa Barbara: ABC-CLIO, 2004).

NEELIMA SHUKLA-BHATT is an assistant professor in South Asia Studies at Wellesley College in Massachusetts. She did her doctoral work in the Study of Religion at Harvard University in 2003. Her research focuses on cultural expressions of devotion in South Asia through poetry, music, and dance. Her writings include essays on the female poet Mirabai and the Gujarati poet Narasinha Mehtra. She is currently working on a project on *garbo*, the goddess-worship dance of Hindu women of Gujarat. Religion and modern media is one of her new interests.

Index

215